The Word of a Woman?

The Word of a Woman?

Police, Rape and Belief

Jan Jordan
Institute of Criminology
Victoria University of Wellington, New Zealand

First published 2004 by
PALGRAVE MACMILLAN
Houndmills, Basingstoke, Hampshire RG21 6XS and
175 Fifth Avenue, New York, N.Y. 10010
Companies and representatives throughout the world

PALGRAVE MACMILLAN is the global academic imprint of the Palgrave Macmillan division of St. Martin's Press, LLC and of Palgrave Macmillan Ltd. Macmillan® is a registered trademark in the United States, United Kingdom and other countries. Palgrave is a registered trademark in the European Union and other countries.

ISBN 1–4039–2169–5 hardback

This book is printed on paper suitable for recycling and made from fully managed and sustained forest sources.

A catalogue record for this book is available from the British Library.

Library of Congress Cataloging-in-Publication Data
Jordan, Jan, 1954–
    The word of a woman? : police, rape, and belief / Jan Jordan.
        p. cm.
    Includes bibliographical references and index.
    ISBN 1–4039–2169–5 (hardback)
    1. Rape – Investigation – New Zealand. 2. Police questioning – New Zealand.
  3. Rape victims – New Zealand. I. Title.

HV8079.R35J67 2004
363.25′9532′0993—dc22   2004047836

10   9   8   7   6   5   4   3   2   1
13 12 11 10 09 08 07 06 05 04

Printed and bound in Great Britain by
Antony Rowe Ltd, Chippenham and Eastbourne

The range of what we think and do
is limited by what we fail to notice.
And because we fail to notice
that we fail to notice
there is little we can do
to change
until we notice
how failing to notice
shapes our thoughts and deeds.

(R. D. Laing, 1970)

Thanks to Taylor and Francis for copyright permission to reprint this extract from Laing, R. D. (1970), Knots, *London: Tavistock Publications.*

Contents

List of Tables

Acknowledgements

Acknowledging all those who helped to bring this book to completion is an impossible task. However, there are some whose particular or timely contributions deserve special mention.

First and foremost, I am indebted to my partner, Chris Wood, who has been a source of constant love, support, wisdom, patience and encouragement throughout this long venture, and always seemed to know when it was time to agitate and time to soothe.

Professor Allison Morris and Dr Jenny Neale each brought their particular strengths to the difficult task of guiding and overseeing the many stages of this research, and I am indebted to them both. Greatly appreciated also have been the comments and advice provided by Professor Liz Kelly, Professor Jeanne Gregory, and Dr Allison Kirkman, each of whom encouraged the preparation of this book. Their opinions I valued immensely, in part because their own writings so inspired.

As well as the above, Margie Barr-Brown and Carol Shand have each played an important 'coaching' role in keeping me on track with what often seemed a daunting venture – I am grateful to them both for believing something would eventually materialise! Guidance from my editor, Briar Towers, is also appreciated and my thanks to her and Jen Nelson for their professional advice and support from afar.

The impetus for this research arose from interviews conducted with women who had been raped or sexually assaulted, and I am truly indebted to all those women who had the courage to share their experiences and who did so in such a full and rich way. I particularly want to acknowledge here the women who were attacked by Malcolm Rewa, whose stories of survival were so compelling and whose honesty and openness touched me deeply.

Much of this research depended on the cooperation of the New Zealand Police, and I acknowledge and respect all those who approved, advised and participated in the studies presented here for their willingness to subject themselves and their organisation to such scrutiny. Some of those who assisted have since moved to other positions or left the Police, but contributed greatly at crucial stages of the research. In particular, I wish to thank staff from the Office of the Commissioner, members of the Offender Profiling Squad (Detective Sergeant Dave Henwood, Detective Russell Lamb and Detective Inspector Peter Mitford-Burgess); and Detective Senior Sergeant Mike Arnerich and Detective Sergeant Darrin Thompson, both from Wellington Central Police Station.

I wish to acknowledge also the support of my colleagues at the Institute of Criminology, and within the School of Social and Cultural Studies, especially Professor Philip Stenning for his encouragement and Lizzy Stanley for her careful reading and wise advice. The support of members of my Victoria University writing group has also been invaluable, and warm thanks is extended to Lise Bird, Deborah Jones, and Sara Kindon, as well as to friend and colleague Devon Polaschek.

I have appreciated the warmth, patience and encouragement of many good friends over the years, some of whom now know more about this topic than they probably ever wanted to! My thanks to all who shared in the project of creating this book by helping me at times to focus on it and, at other times, to *not* focus on it. Both were essential to its completion.

Grateful acknowledgement is made to the Faculty Research Committee of Victoria University of Wellington for contributing to the funding of this research. I also wish to thank the New Zealand Federation of Graduate Women for awarding me their Staff Professional Development Scholarship to contribute to the costs incurred in the transcribing of the many interview tapes. Thanks to Brenda Watson, Tracy Anderson, Marianna Churchward and Sandy Taylor for doing such a wonderful job with these tapes. Warm thanks is also extended to Sandy Taylor for all her secretarial support and professional input at various stages during the production of this book.

To all of you who have helped to bring this book into being – my warm and grateful thanks.

1
Introduction: The Credibility Conundrum

> Man is the hunter; woman is his game;
> The sleek and shining creatures of the chase,
> We hunt them for the beauty of their skins;
> They love us for it, and we ride them down.
>
> (Alfred Lord Tennyson, *The Princess*)

Man/woman; right/wrong; reason/emotion; truth/lies. Dichotomous thinking polarises that which defies polarisation. Yet the crime of rape has been legally defined for centuries in ways which uphold a rigid rape/not rape distinction. Moreover, the societies within which such definitions have been promulgated have reflected patriarchal privileging, with the gender class 'men' being equated with rightness and the 'truth' and the gender class 'women' regarded as wrong, full of falsities and lies. The long history of men's violence towards, and subjugation of, women depended in large part on a woman's protests and accusations being silenced. Little wonder, then, that women came to doubt the worth of their words and the value of their selves. In the quest for survival, the quest for credibility assumed increasing significance.

To be credible is to convey plausibility, to signal truth, to convince by one's words and demeanour that one is authentic. For centuries men's credibility was dependent on continued perceptions of women's lack of credibility, or on what Jocelynne Scutt (1997) has termed the construct of the 'incredible' woman, the woman who is hard to believe, who defies belief. As Scutt says:

> Women's words are rightly accusatory, when women have been raped, bashed, stalked, harassed, sexually exploited, killed. Women's words are rightly accusatory, when they claim these crimes and civil wrongs have been committed against them by men. Men know this. No doubt this is why a male-designed legal system protests so loudly through its written

1

and unwritten laws, rules, practices and procedures that women's words are suspect. That women's words are not credible. That every woman is an incredible woman. (Scutt, 1997, p. 4)

Issues of belief and credibility are more pronounced in the history of criminal justice system responses to rape than they are for any other crime. This has been justified on the basis that rape incidents usually involve no witnesses apart from the key parties involved, thus reducing the situation to one of her word against his. Other crimes, such as robbery, may also depend on the victim's testimony alone but, unlike rape, robbery has not been perceived in such problematic terms. The fact that rape is the word of a *woman* against the word of a *man* is of critical importance. Women's words, historically, have counted for less than men's – if only because men regarded them that way. Throughout the history of patriarchy, men's 'truth' prevailed and women's voice was silenced (Taslitz, 1999). One of the most effective silencing mechanisms, when simply ignoring women was no longer a sufficient control strategy, was to declare women's voices to be lying. Women, it was alleged, either deliberately tell falsehoods, or are so deceived that they do not know their own minds. Either way, the word of a woman counts for little.

This book focuses on the word of a woman in relation to the crime of rape. Whilst the crime of male rape must be acknowledged and is achieving greater recognition legally and socially (Gillespie, 1996; Lees, 1997; Mezey and King, 1992), it is female victims who are the subject of this book. This is not only because of their numerical dominance, but because the history of the crime of rape precluded recognition of male victims until very recently. A major strand of analysis running through this book focuses attention on the patriarchal legacies still present in contemporary thought and practice. Of particular relevance are the ways in which heterosexual relationships have been structured to privilege men and accord them greater rewards and credibility than women. Men's definitions, interpretations and experiences have tended to be accorded the status of 'objectivity' and 'truth'; in contrast, women have traditionally been ignored, subsumed within accounts pertaining to men, discounted as liars, or at best seen as wholly subjective. It was only when groups of women joined together, inspired by feminist visions of gender justice, that these patterns and assumptions began to be collectively challenged.

Feminism and the women's movement

The fact that rape is a crime committed almost exclusively by men, almost exclusively against women, guaranteed it a position of prominence within early feminist campaigns. From the early 1970s onwards, increasing criticism was made of inadequate definitions of rape and responses prejudicial to the rights of victims (Adler, 1987; Brownmiller, 1975; Estrich, 1987; Hall, 1985;

Kelly, 1988; Shapcott, 1988; Toner, 1982). Many of the legal changes introduced in various jurisdictions during the 1980s resulted from earlier campaigning by feminist activists and their supporters, and considerable pressure was placed on the justice system to improve its practices and responses to victims. In New Zealand, for instance, the legal definition of rape was extended to incorporate other forms of sexual violation, spousal immunity was abolished and sentences for rape were increased (Sullivan, 1986). These changes, and the publicity accompanying them, also placed pressure on agencies such as the police to examine their training and procedures. Increasingly, support groups established for rape victims played an advocacy role, and greater liaison was developed between the various agencies involved, bringing together the police, doctors and support agency workers.

The women's movement of the 1970s fundamentally threatened traditional social realities and relationships, in particular men's assumed 'right' of authority and supremacy. Unsurprisingly, centuries of patriarchal rule did not roll over quietly when challenged by feminist activists. By the 1990s, increasing evidence was appearing of a backlash against the gains made by feminists (Enns, 1996; Faludi, 1991; Herman and Harvey, 1993). Some critics have protested that efforts to increase the exposing and reporting of men's abuse and violence have gone 'too far'; the previous climate of denial has, they argue, been replaced by a naïve adherence to such cliches as 'children never lie' and a willingness to always trust and believe the victim (Dershowitz, 1994; Goodyear-Smith, 1995; McLoughlin, 1997; Newbold, 2000). One inference to be drawn from such commentators suggests that it is not men's actions that put them in prison, but women's lies.

Far from being restricted to criticism from those recognised traditionally as being anti-feminist, however, a new breed of sceptical 'feminists' has emerged. Writers such as Katie Roiphe (1993) and Camille Paglia (1992) have argued that women are being encouraged to label all 'bad sex' as rape, with Paglia, for example, advocating that the term 'rape' should be restricted in usage to brutal stranger attacks (Paglia, 1992, p. 69). Their labelling of women's rising resistance to acquaintance rape as a 'hysterical' overreaction effectively reinforces historical images of rape as little more than a product of women's fantastical imaginings.·

Thus the assault on patriarchy has been met with counter-blows from the male-dominated institutions established to safeguard men's social, sexual and political positions of power and control. By the 1990s, groups of men were forming themselves into a men's rights' movement, insistent that they were now a victimised and oppressed minority voice, the 'victims' of feminism (Johnson, 1997).

Within this environment, advocacy and support groups for women in the twenty-first century continue to struggle for resources and recognition. Such services are typically regarded as being of low social status and priority and are forced to spend much of their energy fighting for economic survival rather than being able to focus on service delivery to victims and community education (Foley, 1996; Stirling, 1997). The social position of such agencies parallels strongly the position of those whose causes they champion and represent, providing yet another indicator of the obstacles victims of sexual violence face in their struggle for support and recognition (Kelly, 1999).

Advocacy groups, support agencies, counsellors, psychotherapists and rape researchers have all borne the brunt of recent campaigns aimed at discrediting the voices of those who have sought greater acknowledgement of the extent of sexual victimisation. Years of feminist research and advocacy for rape survivors are in danger of being dismissed as 'victim feminism'. It was, one might argue, to be expected that once the lid was lifted to expose the extent of sexual assault on women and children in the home, there would be some in society who would want to clamp the lid firmly back on the pot. Such 'clamping' was evident throughout the 1990s in two distinct, but related, debates. The 'false memory' debate sought primarily to under- mine survivors' disclosures regarding historical child sexual abuse, essen- tially by proclaiming the unreliability of memory (Loftus, 1992; Porter *et al.*, 1999). The second debate focussed on disclosures by women of adult rape experiences, arguing that perennial silencing favourite – women lie (Macdonald, 1995; McLoughlin, 1997). At a time when women's challenges to patriarchal belief systems seemed to be making significant progress, cre- ating an environment where rape and child abuse could be exposed and con- fronted, these debates emerged as the most recent manifestation of societal repression and denial. The new victims have become not women and chil- dren, but the men they supposedly falsely accuse.

It is within this context that, in recent years, adults recalling abuse from their childhood have been discredited for relying on repressed memo- ries, or on memory at all (Goodyear-Smith, 1995; Loftus *et al.*, 1994; Ofshe, 1994). Therapists, in turn, have been condemned for implanting false mem- ories in vulnerable clients, and for turning rape and sexual abuse into an 'industry' which they manufacture, produce and reap the profits from (Du Chateau, 1993).

> The notion that therapists can implant scenarios of horror in the minds of their patients is easily accepted because it appeals to common preju- dices. It resonates with popular fears of manipulation by therapists and popular stereotypes of women as irrational, suggestible or vengeful. It appeals to the common wish to deny or minimise the reality of sexual violence. (Herman and Harvey, 1993, p. 5)

The notion that abuse survivors are 'making it all up' has been seized upon as a defence by abusers and those who collude with them, and has also been adopted as a panacea to growing societal unease surrounding the safety of the home (Saraga and Macleod, 1997). The memory debate has arisen in the context of resistance to feminist assertions regarding the prevalence and harm of rape and sexual abuse. As such, its own assertions have become important 'props' in the continuation of patriarchal denial of sexual violence. Whilst undermining the voices of the accusers, it reifies the assertions of the accused. The assumption underlying this debate is, by now, chillingly familiar – women and children lie.

Not surprisingly, the media have often become the allies of this movement. The ingredients of a 'good story' are there: drama, suspense, 'truth' and 'lies', families torn apart, innocent men languishing in jail. In the way in which they have seized upon and constructed the 'new issue' of false rape complaints, the media have provided a central strand to backlash arguments of the last decade (Gavey and Gow, 2001). Given dominant discourses and legacies, it should scarcely be surprising that increasing concern about the prevalence and impacts of rape was paralleled by increased denial and suppression of women's testimony. Running throughout is the preservation of the status quo, and the role of the media as reinforcers of existing social relations (Barak, 1994; Howe, 1998; Lees, 1995; Mitchell, 2001).

The 'softer' version of the discourse of denial maintained that, maybe unintentionally, women often made 'mistaken' allegations that they had been raped, possibly encouraged by loose feminist definitions. Thus, in her controversial book, *The Morning After*, Katie Roiphe complains:

> Rape has become a catch-all expression, a word used to define everything that is unpleasant and disturbing about relations between the sexes.... Regret can signify rape. A night that was a blur, a night you wish hadn't happened, can be rape. (Roiphe, 1993, p. 80)

Media reporting of what are believed to be false rape allegations has become a fashionable area of inquiry and speculation in recent years. The coverage given to rape reports which are believed to be false is extensive, and articles centred round the theme of women lying appear to be positioned with greater prominence and emphasis than stories covering rape charges that end in conviction (Gavey and Gow, 2001; Hamlin, 1988). Writing in the context of the United States, John Hamlin has noted that:

> The resurgence or perpetration of the myth that women are liars and the willingness of the public to accept the idea that women lie wherein rape is concerned, is partially shaped by press coverage. (Hamlin, 1988, p. 224)

As depictions of rapists as two-headed beasts come to be replaced with more benign images of 'ordinary' men, and increasing attention is given to rapes perpetrated by husbands, acquaintances and professional men, it is scarcely surprising that vigorous campaigns of resistance will be mounted to, yet again, undermine women's accusations concerning men's violence. Within this climate, a new breed of rape 'victim' has been championed: the falsely accused man. In a recent book, Greg Newbold claimed to have evidence of a

> ...mounting number of cases where women or girls, out of malice, jealousy or simple caprice, have falsely accused men of sexually violating them. (Newbold, 2000, p. 137)

Subsequent analysis of the 'evidence' on which this assertion was supposedly based has exposed the falseness of the claims, yet the author remains an oft-quoted media 'expert' (Buckingham, 2004).

Enns (1996) has argued that cycles of awareness and denial of abuse have occurred throughout the twentieth century. One such cycle was evident when Freud first articulated his views concerning the prevalence of child sexual abuse. In treating women patients who presented with symptoms of hysteria, Freud was both surprised and appalled as they repeatedly disclosed accounts of sexual abuse. Although relatively trivial incidents often appeared to trigger such symptoms in his patients, investigations typically revealed major episodes of trauma in their childhoods (Herman, 1992). Freud presented, with great professional pride, his paper on *The Aetiology of Hysteria* in 1896, confident that his work represented a major breakthrough (ibid.). His assertions were rejected so vigorously by his contemporaries that, to save face and retain professional acceptance, he felt compelled to backtrack. Since he could not deny that women patients were disclosing high levels of childhood sexual abuse, Freud sought an alternative explanation and proposed that such abuse was the invention of fantasising or delusional women. His repudiation of his theory came swiftly, and has been attributed also to the profound social unease he felt as the daughters of men from a range of backgrounds, including those from Vienna's most respectable bourgeois families, revealed that they had suffered familial sexual abuse (ibid.). Ultimately, the climate of denial at the time was so strong that it silenced women's disclosures of sexual abuse. It was to take another century of social and political change before the voices of women and children would begin to be heard.

Like Enns, Herman (1992) has maintained that issues of domestic and sexual violence were debated only when political movements became strong enough to challenge society's denial of abuse, with such attention waning when more conservative trends assumed power. Denying the existence, extent and effects of sexual violence is an established social phenomenon (Taslitz, 1999). As one writer commented:

> The instinctive reaction to terrible news, by either an individual or a society, is denial and dissociation, framed in the terms of everyday realism and common sense – it cannot be true, it is too implausible....

Societies dissociate their knowledge of trauma – massive injustice, torture, genocide – preferring to live in the 'bleached present' of conventional disbelief and logical denial. (Wylie, 1993, quoted in Enns, 1996, p. 361)

Whether societal denial and dissociation mirrors individual victims' denial and dissociation, or vice versa, is a moot point; what is clear is that, just as those victimised by rape may minimise their experience (Kelly, 1988, 1996), so do many in society minimise the prevalence of, and harm caused by, sexual violence.

This book presents the results from a series of academic studies specifically oriented towards evaluating the credibility conundrum. Consideration of international research reveals strong similarities in women's experiences of rape and responses to it by the criminal justice system. Women who have been raped struggle to have their voices heard and their words believed in countries as diverse as Norway and Nigeria, Nicaragua and New Zealand. In a world forced increasingly to recognise both the commonalities and diversities of human experience, this is a study with global significance.

The studies

Internationally, there has been comparatively little research conducted on complainants' experiences of reporting rape to the police since the significant reforms to law and procedures which took place in many jurisdictions during the 1980s. New Zealand was one of the first countries to attempt major reforms of its rape laws and, amongst other developments, introduced an expanded, gender-neutral definition of 'rape' in 1986, as well as abolishing married men's 'right' to spousal immunity from prosecution for rape (Sullivan, 1986). Whilst some important, recent studies have been undertaken in England (Gregory and Lees, 1999; Kelly, 2002; Temkin, 1997, 1999); Canada (Walby and Myhill, 2001); the United States (Tjaden and Thoennes, 1998, 2000) and Australia (Easteal, 1998a; New South Wales Department for Women, 1996), this book is based on developments in New Zealand in the years following the first documented study of rape and the criminal justice system in this country (Young, 1983).

New Zealand, as a nation with a recent history of colonisation, is essentially governed by laws and courts of justice imported from Britain in the nineteenth century. This provides a suitable basis for comparisons between it and other countries with criminal justice systems derived from British law, such as Australia and Canada. Additionally, New Zealand's pattern of colonial development resulted in the establishment of a single, centralised, national police force, thereby providing a relatively uniform context for data collection and analysis.

In order to analyse police responses to female complainants of rape and sexual assault, this book presents a series of related studies on rape. The specific aims of this research were as follows:

- To identify and examine the factors which inform police decision-making in relation to female rape complainants;
- To understand why police officers express doubts as to the authenticity of women who make rape complaints;
- To gain an understanding, from the complainant's perspective, of police practices, and the attitudes necessary to establish positive police–complainant relationships.

The first study documented here, in Chapter 3, involved the interviewing and analysis of 48 women's experiences of reporting rape and sexual assault to the police. One significant finding emerging from this study was the centrality of issues of belief and credibility as they related to police perceptions of rape victims. The identification of this issue informed the decision to embark on three subsequent studies: the first of these involved an analysis of police files to determine the factors affecting investigative decision-making (Chapter 4); the second involved interviews with experienced detectives to elicit their views on rape investigations and aspects of victims' credibility (Chapter 5); and the third involved interviews with a group of women deemed highly credible – the victims of a serial rapist – in order to ascertain the extent to which 'perfect' victims receive 'perfect' policing, and what might be learned from their experiences (Chapter 6).

Methodological considerations

Research is clearly undertaken by researchers, each of whom bring their own subjectivities to the research task. As Liz Stanley and Sue Wise pointed out so cogently, research emerges from, and in turn is experienced by, the researcher and is not simply the outcome of detached, 'objective' practices (Stanley and Wise, 1993). As a criminologist with a background in sociology, I consider it essential to contextualise individual acts within their social structural location. This 'location' is, for me, not a fixed, static entity but a fluid concept that evolves and mutates through time. Any understanding of contemporary dynamics must acknowledge the legacy of the past, ever present even if slightly obscured or more nuanced. As a feminist, I am particularly aware of the critical impact of gender and of the significance of living in a society marked by gender differences and inequalities. And as a woman who is passionate about social justice, I am motivated to probe beneath surface realities to ascertain the truths and to strive for fairness and equity. It is from such standpoints and perspectives that these studies were conducted, and this book emerges.

Interviewing dynamics

Much of the data gathered for this book was obtained through in-depth interviews with either police detectives or women who had been raped or sexually assaulted. These interviews were all based on semi-structured schedules, using predominantly open-ended questions. Such an approach was favoured for its flexibility and responsiveness and for the ways it encourages those being interviewed to tell their realities in their own words (Reinharz, 1992). Kenneth Tunnell has observed, in relation to interviewing criminal offenders,

> A sociological verstehen [understanding] of crime means accepting the subjective viewpoint and understanding actors' states of mind while rejecting the notion that science can deliver a complete or ontological reality. It also implicitly means that empirical knowledge is subjective and typically reflects (among other things) investigators' interests, values and biases. (Tunnell, 1998, pp. 214–15)

The theoretical foundations and methodological infrastructure of this book inevitably reflect my biases and subjective impressions as well as those of all the many participants in the research process. These must be acknowledged, rather than hidden behind a façade of 'scientific objectivity' that can never be sustainable in the value-laden world of social research. To quote Tunnell again,

> Sociology, happily, is not value free, but is filtered through human qualities and emotions and, as a result, is both limited and liberated by the human state. (Tunnell, 1998, p. 217)

Acknowledging my own background was, therefore, central to the process of negotiating and establishing rapport with the interview participants. Early feminist researchers often commented about how easy it was for women to interview women (Bell and Roberts, 1984; Finch, 1984; Oakley, 1981). Subsequent writers have qualified this to some extent, noting that gender-identification alone may not be sufficient to overcome the structural divisions of race and class (Edwards, 1993; Horn, 1995). In my case, it seemed to be very easy to establish a good rapport with the women I interviewed, and this may have been aided by, in most cases, our sharing not only a common gender but also common ethnicity and similar class positions. However, rapport also seemed to be just as easy to gain with those women from a different ethnic or class background. What appeared to be more important was the women's sense of where I was coming from, what my credentials were and why I was doing what I was doing. One, for example, asked to see a copy of other research I had published on rape and, during some of the interviews, it seemed appropriate at times for me to acknowledge that I, too, knew some of the realities of sexual victimisation. From what some of these women said, it seemed that in telling their 'stories' I was doing what many of them had hoped would happen, so we shared a common goal. Many made comments suggesting the interview to be the first occasion where they felt they were given the space to present their own version of events and to stress what was important to them, as supposed to satisfying police requirements or reassuring family members. This is consistent with observations made elsewhere suggesting survivors' experiences of telling and retelling their stories may be empowering and transformative (Culbertson, 1995; Ford and Crabtree, 2002). Ultimately, the fact, which I believe the women could sense, that I respected them and was committed to representing them accurately meant that I was privileged to have them share with me what were often very personal, and sometimes still emotionally raw, experiences.

The interviews that I conducted with the police officers could have been quite different. To begin with, most were male and I was not, and they were 'police' and I was not. What may also have counted against me was my status as an academic, since the latter rarely rank highly in the eyes of many police. However, as both Edwards (1993) and Horn (1995) have said, it is possible to acknowledge structural differences and turn them into advantages. Thus I tried to ensure that I approached these interviews in a way that communicated my position as someone who knew very little about the world of policing and was dependent on them clarifying my understanding. This was not hard to do, since at times my ignorance was palpably obvious! What was particularly important was the need to convey respect for the officers concerned and, on those occasions where I felt such respect waning, to consciously try to place myself in the shoes of that particular detective and try to understand the world from his or her vantage point. I believe this helped immensely both in maintaining rapport and advancing my understanding and awareness.

Conducting research with both rape complainants and detectives impressed upon me the existence of diverse 'truths' and social realities. My experiences reaffirmed that there is no one, single, absolute Truth 'out there' waiting for the intrepid social scientist to discover it (Stanley and Wise, 1993, p. 113). Instead, competing and contradictory accounts were encountered and had to be negotiated, as the realisation grew that 'lies' were sometimes told in a bid to have the truth believed, and apparent 'truths' were maintained in ways that led to false conclusions being reached.

Ethical issues

Any research involving people has ethical implications, and research involving persons who are traumatised and potentially vulnerable carries with it particular ethical responsibilities. Even the initial decision as to whether or not it is justifiable to interview women who have been raped is a difficult one to make. Of major concern is the potential for the research process to impact detrimentally on participants, and the fear that it may itself become a victimising experience. Involvement with an earlier study (Jordan, 1998a) had sensitised me to the paramount importance of these issues, and also persuaded me that sensitive, ethical, constructive research was possible in this area. It is also essential, and desirable, as a means of ensuring that the voices of rape complainants themselves could be heard. For this to be achieved, however, it was important that certain safeguards were adhered to, along with a commitment to placing the women's welfare first and my research results second. In the case of the women interviewed who had been attacked by the same serial rapist, the initial impetus came from some of the women themselves and there was a process of consultation between them and myself prior to any agreement that a study would be undertaken. Considerable effort was also taken by me, as the researcher, to minimise the risk of retraumatisation in interviewing the women. The procedures adopted are outlined further in Chapter 6 of this book.

Deciding whose voice to privilege

Interview subjects are not all positioned equally, and that is especially true when the research involves gathering material from different sets of respondents. In this case, the police occupy a position of authority in a system which redefines victims as witnesses, making it additionally important for a researcher to be aware of potential power imbalances. It is against this backdrop that the question arises of whose account to privilege or situate in the most influential position. This is not necessarily the same as inferring one particular position to be more truthful than another, because the 'truth' of any particular context may be somewhat different for the parties involved. As will be seen in the research results, the narratives of rape adhered to by the police may be ostensibly about the same incident as that reported by the victim, yet appear quite different in emphasis and interpretation. Subjective experiences differ, and the issue for the researcher becomes one of whose subjective experience to position more centrally. In the research presented here, it is the voices of the victims which are privileged by using accounts from raped women themselves to both begin and end this book. The data obtained from the police are, in effect, sandwiched between the studies conducted with the women themselves, whose perceptions of how they were treated lie at the heart of this endeavour.

'Victims' and 'survivors'

Considerable debate has surrounded the use of the terms 'victim' or 'survivor' in relation to women who have experienced sexual violence. The term 'victim' was criticised, often rightly so, for reinforcing a sense of women's passivity and consolidating her victim-status. The preference for 'survivor' was equated with recognition of women's active resistance and sense of agency (Kelly, 1988; Stanko, 1985). More recently, however, the 'victim' or 'survivor' debate itself has appeared to be in danger of reinforcing a binary opposition which negates the complex realities of women's experience (Naples, 2003). An unintended consequence resulting from over emphasis of the survival aspects can be a silencing of the victim's voice, and a minimising by some women of the effects of sexual violence. Women whom I interviewed often expressed divided views on this issue, with some explicitly rejecting being told, as they saw it, that they 'had to call themselves survivors'. In this book, therefore, I use both terms at different times, consciously choosing the term 'victim' either when acknowledging that a person has been criminally offended against, or when it is important to ensure adequate recognition of the effects of men's violence and victimisation on women as well as women's capacity for survival.

Outline of chapters

The subject of rape traverses a series of contested and highly disputed terrains. Sex, power, privilege, law and religion are all evident in discussions of rape through the ages, which makes charting a course through the literature a complex and potentially hazardous task. What is included in Chapter 2 represents my attempt to consider the ways in which themes evident in the literature on rape and on the nature of women combine to influence responses to women who make complaints of rape.

Chapter 3 outlines criminal justice system responses to rape, focussing in particular on women's experiences of reporting incidents of rape and sexual assault to the police. Data obtained from extensive interviews with New Zealand women who had been raped are included, and illustrate the importance to the women of feeling they were believed by the police.

An analysis of police rape investigation files is presented in Chapter 4 and serves to identify the key factors affecting police decision-making processes in relation to rape complaints. Emphasis is placed on understanding how evidence in sexual assault cases appears to have been evaluated and why the investigation of cases was so often terminated.

Chapter 5 documents the findings that emerged from interviews with detectives concerning their experiences in sexual assault investigations in New Zealand. This study sought to identify commonalities and differences in detectives' perceptions, and advance understanding of the ways in which police officers view and assess the credibility of rape complainants.

In Chapter 6, the focus shifts to a consideration of the experiences of one group of rape victims in particular and their interactions with the police. Their status as the victims of a serial rapist meant that few of these women encountered disbelieving attitudes or negativity from the police. Moreover, their importance to the success of the investigation was recognised and conscious efforts were made by the police to treat them with consideration and respect. For these reasons, they provide a good opportunity for gaining further insights into factors affecting the quality of police–complainant relationships.

The implications of the findings from the various studies presented are explored in Chapter 7. The themes emerging are discussed, and the implications of this research, for the police in particular, are outlined.

The book ends with the proposition that adherence to particular myths and 'lies' about women will frequently continue to mask the 'truth' behind any one case being recognised and justice delivered. What indeed does it take for the word of a woman to be believed?

2

'She stings while she delights': Rape Definitions and Representations

> We're trapped inside a legacy, and its core is patriarchal.
>
> (Johnson, 1997, p. 4)
>
> From seduction to rape, from rape to seduction, an easy and endless patriarchal loop.
>
> (Taslitz, 1999, p. 57)

Introduction

To understand current manifestations of the credibility conundrum necessitates awareness of the broader social and historical context surrounding women's experiences of rape. The material presented in this chapter derives from an examination of both historical and contemporary literature on rape, as well as providing a brief review of changing representations of the nature of women. Issues pertinent to definitions of rape are presented first, in order to provide an overview of the principal subject matter at the heart of this book. However, the ways in which rape has been defined in law have reflected dominant ideological discourses, a key strand of which involves underlying assumptions and beliefs concerning the nature of women. Accordingly, the second section of this chapter explores these representations of women, with particular emphasis on perceptions of women's veracity, since this impacts significantly on responses to women as rape complainants.

Rape: nature, definitions and history

What is rape?

Defining rape is a difficult task (Bourque, 1989; Box, 1983; Katz and Mazur, 1979; Kelly, 1988; Los, 1994). While simple definitions can be advanced, such as rape is sex forced on a woman without her consent, these attempts to define rape ignore the fraught minefields that surround the categories 'sex', 'force', 'woman' and 'consent'. Take the concept of 'sex', for example.

If sex is equated with acts of intercourse involving penetration by a male's penis of a woman's vagina, then this effectively limits the accepted understanding of what is sexual to practices reflective of masculinist and heterosexist assumptions. In other words, the view of sex which prevails is one formulated by men to describe sex with women, as viewed from their subjective standpoint. Moreover, if definitions of rape are predicated on such assumptions, only those offences are acknowledged which involve the penetration of a woman's vagina by a man's penis, with the added ingredient of 'force', on his part, and/or 'lack of consent', on hers. Many women's experiences of sexual victimisation are excluded by this approach, and even those who are included may find such definitions used to minimise the trauma of their experience. In writing about the 'legitimate victim', Weis and Borges noted:

> The widely held conception that rape is primarily a sexual act easily leads to the argument that for sexually experienced women, one more act should not matter. If, however, rape is understood as humiliation, violation of self-determination and an intimate attack on the woman's personhood, then the extent of her previous sexual experience should bear little impact on the treatment she deserves as an authentic rape victim. (Weis and Borges, 1975, pp. 122–3)

Much feminist debate has railed over the issue of whether or not rape is a sexual act (Bell, 1991; Brownmiller, 1975; Cahill, 2001; Donat and D'Emilio, 1992; Griffin, 1975; Howe, 1998; Los, 1994; Muehlenhard *et al.*, 1992) and over the extent to which an emphasis on the sexual aspect conceals the power and coercion aspects involved and obscures acknowledgement of rape as an act of violence (Howe, 1998; Kelly, 1988). To remove or obscure the power dimensions reduces rape to an act of clumsy seduction or presents it as resulting from poor communication on the part of a lust-driven male, thereby privileging the voices of self-justifying men over their victims. Feminists' acknowlededgment of the relationship between 'sex' and 'power', however, can also differ in emphasis and interpretation. While some have stressed men's use of their power to achieve sexual satisfaction (e.g., Barry, 1979), others have shown how sex is used to establish or maintain power (e.g., Kelly, 1988). To complicate things further, feminists themselves have adopted contradictory standpoints on this issue. While some, such as Brownmiller (1975) have urged that rape be recognized as an act of violence, others, such as MacKinnon (1989), have argued that it can best be understood as an extension of compulsory heterosexuality, barely distinguishable from 'normal' sexual intercourse. Jocelynne Scutt expressed it this way:

> Far from rape *not* being 'about sex' as some are wont to argue, rape is directly relevant to 'sex'. Certainly for the victim, it is nothing to do with

loving, caring, consideration which *we* see as *consensual* 'sex'. But it is 'about sex': the 'sex act' is intimately linked with power and violence in the act of a rapist....Rape is a manifestation of power, aggression, violence and brutality specifically directed *through* sex. It is not 'not sex'. (Scutt, 1993, p. 182) [Emphasis in original]

What seems particularly important is preserving a sense of the structural interconnectedness of sex and violence within heterosexual relationships in a patriarchal society, in a way which acknowledges the diverse forms and manifestations such violence may take. Within this, recognition must be given to women's own processes of perceiving, defining and responding to sexual violence. This approach will inevitably expand and complicate traditional legal definitions, stressing as it must the diverse and even contradictory ways in which sexual violence is experienced and understood.

This raises the critical question of deciding whose voice to privilege, whose perspective to speak from. Rape as defined by the victim will be a very different phenomenon from rape as defined by the perpetrator. Rape as defined by the victim may also differ markedly from its definition in law or, for that matter, in much of criminology or even feminist theory. Moreover, those who have been raped may define rape very differently from those who have not; and even this is not straightforward. For many victims of rape themselves, the definition of rape is a vexed issue, particularly in relation to naming their own experience as rape (Basile, 1999; Gavey, 1999; Kelly, 1988; Myhill and Allen, 2002; Patton and Mannison, 1998; Wood and Rennie, 1994). Rape itself is an emotive word, and has traditionally borne its own cloak of stigma. Many sexual assault victims struggle to make the decision to report the offence; the majority never do (Bachman, 1993; Burt and Katz, 1985; Du Mont *et al.*, 2003; Epstein and Langenbahn, 1994; Freckelton, 1998; Koss *et al.*, 1987; LeDoux and Hazelwood, 1999; Myhill and Allen, 2002; Russell, 1984). The reluctance to define oneself as a rape victim can be linked to various concerns, including fear of being blamed or ostracised, fear of the perpetrator and/or consequences, mixed emotions towards the perpetrator (who is typically already known by the victim and may be her boyfriend or partner), and a general reluctance to admit to being sexually violated (Holmstrom and Burgess, 1991; Kelly, 1988; Wood and Rennie, 1994). What is fundamentally difficult for all sexual assault victims is acquiring and maintaining a sense of their own legitimacy within a context defined by, and reflective of, men's definitions and perspectives.

In recent years, there has been extensive challenging by feminists of the traditional definitions of rape for being so narrowly restricted to one particular sexual act and of the law generally for being biased in favour of men (Cahill, 2001; Donat and D'Emilio, 1992; Kelly, 1988; Mason, 1995; Taslitz, 1999). To define rape in law as penetration by the penis of the vagina, without consent, excludes the possibilities of men being victims or women the perpetrators of sexual assault, and prevents recognition of other sexual acts which may be experienced as equally violating. The argument has been advanced that the traditional definition derives from heterosexual men's obsession with, in effect, one object and one opening (Howe, 1998; Walklate 1995).

Any woman who has had a bottle or hairbrush rammed up her, or had a penis forced down her throat to the point where she wanted to gag, or had objects thrust up her anus, knows only too well that sexual violation comes in many forms. The force accompanying sexual violation may also be more subtle than these examples would indicate. The presence of weapons or threats may be used to secure victims' compliance; or compliance might be obtained by the implicit threat of withdrawal of funds, or by promises of protection or favours. While gender inequality continues at a social level, women will remain vulnerable to sexual and physical violence in their relationships with men.

The dichotomous thinking of the law bears little resemblance to the continuum of experiences described by women as sexual assault. Formal laws reflect the polarised thinking characteristic of the Western philosophical tradition: black and white, either/or, binary opposites, a choice of one or the other, not a mixture, not 'both/and' but 'this or that'.

> In particular, legal discourse tends to assume that there is a fine line between consensual and non-consensual sexual intercourse: that is, behaviour which might look like rape can become consensual in the blink of an eye .... [The] line drawn between rape and legitimate sexual behaviour has been drawn in a location which erases the experiences of the majority of victims of sexual assault. (Young, 1998, pp. 145–7)

When women speak in their own voices, they detail a much broader range of sexual experiences that feel coercive, and bring with them the violation and traumatising effects of coerced sex, than those legally defined as rape/attempted rape (Kelly, 1988; Young, 1998). Even within the law itself, the difference between sexual violation and indecent assault, for example, is often blurred, with some of the incidents classified as indecent assault being described in very similar ways to others classified as attempted rape or sexual violation (Gregory and Lees, 1999; Walklate, 1995; see also examples in Chapter 4 of this book).

Accordingly, many feminists argue that legal definitions do not resonate with women's experiences (Kelly, 1988; Scutt, 1998; Smart, 1989; Young, 1998). If we accept the high incidence and prevalence figures, we can see that rape is not a rare, aberrant act, but is what Walklate terms an 'ordinary' experience, and one that is far more common than generally supposed.

> Rape is the ordinary product of ordinary (male, heterosexual) behaviour. That helps explain the emotiveness of the issue. It touches upon all our

experiences both male and female. It is its ordinariness which renders it so difficult to grasp and embrace. It challenges us all to examine ourselves and our relationships very carefully. In so doing, it can make us all uncomfortable. And so it should. (Walklate, 1995, p. 85)

This point has been further reinforced in a recent survey of college women in the United States, the results of which led the author to conclude:

> ...the finding that most women had been sexually victimized in some manner by age 20 combined with the finding that the most common perpetrators of rape were boyfriends and male friends points to a need to consider whether sexual aggression may in fact be a *normative* aspect of male–female relationships in our society. (Stepakoff, 1998, p. 122) [Emphasis in original]

It is, therefore, apparent that legal definitions of rape do not necessarily reflect women's experiences of sexual assault and violation. The law assumes a clear dividing line between rape and not-rape, a distinction which primarily only some male judges and lawyers seem able to uphold. For most victims of sexual assault, the black and white categories of the law fade into multiple shades of grey. The legal definitions seldom come close to what women experience, and how women feel. Thus, as Liz Kelly has so clearly set out, women's experiences are depicted much more easily along a continuum of sexual violence than they are encapsulated within the law's unyielding categories (Kelly, 1988). As she expresses it:

> The male definitions of sexual violence which are encoded in laws and which underlie the stereotypes are limited and draw on the extremes of the continuum of sexual violence. (Kelly, 1988, p. 157)

Criticism of narrow legal definitions of rape has led to many jurisdictions introducing legal reforms in this area.[1] In New Zealand, the most significant changes occurred in 1986, when legislative amendments were introduced which, amongst other changes, expanded the definition of sexual assault to make rape, as traditionally defined, one category of a new offence of 'sexual violation' (Sullivan, 1986). These changes acknowledged that the penis was not the only weapon of sexual assault, nor the vagina the only orifice able to be invaded. Hence, sexual violation offences were redefined to include forced anal and oral sex (using any object able to be used for that purpose), and the concept of 'rape victim' was expanded to apply to both male and female victims of sexual assault. One other major change introduced at this time involved the abolition of spousal immunity. Previously, rape charges could not be laid by a wife against her husband; as discussed further in this chapter, there was legally no such act as rape in marriage. The abolition of spousal immunity removed the husband's prerogative, making it legally possible, at least, for men to be charged for acts of sexual violence perpetrated against their wives. Within this book, the terms 'rape' and 'sexual violation' are used synonymously, reflecting legal acknowledgement of the expanded concept of rape.

Measurement of rape

The measurement of rape has been a vexed issue, partly because of definitional debates, and also because of the profound methodological difficulties associated with the quest for reliable data in this area. One major difficulty associated with the measurement of rape arises from the fact that not all studies define rape in the same way (Kelly, 1988; Walklate, 1995). Some researchers use definitions which equate with legal definitions in order to facilitate comparisons with police statistics (e.g., Russell, 1990; Warshaw, 1988); others allow respondents to define their own experience (e.g., Hall, 1985; Kelly, 1988).

Official crime statistics have long been recognised as notoriously unreliable indicators of the incidence of rape. Most rape victims do not report (Bureau of Justice Statistics, 1991; Feldman-Summers and Norris, 1984; Kelly, 1988, 2002; Kilpatrick *et al.*, 1987; Koss *et al.*, 1988; Myhill and Allen, 2002; Williams, 1984), or minimise the severity of the incident (Kelly, 1988; Kelly and Radford, 1996; Wood and Rennie, 1994). Results from one U.S. study, for example, showed that between 5 and 8 per cent of adult cases of sexual assault were reported to the police, compared with 61.5 per cent of robberies and 82.5 per cent of burglaries (Kilpatrick *et al.*, 1987). Even if reporting rates were higher, police in different jurisdictions often have different recording practices, even between districts within nations, let alone on an international basis. One approach taken by researchers is to estimate the *incidence* of rape, that is, the total number of incidents occurring in a specified time period or, expressed slightly differently, the number of new episodes of an event occurring during a specific time period. For example, the 2000 British Crime Survey offers an incidence estimate of 61 000 sexual offences against women for the 12 months preceding survey participation, of which 18 per cent were reported (Myhill and Allen, 2002).

An alternative measurement strategy has involved estimating *prevalence* rates, that is, the number of individuals who experience victimisation within a specified time frame. Examples of these include Hall's prevalence study (1985), which reported that one in six women had experienced rape, and one in three sexual assault, in their lifetime, and also studies by Russell (1990) and Painter (1991), who both reported a prevalence rate of one in seven for women who had experienced rape in marriage. A recent international review of more than 500 studies concluded that 'at least one in three women all over the world has been beaten, forced into sex or abused in her lifetime' (United Nations Population Fund, 2000).

It was hoped that many of the measurement difficulties associated with the traditional reliance on official statistics would be circumvented by victimisation surveys, but they also have questionable validity. For many years, for instance, the British Crime Surveys yielded exceptionally low rates of sexual abuse and violence, a finding acknowledged to emanate from the methodology of the survey rather than from low rates of sexual assault per se (Gregory and Lees, 1999; Maguire, 1994; Myhill and Allen, 2002; Stanko, 1988).

The practice of including a few questions on rape and family violence in the middle of a general crime survey came to be criticised, especially when it was possible that interviewers were asking such questions while other family members, and possibly perpetrators, were also present (Gregory and Lees, 1999; Stanko, 1988). Statistics Canada used telephone interviews when conducting a national survey, based on a random sample of 12 300 women, on violence against women (Walby and Myhill, 2001). This study included the finding that over one in three women had experienced a sexual assault in their lifetime, most of which (81 per cent) were perpetrated by known men, and of which only 6 per cent were reported to the police (ibid.). The New Zealand Survey of Crime Victims 2001 attempted to address the disclosure issue by using computer-assisted self-interviewing to obtain information on sexual victimisation. The results showed significant differences in men's and women's experiences of sexual interference or assault over their lifetime, with 5 per cent of men reporting this compared with one in five women (Morris and Reilly, 2003).

Some researchers designed specific sexual victimisation surveys, worded carefully and administered in potentially safer and less compromising environments than many of the generic victimisation surveys. Probably the best known of these, in relation to rape and sexual assault, has been the Sexual Experiences Survey (Koss *et al.*, 1987). The questions were worded in 'neutral' language that asked women to describe different sexual experiences, which were then assessed by the researchers to determine whether these incidents, as described, met legal definitions of rape, attempted rape, and so forth. The survey was conducted on college campuses in the United States of America. The results showed that over one-quarter of the respondents (27 per cent) recalled an incident that had occurred since their fourteenth birthday and that met the legal definition of rape, or attempted rape. Eighty per cent of these incidents involved someone whom the victim already knew, with 57 per cent involving someone they were dating at the time.

The Sexual Experiences Survey was replicated with a smaller sample of university undergraduate students in Auckland, New Zealand, and yielded strikingly similar findings (Gavey, 1991). The results showed that 25 per cent of the participants had been raped or had experienced attempted rape, with perpetrators known by the victim accounting for 83 per cent of the sexually abusive incidents reported overall by participants.

One could argue that it may be misleading to extrapolate the findings of these surveys to the general population, given that these figures are drawn from small, population-specific studies and could be overestimates; alternatively, the likely higher than average education and socio-economic levels of the participants may result in higher than average rates of defining and disclosing rape, with estimates based on such samples tending to underestimate overall prevalence.

Whilst victimisation surveys, if administered sensitively, can provide potentially more reliable estimates of prevalence rates, it is likely that they will still underestimate the extent of sexual victimisation. The reluctance of many women to define and name what they experienced as violence, minimise its severity, or simply 'forget' and try to erase it from their memory, means that, as Kelly has noted, 'all estimates of prevalence are likely to be underestimates' (Kelly, 1988, p. 158). This is especially so in relation to sexual violations perpetrated by men who are known by the victim who, as the research cited above shows, make up the majority of sexual assault victims.

Consideration of how rape is defined and measured raises issues regarding who decides what is recognised and counted as rape, and on the basis of what assumptions. This necessitates examination of the historical and socio-cultural contexts which gave rise to legal definitions and criminal justice system practices.

The history of rape

When we consider the changing legal responses to rape over the centuries, we see before us a microcosm of gender relations in the social world.

The oldest written laws making rape a crime date back to the early part of the seventeenth century before Christ, contained within the Code of Hammurabi (Smith, 1974). As Smith says:

> Rape is no doubt as old as the human race. We know it to be as old as our brief six millennia of recorded history, also that it is embodied in the legends of the pre-record era. (Smith, 1974, p. 188)

Deuteronomy, Chapter XXII, spells out early Hebrew penalties for rape: If a man forced a betrothed damsel 'in the field', the penalty would be death to him and no punishment would be given to her (the assumption being that, if she was in a remote place, her cries for help would be in vain). If, however, a man in the city lay with a woman, who was betrothed and a virgin, and she failed to cry out, then the penalty was death to them both (Smith, 1974). Moses was, in effect, the lawgiver, the judge and the jury; through him the invisible god Yahweh spoke. This one-god was wholly masculine, meaning that no longer would the goddesses who embodied feminine essences of love, passion and fertility be worshipped (Smith, 1974). This appropriation of power by men heralded a vast change in attitudes persisting to today; as men's 'rights' prevailed, so the status of women fell. When God became male, the man became god.

The early rape laws were passed to protect virginity, with greater concern apparent for the man whose daughter/property may be sullied by rape than for her as a person in her own right. In many ways, this is understandable given that women were not viewed as autonomous social beings (Brownmiller, 1975; Clark and Lewis, 1977). As the property of men, women were items of exchange, commodities whose social value lay in their reputation and reproductive abilities. From women, the sons and heirs of men were born. In a patriarchal, patrilineal society, men sought to ensure the legitimacy of their offspring and the continuance of their bloodline. Against this backdrop, the crime involved in the rape of a woman derives from one man defiling the property of another man; the victim of rape is accordingly seen, not as the woman who has been violated, but as the man to whom she 'belongs' (Brownmiller, 1975).

The history of rape and the history of marriage are inextricably entwined. The earliest references to rape depict a social process by which men were condoned in their taking of a woman by force in the context of acquiring a spouse. Bride capture literally meant the capture and forcible rape of a woman whom the man desired to possess as his wife (Brownmiller, 1975). An episode from the early history of ancient Rome illustrates this well. According to legend, Roman men decided to hold a festival to which they would invite the neighbouring Sabines; at an arranged signal from Romulus, the men all seized a woman violently to take as their wives. This event inspired many artists to depict its scale in canvas, the most famous being Nicholas Poussin whose Rape of the Sabines (painted in Italy in the 1630s) portrays an epic, heroic scene in ways that simultaneously glorify and sanitise mass rape (Wolfthal, 1999).

To take possession of a woman's sexuality meant that a man had control of her for life. As Brownmiller comments:

> Forcible seizure was a perfectly acceptable way – to men – of acquiring women, and it existed in England as late as the fifteenth century. (Brownmiller, 1975, p. 17)

Although such a practice has long been rejected for its violent origins, its legacy has lived on for centuries in marriage ceremonies and legal codes. In New Zealand, a woman was prohibited from making a claim of rape against her husband until 1986, precisely because the husband was viewed in law as the sexual master of his wife. When she said 'I do' in the wedding ceremony, and promised to 'love, honour and obey', she was effectively consenting to sex on demand – his demand – for the rest of her life. There was no right of refusal, no choice for her – the choice was all his. Her 'no' had no meaning in the context of a relationship where, legally, it was only his 'yes' that counted. To try and avoid sex, women often resorted to appeals to what they hoped was his better nature, his non-sexual nature.

Wives, historically, have long been regarded as the property of their husbands; in New Zealand, for example, it was not until 1868 that wives were legally allowed to own property in their own right (Sutch, 1973). Moreover, the presumption of coverture stipulated in effect that, if a woman committed a criminal offence in the presence of her husband, he (not she) was to be held criminally liable for that act, since she was not an autonomous legal actor (Sutch, 1973). Lacking legal autonomy was consistent with married women's lack of sexual autonomy – raping one's wife was not rape, it was a husband's right within the law.

At the heart of such an edict lay the conviction that it was a woman's wifely duty to obey and be submissive to her husband. This extended to her speech – in early England a wife who scolded her husband committed a common-law offence, for which she could be tried in court by a jury, a practice persisting to the mid-eighteenth century (Faith, 1993).

> The woman who criticized her husband, who bossed him, who insulted him, or who in any way showed her rejection of his authority, was a shrew, or a scold, subject to public humiliation. She could be locked into the pillory, or run through town while being lashed. She could also be chained and whipped in a public square, demonstrating to other women the penalty for betrayal of the gendered role. She could be made to wear the 'brank' (or 'scold's bridle'), a metal apparatus which fit over the head and into the mouth, with sharp points that cut into the woman's tongue if she attempted to speak. (Faith, 1993, pp. 29–30)

A wife's words could be silenced, her speech be cut from her mouth. Even a woman's tongue was not her own.

The notion of the wife being the property of the husband clearly underpins the spousal exemption from rape laws which, in effect, licensed husbands to rape. This notion is said to date at least from the days of William the Conqueror when legal rules allowed victims of rape to 'forgive' the man by consenting to marry him (Easteal, 1998b; Snelling, 1975). Such thinking was still evident in the eighteenth century in Lord Matthew Hale's famous pronouncement:

> The husband cannot be guilty of a rape committed by himself upon his lawful wife, for by their mutual matrimonial consent and contract, the wife hath given up herself in this kind unto her husband which she cannot retract. (Hale, 1736, quoted in Easteal, 1998b, p. 108)

Hale came to be recognised as the most cited authority on rape in England, and his assertion prevailed in many international legal codes until recently.

Spousal immunity was abolished in New Zealand in 1986, in Australia in 1991 (Heath, 1998); in the United Kingdom in 1991 (Kennedy, 1992) and in the United States of America in 1993 (Bergen, 1996).[2] The rape of women in marriage, however, continues (Easteal, 1998b). As Susan Griffin observed:

> The laws against rape exist to protect the rights of the male as possessor of the female body, and not the right of the female over her own body. (Griffin, 1975, p. 33)

Rape laws may have changed; the reality of rape has not.

Changing perspectives on rape

Examination of published works on rape reveals a chronological develop-ment that parallels closely shifts in social movements and attitudes. During the 1950s and 1960s, most literature dealing with rape focussed on the rapist (Walklate, 1995). Men who raped were typically portrayed as either mentally or sexually disordered (Scully, 1990), and the notion of victim precipitation was also strongly apparent (Amir, 1967; Box, 1983; Katz and Mazur, 1979). Concern was voiced, not regarding women's vulnerability to being raped, but over men's vulnerability to unfounded charges of rape (e.g., Firth, 1975). Increasingly, men were presented as the victims of either their own or of women's disordered states. As Elizabeth Kemmer notes in her bibliography of rape:

> From approximately 1965 to 1968, rape literature focussed on the offender and the unjust system that convicted the falsely accused male of so heinous a crime. The sympathy of the public was with the offender, thus making the victim the guilty party in a rape situation. This attitude is reflected in statistics and literature concerning the incidence of rape, in rape reporting, and in rape convictions for the years mentioned. Rape was still a fairly silent, secret crime – a crime whose victims were the most silent of all. (Kemmer, 1977, p. xii)

The growth of the Women's Liberation Movement, from the late 1960s onwards, encouraged women to engage increasingly in critical reflection of their position in society and their relationships with men. As what Marilyn French called 'the slime under the rug of patriarchy' began to be exposed (French, 1992, p. 198), dominant myths about rape were questioned and debated (Burt, 1980; Kelly, 1988; Shapcott, 1988; Smart, 1976). The notion of victim precipitation was criticised for its victim-blaming implications (see e.g., Smart, 1976; Weis and Borges, 1975) and feminists' awareness of the issues associated with rape, child abuse and domestic violence grew through-out the 1970s and 1980s (Adler, 1987; Bourque, 1989; Herman, 1992; Kelly, 1988; Morris, 1987; Smart, 1989; Stanko, 1985). Critical social analysis was accompanied by political and legal strategies aimed at improving the status of women and reducing their vulnerability to such practices (Gregory and Lees, 1999; Smart, 1995; White and Perrone, 1997). Victims of rape were portrayed as deserving of sympathy; support and crisis centres were established in the 1970s; and campaigns were launched which aimed at achieving social and legislative reform (Kelly, 1988; Kemmer, 1977).

The perception of rape as a sexual act was challenged by early feminist writers such as Brownmiller (1975) and Griffin (1975), who argued that such an emphasis obscured the violent and aggressive dimensions of the assault (Walklate, 1995). Thus radical feminists (e.g., Barry, 1979; Dworkin, 1982) strove to have rape recognised as being different from simply unwanted sex; since traditionally no 'good' woman wanted sex, unwanted sex had been regarded as the norm and not something to complain about. Instead, rape was now increasingly defined in terms of violence and attention was focussed on issues of men's power and control.

Redefining rape as primarily an act of violence and control, however, can deny the sex-specific nature of the act. The act of raping a woman is both similar to, and different from, physically beating her. While most rapes are not accompanied by visible, physical injuries, the intrusion and violation of self is acutely felt and experienced. It is precisely because of what sex represents that the rapist chooses to exert control in this way. Thus later writers, such as Kelly (1988), MacKinnon (1989), and Smart (1989, 1995), tried to reinstate the sexual dimension to analyses of rape and sexual assault. Sexual violence is both sexual *and* violent, not simply one or the other. The question then becomes: why do men so frequently choose to be violent in sexual ways?

Greater awareness of the pervasiveness of sexual violence necessitated changed images and representations. Stereotypes of deranged stranger assailants began to be challenged, and from the mid-1980s onwards, increasing acknowledgement was given to date and acquaintance rape (Bohmer, 1991; Estrich, 1987; Warshaw, 1988). The 'ordinariness' of men who rape came to be stressed (Allison and Wrightsman, 1993; Kelly, 1988; Stanko, 1985), with the earlier psychopathological explanations being at least supplemented, if not replaced, by sociological and criminological accounts emphasising societal and structural variables (Smart, 1989).

During the 1990s, increasing emphasis began to be placed on the relationship between men, rape and masculine identity (Jefferson, 1997). Scully and Marolla (1993), in their studies of men convicted of stranger rape, identified a range of motivations underlying rape, from a stated desire to put women in their place, to viewing rape as impersonal sex with added risk and excitement. One man referred explicitly to the feelings of mastery and conquest he felt whilst raping a woman, likening it to the sense of supremacy felt after 'riding the bull at Gilleys'.[3] Scully and Marolla suggest that such statements reveal the cultural roots of rape to be linked to the masculine quest for control, as expressed through conquest and penetration. Other writers (e.g., Cameron and Frazer, 1987), have suggested that this search for control lies at the heart of masculinity, and can be linked to notions of 'male sexual propriety' and ownership, not only in relation to rape but evident also in domestic violence and in spousal homicide statistics (Polk, 1994; Stanko, 1985; Wilson and Daly, 1992). As Sandra Walklate says,

> Recasting rape in these terms helps an understanding of why it is difficult to see the 'ordinariness' of rape and sexual assault. Women say 'no'; men fail (or refuse) to hear it. There is little in the heart of the cultural expectations associated with masculinity to encourage them to hear it. This does not mean that they cannot. (Walklate, 1995, p. 84)

Writers such as MacKinnon (1987) asserted that sexual violence was an inevitable feature of heterosexual relationships in a patriarchal society, in an argument that effectively reduces all heterosexual sex to rape, irrespective of whether either of the parties involved defined or experienced it as such. More recently, concern has been raised in some quarters that such an emphasis is reductionist and that, in reducing all heterosexual sex to violence, this approach ignores the diversity of both men's and women's attitudes towards, and experiences of, sex (Cahill, 2001; Walklate, 1995).

Walklate (1995) maintains that the presumption that sexual violence is inextricably entwined in men's sexuality within heterosexual relationships removes the capacity for either women to be sexually violent or for men to be the victims of sexual violence. Nevertheless, early radical and lesbian feminists managed very effectively to shake the foundations of heterosexual supremacy by challenging the stereotypes and assumptions underlying dominant conceptions of men, women, sex and violence (Barry, 1979; Daly, 1979; Dworkin, 1982; Kelly, 1988). What also needs to be acknowledged, however, are the different ways in which gender mediates women's and men's experiences, such that the experiences of either abusing or being abused will differ for each, and warrant separate structural, as well as individual, analysis. While the critical gaze first fell upon social constructions of femininity, increasingly that gaze is being turned towards deconstructing masculinity (Baker, 1999; Carrington and Watson, 1996; Jefferson, 1997; Smart, 1995). Whereas the male was assumed to be the norm, and women were defined in relation to this male norm, no longer is this practice justifiable. The question inevitably arises: why should men be accorded the subject position, the active voice and the defining gaze? The power of such privileging cannot be denied. As John Berger so acutely observed:

> *Men act* and *women appear*. Men look at women. Women watch themselves being looked at. This determines not only most relations between

men and women but also the relation of women to themselves. The surveyor of woman in herself is male: the surveyed female. Thus she turns herself into an object – and most particularly an object of vision: a sight. (Berger, 1977, p. 42) [Emphasis in original]

A woman who has been raped comes under particular surveillance by men, whilst in turn seeing herself through a male lens. She is an object of shame, and accordingly prone to self-blame.

Understanding sexual violence within a patriarchal society involves understanding social constructions of heterosexuality and the ways in which these have privileged men's subjective realities. Cossins puts it this way:

Through the eyes of the sense common to men, a woman, as a constructed gendered subject, is considered to readily invent allegations of sexual assault, or say no when she means yes, conforming to a prevalent cultural belief that women should generally be sexually available to men ....

In fact, wherever there has been heterosexual intercourse, historically, it has been *assumed* to be consensual unless a complainant can prove otherwise. In light of this assumption, the spectre of the lying, immoral woman and the man falsely accused is a particularly potent cultural image that continues to undermine the administration of justice. (Cossins, 1998, p. 100) [Emphasis in original]

Similar analysis needs to be conducted in the area of sexual violence as Ken Polk undertook in relation to men, masculinity and murder (Polk, 1994). In his book, Polk sought to unravel the complex threads involved in ways which incorporated the dynamic nature of social and sexual relationships, rather than depicting these as fixed, static entities. Applied within the context of heterosexual relationships, it is clear that men's and women's understandings of sex and marriage at the beginning of the twenty-first century were qualitatively different from views held a century, or even half a century, earlier. At the same time, paradoxically, the structures of heterosexuality have essentially remained intact. So how has change occurred, and how can we better understand the processes involved in the construction of masculine and feminine identities? What do such changes mean? Can we influence these in ways that reduce the most destructive dimensions and enhance the more positive aspects of our social and sexual relationships? If the structures really are immutable, no change is possible, but to accept this is to bid the hope of a society free of rape goodbye.

Rape and the law

Studying the laws of a land reveal much of import regarding what is prized and valued in that society. Traditionally, considerable effort was spent on attempting to establish law's supremacy and portraying its origins as divine and other-worldly. As such, the law was unquestionable, and its decrees absolute (Smart, 1995).

The history of rape legislation provides an illuminating window into the history of male–female relationships. Prior to the nineteenth century, rape was defined as carnal knowledge of a woman against her will; by definition, this act necessitated the use of force or threat by the accused and resistance by the victim (McSherry, 1998; Vigarello, 2001). From the mid-nineteenth century onwards, after rape ceased to be a capital offence, the courts in England began to use the concept of 'lack of consent' to include situations where the victim of rape was asleep or inebriated or where there was fraud as to the nature of the act (cases cited in McSherry, 1998, p. 27).

Traditionally, the law has made the issue of consent the central concern. This effectively places the burden of proof on the victim (Adler, 1987; Edwards, 1981; Kennedy, 1992; Lees, 1996, 1997; Scutt, 1997; Smart, 1989; Stuart, 1993). She has to demonstrate that her lack of consent was apparent, preferably by physical resistance. Commentary in a medical article from the early twentieth century illustrates the dominant discourse at that time:

> The question whether or not an adult female can be forcibly induced against her will to submit to sexual intercourse was at one time seriously debatable, but the present consensus of opinion amongst those who should know is that so long as the woman remains conscious she cannot be compelled by force to acquiesce, no matter how physically strong the male nor how physically weak (within certain limits) the female. In other words, so long as the woman is physically capable of resisting the attack, accomplishment of the act is manifestly impossible, since it has been amply demonstrated that the male cannot successfully fight and copulate at one and the same time. (Mapes, 1906, pp. 928–9)

The legal presumption of consent assumes 'normal' heterosexual sex is centred around the act of penetration, and that women enjoy being coerced or persuaded to engage in sexual intercourse. Sexual intercourse is presented as a hunt by the man, who chases, corners and conquers a demurely protesting female. In what has been termed the 'penetrative/coercive model of sexuality' (McSherry, 1998, p. 28), women are presented as passive and submissive in sex, assumed to be acquiescing unless they physically resist. Evidence of resistance will be observable, manifest in the visible, physical injuries that will supposedly accompany any genuine rape allegation (Bronitt, 1998; Edwards and Heenan, 1994; Harris and Grace, 1999; Kennedy, 1992; Temkin, 2002).

In discussing rape in France under the *ancien régime*, Georges Vigarello illustrates this assumption through an analysis of case law and legal treatises, as well as showing concurrence in the views of Enlightenment philosophers (Vigarello, 2001). Voltaire, for instance, described unequivocally the physical obstacles to rape, commenting:

> For girls or women who complain of having been raped, all that is needed, it seems to me, is to tell them how, long ago, a queen frustrated an accusation of rape. She took a scabbard and, constantly shaking it, she made the complainant see that it was then impossible to put a sword in the scabbard. It is the same with rape as with impotence: there are some cases which ought never to come before the courts. (quoted in Vigarello, 2001, p. 43)

What such reasoning demonstrated, as Vigarello himself remarked, is that

> Bodily physique was sufficient to convince the judges. The thesis of consent was naturalized, intuitive anatomy transformed into a criterion of truth. (ibid., p. 43)

The twentieth century equivalent of the sword and scabbard became the pencil and the coke bottle[4] – defence lawyers used this example to infer that rape is impossible if the woman displays any physical motion or resistance (Shapcott, 1988).

The extension of such thinking effectively equates visible evidence of physical resistance with non-consent. Anything less than this betrays a woman's supposedly 'real' desires and inclinations. Her saying 'no' cannot be construed as adequate proof of lack of consent, since it is expected that women will say no when they mean yes (Lees, 1997; Scutt, 1997, 1998; Taslitz, 1999; Temkin, 2002). According to this view, the word of a woman is not to be trusted. Women do not tell the truth; moreover, they are so deceived that it is impossible for them to even know the truth. What, indeed, is 'truth' to a bent rib whose carnal and deceptive nature caused the downfall of the human race?

If an alternative subject-position is adopted here, then other questions assume relevance. For example, when rape is described as a crime of passion, whose passion is being talked about? The language of sex has traditionally privileged men's voice over women's. Sex only counts if *he* penetrates her; sex is not complete until *he* has ejaculated; sex is not satisfying unless *he* is satisfied. According to this perspective, men need sex and women need men. To attract men, and to keep their man, women must satisfy them sexually. Men's sexual needs predominate; women's are denied, sublimated or misinterpreted.

Viewed from this perspective, it is not surprising that until very recently, the law did not even acknowledge the various violent and coercive contexts in which women may be raped; for example, the presence of weapons or threats, or the impact of perpetrators occupying authority positions (such as priests or professors).[5] Recognition is still seldom given to the paralysing impact of fear on prospective rape victims, rendering physical resistance impossible. As Liz Kelly's research so clearly established, at the time of the attack, many rape victims become terror-bound, fearing they are about to die (Kelly, 1988). Sandra McNeill's research showed that women confronted by flashers can also fear death in such an unpredictable encounter (McNeill, 1987). Men's displaying of their penises, in a society where many use the penis as a weapon, can produce reactions as potent as if they had pulled a gun. Furthermore, the prevalence of sexual abuse and rape is so common that, frequently, a rape victim will recall previous violations and, as a survival strategy, may dissociate[6] from the experience or decide to 'get it over with' as quickly as possible (Kelly, 1988). How can the law then, based as it is primarily on men's perspectives, reflect the diversity and complexity of women's realities and experiences? Kaspiew expresses this view well:

> Women are the outsiders because rape law has for centuries reflected the patriarchal view of human relationships and sexuality which defines woman as 'other', and that which is possessed. Rape law reflects a construction of sexuality which discounts women's subjectivity and privileges the male perspective. (quoted in Easteal, 1998a, p. 1)

Or, as Catharine MacKinnon (1983) has succinctly asserted:

> The law sees and treats women the way men see and treat women. (MacKinnon, 1983, p. 635)

One area within which such a bias has been evident is in relation to the law of recent complaint, also known as the 'fresh complaint' rule. This law governs the evidential significance of when a victim tells others (especially the police) about the rape or abuse, and attaches differential weighting to complaints which were made at the first opportunity, compared with delayed complaints. The underlying assumption has been that the 'reasonable' victim should report sexual abuse immediately; delay or failure impacts negatively on the apparent truthfulness of the victim as a witness (LaFree, 1981; Maclean, 1979; Peters, 1975; Temkin, 2002; Torrey, 1991). As far back as the Book of Deuteronomy, rape victims were expected to cry out during the assault unless they were in a field and beyond earshot. Likewise, medieval common law ruled that victims of violent crime (including rape) were expected to make a 'hue and cry' immediately upon violation (Bronitt, 1998; Brownmiller, 1975; Freckelton, 1998; Temkin, 2002; Wolfthal, 1999). In England, Henry de Bracton's thirteenth-century law code stipulated that a victim of rape

> must go at once and while the deed is newly done with the hue and cry ... show the injury done to her. (quoted in Wolfthal, 1999, pp. 42–3)

Victims of rape were expected to travel around their locality displaying injuries sustained in the attack to 'men of good repute' and law enforcement officials (Bronitt, 1998).

> Indeed, making a complaint of rape without raising a 'hue and cry' automatically resulted in the allegation being dismissed and the victim being prosecuted for making a 'false appeal'. (Bronitt, 1998, p. 44)

Similar edicts existed in secular law codes across Europe, as well as in canon law, inquisition testimony and court records (Wolfthal, 1999).

By the eighteenth century, the requirement of 'hue and cry' had been repackaged into a rule of evidence relating to the truthfulness of women who complained of rape. Blackstone's Commentary in 1769 clarifies the legal position:

> [I]f the witness be of good fame; if she presently discovered the offence and made search of the offender; if the party accused fled for it; these and the like are concurring circumstances which give greater probability to her evidence. But on the other side, if she be of evil fame, and stand unsupported by others; if she concealed the injury for any considerable time after she had opportunity to complain; if the place, where the fact was alleged to be committed, was where it was possible she might have been heard, and she made no outcry; these and the like circumstances carry a strong but not conclusive, presumption that her testimony is false or feigned. (quoted in Bronitt, 1998, p. 45)

The law of recent complaint presumes that victims of rape and sexual abuse are capable of reporting their violation to others at the first opportunity; otherwise the complaint is perceived to be suspect. Underpinning this doctrine is a basic distrust of the testimony of women. Thus, Bronitt says,

> From a forensic perspective, both the timing and circumstances of the complaint provide the key to identifying false accusations. (Bronitt, 1998, p. 49)

In court, the prosecution may present a case to explain the victim's delay in reporting; or the jury is left to use 'common sense' to determine the significance or otherwise of any time lag. What is asserted is the 'naturalness' of prompt reporting, contrary to the findings of empirical research demonstrating that the more typical, 'normal' response to rape is for women not to report it at all (Burgess and Hazelwood, 1999; Kelly, 1988; Painter, 1991; Russell, 1984; Torrey, 1991; Walby and Myhill, 2001). A senior New Zealand detective interviewed in 1976 expressed it this way:

> If a girl complains very soon after the event this shows consistency of behaviour – that's how you'd expect a woman who'd been raped to act.

If she doesn't complain for several weeks, perhaps until she's discovered she's pregnant, then that's less convincing. It could look as if she's complaining about being pregnant rather than about being raped. (quoted in Lloyd, 1976, p. 35)

A related area, which has also been the subject of recent reforms, concerns judicial warnings to the jury regarding a lack of corroboration in most rape allegations (Edwards and Heenan, 1994; Kennedy, 1992; Lees, 1996; Scutt, 1997; Temkin, 2002). In the seventeenth century, Chief Justice Matthew Hale ruled that rape was a charge

... easy to be made and hard to be proved, and harder to be defended by the party accused, tho' never so innocent. (quoted in Lees, 1996, p. 131)

The legacy of this ruling continued formally within the courts until very recently, and persists informally, at an attitudinal level, still today (Lees, 1996). The fact that most rapes happen in private settings, with no witnesses, was offered as justification for the requirement for judges to warn juries of the possible dangers associated with convicting defendants who had been accused in such circumstances (Mack, 1998). In a book entitled *Sex and the Law*, an American judge asserted:

There are few crimes in which false charges are more easily or confidently made than in rape. Experience has shown that unfounded charges of rape are brought for a variety of motives. The adage, 'Hell hath no fury like a woman scorned', is frequently encountered in rape prosecutions. (Ploscowe, 1951, p. 187)

Not only were rape allegations believed to be easy to make, but they were based on the word of a woman, which was viewed as no word at all. Carol Smart thus refers to the corroboration warning within the legal system as an example of the 'disqualification of women and women's sexuality' (Smart, 1989, p. 26). Judges would warn juries not to convict on a woman's testimony alone, a sentiment clearly espoused in the words of an Australian judge:

[I]n cases of alleged sexual offences, it is really dangerous to convict on the evidence of the woman or girl alone ... because human experience has shown that girls and women in these courts do sometimes tell an entirely false story which is very easy to fabricate but extremely difficult to refute. Such stories are fabricated for all sorts of reasons, which I need not now enumerate, and sometimes for no reason at all. (L. J. Salmon (1968) quoted in Mack, 1998, p. 61)

More recent critics have pointed out that no such warning is given in relation to other crimes, such as robbery, which are also likely to occur without the presence of witnesses (Bargen and Fishwick, 1995). The corroboration warning given in rape cases appears to be based, then, not only on the private nature of the crime but on the historic beliefs outlined earlier in this chapter regarding women's deceitfulness and lack of credibility (Mack, 1998; Smart, 1989; Temkin, 2002). If women are neurotic, irrational, liars and prone to fantastical imaginings, why should their word count against that of a man? The main problem with rape allegations, it seems, is that women make them against men.

Effects of rape

In relation to the effects of rape on victims, for many years these were minimised and the notion was even purported that not only were women minimally harmed by rape, but some even found the experience pleasurable. In 1971, the results of a supposedly academic survey from the University of Michigan were released which stated that nearly one-half of women who were raped experienced an orgasm during the attack, a 'fact' which was used to support the notion that fear has 'a sexually exciting quality for most women' (quoted in Shapcott, 1988, p. 152). This survey was subsequently revealed to be a 'pornographer's invention' (ibid.), but the very act of its creation is a telling indictment.

More commonly asserted was the view that rape was only traumatic for women who were sexually inexperienced; hence the rape of a prostitute was assumed to cause little distress, other than financial, and have negligible impact (English Collective of Prostitutes, 1997). Assumptions regarding the improbability of women who were not virgins being harmed by rape confirms again the confusion that arises when rape is perceived in fundamentally sexual terms.[7] The traumatic effects of rape are minimised or negated when the violence within rape is ignored, along with the way it violates a woman's being and removes her sexual autonomy.

Since the mid-1970s, feminist work and research with victims of sexual violence has documented the extensive and often devastating effects of rape on the survivors (Burgess and Hazelwood, 1999; Crowell and Burgess, 1996; Goodman *et al.*, 1993; Kelly, 1988; Kilpatrick *et al.*, 1987; Koss, 1990; Koss *et al.*, 1994; Resick, 1993; Wiehe and Richards, 1995). In many jurisdictions Victim Impact Statements were introduced to inform sentencing decisions (Callihan, 2003), and the seriousness of the offence has to some extent been recognised by the state in extending the penalties available. Increasing recognition has been given to the effects of rape on victims of acquaintance and marital rape with a growing body of research documenting that the extent of the harm caused by rape appears to be little affected by the nature of the victim–offender relationship (Koss *et al.*, 1988; Riggs *et al.*, 1992; Wiehe and Richards, 1995). In other words, rape trauma is an effect of rape irrespective of whether the rapist is a stranger or the woman's husband. What may differ is not the fact of trauma but some of the particular manifestations it assumes – for instance, the violation of trust is felt in distinctive ways when sexual violence occurs within intimate relationships (Frazier and Seales, 1997; Kelly, 2002; Wiehe and Richards, 1995).

Rape trauma itself has come to be defined as a 'syndrome', diagnosed when the common aftereffects of rape are present and when a complainant's behaviour can be interpreted as consistent with having been raped (Burgess and Hazelwood, 1999; Frazier and Borgida, 1999). The concept of 'rape trauma syndrome' has been used to describe an acute phase of reaction followed by a longer period of reorganisation and recovery, during which time behavioural, somatic and psychological effects may be observable (Burgess and Hazelwood, 1999). Some writers have argued, however, that rape trauma syndrome has tended to be overused as evidence of rape having *occurred*, rather than to educate the judge and jury regarding the *effects* of rape on complainants (Bronitt, 1998), and the variability of those effects. Moreover, the naming of the effects of rape as a 'syndrome' raises concerns that such a label may serve to portray rape survivors as psychiatrically disturbed and unstable, rather than as women displaying typical reactions to a traumatic event (Gregory and Lees, 1999; Koss *et al.*, 1994). 'Deviancy' lies in the actions of the rapist, rather than in the reactions of the victim. A focus on individual responses to rape deflects critical attention away from the gendered, socio-cultural context within which rape attacks are spawned. Also of concern is the possibility that lawyers or doctors appearing for the defence will use the absence of particular symptoms as 'proof' that the complainant could not have been raped (Bronitt, 1998; Gregory and Lees, 1999).

Greater education is clearly still needed concerning the diversity of ways in which sexual assault may impact on victims, often in ways which may appear at times to be irrational, bizarre and contradictory (Bronitt, 1998; Burgess and Hazelwood, 1999; Freckelton, 1998; Kennedy, 1992). Deeper understanding is required of the various reasons underlying the reluctance of sexual assault victims to tell others about the rape/assault, and to enhance awareness of the psychological processes of avoidance, denial and dissociation. In addition, the structural reasons which may be associated with delayed reporting also need to be addressed. These include the victims' perceptions of the police and criminal justice system, the extent to which they feel they will be believed and supported and how much they fear being blamed by those around them (Jordan, 1998a; van de Zandt, 1998).

Much of the history of rape and rape legislation has been built upon a foundation of misogynist beliefs and assumptions concerning the 'nature' of women.

Nature of women

Dominant images and discourses

From the Biblical account of the Fall, women have been presented by men as deceitful, as natural born liars (Cavanagh, 1971; Easteal, 1998a). The devil tempted Eve, but it was Eve who seduced, deceived and manipulated Adam, using her feminine wiles to beguile and lead him into sin. This account emphasises two parallel and paradoxical themes that have been significant in the history of male–female relationships. First, one strand leading to the Fall was woman's weakness and openness to manipulation by the devil; the second strand stressed men's weakness and openness to manipulation by women. When Eve tempted Adam, not only did Adam suffer the consequences but, according to the story, her actions impacted on the entire human race. As depicted by patriarchal religions, all the woes and afflictions of humanity derive from this one source – the deadly charms of a woman. Judeo-Christian doctrines portray women's sexuality in dualistic terms, juxtaposing the virtue of the Madonna with the contemptibility of the whore (Easteal, 1998a; Summers, 1975).

Given the pre-eminence of patriarchal thought historically and cross-culturally, it is difficult to conceptualise even the possibility of alternatively based social systems. How, when one's vision and perception is channelled so narrowly through a patriarchal lens, can we imagine what life would be like in societies which did not depend on women's subjugation for their economic and social survival? While this topic is hotly debated, nevertheless there are many who argue that very early societies regarded women more positively than those of more recent times (Eisler, 1987; Gimbutas, 1989). Whilst there has been considerable romanticism concerning a golden age of matriarchy, nonetheless archaeological evidence from pre-Judeo-Christian times suggests the possibilities of a time when women were revered and respected as nurturers and givers of life (Gimbutas, 1989; Wilshire, 1994). Very early mythological thinking, for example, posited creation stories in which, out of Nothingness, came Gaia[8], giver of life (Highwater, 1990). From her body the land and sea were formed, and from her fertile abundance came life itself. Gaia was prayed to as supreme being, the source of life and death, the Earth Spirit and the Great Mother.

Women's life-giving properties were regarded as a source of awe and mystery but were also feared for these same reasons. As men's fear of these mysterious womanly powers grew, the more likely they were to perceive women as a threat (Cavanagh, 1971). Myths and legends changed to depict women as unruly and in need of subjugation.

In time, the power of Gaia was usurped by an Olympic world of superior male gods, and Gaia's name was replaced in Delphi by that of the rational male deity, the sun god Apollo (Highwater, 1990). Jane Ellen Harrison's anthropological research similarly maintained that the concept of a male supreme being is a comparatively recent invention, which could be traced back to Zeus, about 2500 BC and later, about 1800 BC, to the writings of Abraham, the first Old Testament patriarch (Harrison, 1903, cited in Highwater, 1990).

The defeat of the mythical supremacy of the Mother Goddess was supposedly further signified in two events. For giving men the gift of fire, the Greek god Zeus first bound Prometheus to a rock, then punished the offspring of Prometheus by creating women (Highwater, 1990). Hesiod wrote that when Hephaestus created the first woman, Pandora,

> Into her heart he put lies and false words and treachery... so she might be a sorrow to the men of the earth. (Hesiod, quoted in Highwater, 1990, p. 57)

As Highwater comments:

> The transformation of a pre-Hellenic earth goddess into such a destructive demon as Pandora provides a fascinating insight into the workings of the patriarchal Greek mind. According to the famous myth about this first woman, all possible torments and evils, all wickedness and sorrow were contained in a box. Despite warnings not to touch the box, Pandora opened it, unleashing endless disaster upon men. Like Eve after her, it was Pandora's beguiling sexuality that allowed her to bring about the Fall. Thus Hesiod reflected the Greek attitude toward women when he wrote: 'Do not allow a sweet-tongued woman to beguile you with the fascination of her body'... Thus, the power of women had been villainized. (Highwater, 1990, pp. 57–8)

Likewise, Cavanagh has observed:

> From the time of the myth of Pandora, woman has been characterized as mischief-maker. (Cavanagh, 1971, p. 268)

Anthropologists and archaeologists have thus suggested that a rich oral tradition of myth-making pre-dated the efforts of Homer and Hesiod in the seventh century BC to document the classical myths (Highwater, 1990). Similar patterns occurred in other parts of the world, as Goddesses became devalued in many cultures, to be replaced by male gods (Gimbutas, 1989; Wilshire, 1994).

Men expressed doubts regarding the extent to which a woman's word could be trusted. This is exemplified in the legend of Cassandra, whose name means 'she who entangles men' (Mills, 1991, p. 40). Apollo gave Cassandra the gift of prophecy, for which he expected sex in return. She refused him and, in a fit of pique, he ensured that although her prophecies would be true, no one would believe her. One of her warnings, which went unheeded, was that the Greeks would use a wooden horse to bring about the fall of Troy. Mills writes that:

> Cassandra symbolises a patriarchal refusal to trust in the words of women. (Mills, 1991, p. 40)

The influence of Judeo-Christian thinking played a major role in reconstructing the portrayal of women. Eve, the first woman in the Bible, was formed from the bent rib of a man, and her inherent defectiveness, sealed forever (Cavanagh, 1971; Highwater, 1990). She was depicted as the source and fountain of man's oppression (Griffin, 1975; Tong, 1984). Reflecting this image of the woman being a lying temptress, Tertullian stated in a letter to his wife:

> In pain shall you bring forth children, woman, and you shall turn to your husband and he shall rule over you. And do you not know that you are Eve? God's sentence hangs still over all your sex and his punishment weighs down upon you. You are the Devil's gateway; you are she who first violated the forbidden tree and broke the law of God. (quoted in Tong, 1984, p. 99)

Women were sealed in their status as chattels, as the property of men to be given, traded, stolen and discarded. Such beliefs ensured men's social and sexual status, guaranteeing them ownership as well as easy access (Dworkin, 1982). While such an arrangement was in men's interests, it clearly worked to the detriment of women, who were not only treated as disposable chattels, but liable to be branded as whores once men had no further use for them. In this climate, the division of women from each other further reinforced men's social position and control (Summers, 1975), with the Old Testament clearly delineating men's rights to abduct and rape women under certain conditions.[9]

The notion that, underneath, women *wanted* to be taken forcefully helped men appease their consciences. Writing in 500 BC, Herodotus, known as the Father of History, declared:

> Abducting young women is not, indeed, a lawful act; but it is stupid after the event to make a fuss about it. The only sensible thing is to take no notice; for it is obvious that no young woman allows herself to be abducted if she does not wish to be. (Herodotus, quoted in Dworkin, 1982, p. 28)

Likewise, Ovid wrote:

> Women often wish to give unwillingly what they really like to give. (quoted ibid., p. 28)

Misogynist sentiments continued throughout New Testament writings, evident especially in Paul's epistles. Women's carnality meant they were to be excluded from the possibilities of priestly status (Cavanagh, 1971), and their roles as men's subordinate wives and helpmates were secured. Woman's hope comes with the resurrection, when to equip her for a state 'suited to glory rather than to shame' (Augustine, cited in Tong, 1984, p. 100), she will be effectively reborn without the organs associated with intercourse and reproduction. As many of the Church Fathers went on to proclaim:

> Because of her sexual being and reproductive function, woman was less rational and less spiritual than man; that is, less able to distinguish between truth and falsity and less able to discern between good and evil. (Tong, 1984, p. 100)

Early Christian writing by St Augustine posited the division of women into the polarised categories of Madonna and whore (Summers, 1975; Tong, 1984). The emphasis in Christian thought on the virtues of the Virgin Mary elevated one woman in status whilst simultaneously condemning all 'ordinary' women for failing to attain such purity (Bullough, 1974). Women were increasingly despised and reviled, and portrayed as the embodiment of evil. Examples of common sayings about women from the Middle Ages provide graphic examples of such sentiments:

> Wouldst thou define or know what a woman is? She is glittering mud, a stinking rose, sweet poison, ever leaning towards that which is forbidden her.
>   Woman was evil from the beginnings, a gate of death, a disciple of the servant, the devil's accomplice, a fount of deception, a dogstar to godly labours, rust corrupting the saints; whose perilous face had overthrown such as had already become almost angels. (quoted in Bullough, 1974, pp. 173–4)

Sayings such as these, and comments about women's general inferiority, have not been confined to single nations or particular epochs. The patterns of social control which emerged have assumed diverse forms historically and cross-culturally, although with similar underlying systems of belief and essentially common goals. In China, for instance, women's social status was painfully controlled from approximately 1000 AD through the practice of foot binding, a custom which ensured women's complete dependence on men for their survival (Daly, 1979; Dworkin, 1982). Men defined as erotic a practice which deformed women for life.
    Likewise, the witchcraft purges of the fourteenth to seventeenth centuries were directed predominantly at women (Daly, 1979; Hester, 1992), and were expressly linked to women's sexuality. In 1486, the German monks, Kramer

and Sprenger, graphically described in the *Malleus Maleficarum* (The Witches Hammer) how women were defective from the start, formed as they were from a bent rib. Not only were women imperfect, they were also inherently deceptive. Thus the *Malleus Maleficarum* depicted women as cunning, evil and prone to consorting and copulating with the devil. Of women's voice the monks said:

> For as she is a liar by nature, so in her speech she stings while she delights us. Wherefore her voice is like the song of the Sirens,[10] who with their sweet melody entice the passers-by and kill them. (Kramer and Sprenger, 1486, translated by Summers, 1971, p. 46). [Note added by author]

The threat of being labelled a 'witch' was a powerful measure of social control, which effectively limited and constrained all women's behaviour (Hester, 1992). What provided the context for such fears to flourish was the belief that women were 'inferior and sinful', a conviction utilised to curtail changes to women's economic position as well as their social status (Hester, 1992, p. 200).

Much of the *Malleus Maleficarum* may be dismissed as fantastical superstition; nevertheless, many of the ideas underlying its edicts echo the views espoused about women since the dominance of patriarchal thinking was established. This is evident in pronouncements made by prominent philosophers whose thoughts on the nature of men and women have been hailed through the centuries for their greatness. For example, writing in the fourth century BC, Aristotle claimed that 'the nature of man is the most rounded off and complete', whilst a woman is:

> more jealous, more querulous, more apt to scold and to strike. She is, furthermore, more prone to despondency and less hopeful than the man, more void of shame or self respect, more false of speech, more deceptive, and of more retentive memory. (Aristotle, quoted in Agonito, 1977, p. 49)

Centuries later, commenting specifically on women's ability to resist physically a man intent on rape, Rousseau[11] alleged that women were naturally prone to deceit and 'false surrender':

> a choice deliberately to delude, an artifice inherent in the feminine being who seeks 'to provide herself beforehand with excuses and the right to be weak if she chooses'. (quoted in Vigarello, 2001, p. 43)

In a similar vein, Balzac[12] asks:

> Have you ever observed a lie in the attitude and nature of women? Deceit is as easy to them as falling snow in Heaven. (quoted in Larson, 1969, p. 18)

Likewise, Schopenhauer[13] asserts:

> Nature has given women only one means of protection and defense –
> hypocrisy, this is congenital with them, and the use of it is as natural as
> the animal's use of its claws. Women feel they have a certain degree of
> justification for their hypocrisy. (ibid., p. 18)

Schopenhauer also stated that a perjury in a court of justice is more often
committed by a woman than a man, and that indeed it could generally be
questioned whether a woman ought to be 'sworn' at all (ibid., p. 20).
Arguing along similar lines, Nietzsche,[14] in *Beyond Good and Evil*, claimed:

> [Woman's] great art is the lie, her highest concern is mere appearance and
> beauty. (quoted in Cavanagh, 1971, p. 275)

Artists provided powerful representations of how these attitudes affected
women's testimony in criminal law cases. During the fifteenth and sixteenth
centuries, for example, huge Justice Paintings adorned many European
courtrooms. Images suggesting women's words were unreliable abounded,
such as the sculpture adorning the ceiling of the town hall of Courtrai, in
France, showing a woman with padlocked mouth, and paintings and wood-
cuts portraying women falsely accusing men of rape (Wolfthal, 1999). Such
works both reflected and reinforced dominant ideologies. Art historian
Diane Wolfthal writes:

> The idea that women falsely cry rape struck a particularly receptive chord
> and was illustrated in numerous images. ... It is critical to understand how
> these misogynist elements functioned in the courtroom context, particu-
> larly during rape trials. (ibid., p. 118)

The same point emerges from Vigarello's analysis of rape trials in early
modern France, in which he refers to the use of criminal proceedings as

> a way of judging the complainant; they reinterpret her gestures so as to
> imprison her in lies. Everything indicates that she was not a subject; her
> attitude was predetermined, her defence was unheard. The reasoning was
> circular: a relative insensitivity towards brutality, an insensitivity all the
> greater because the victim was not believed. The procrastination of the
> judges was aggravated by their suspicion of the complainant. This suspi-
> cion extended well beyond cases of rape: 'As the testimony of women can
> be more fickle and more subject to variation, one generally attaches less
> weight to it than to that of men.' (Vigarello, 2001, p. 45, quoting
> Denisart, Collection de décisions nouvelles, vol. 2, p. 315)

Similar views were reflected in early criminological writings by Lombroso and Ferrero whose late-nineteenth-century book, *The Female Offender*, stressed the underlying weaknesses of women which influenced them to lie and deceive. Similarly, Otto Pollak's influential book, *The Criminality of Women* (1961),[15] also depicted women as vengeful, arguing that women's physiology predisposes them to crime and deception. Lying comes naturally to women, since not only do they learn early in life to conceal what they are ashamed of (menstruation), but women are also able to fake orgasm in ways men cannot. No wonder then, argued Pollak, that women are so skilled at crimes involving deception and concealment, since

... for women deceit ... (is) ... a socially prescribed form of behaviour. (Pollak, 1961, p. 11)

The combination of such beliefs about women with masculinist representations of men's sexuality contributed to an environment within which raped women had scant chance of having their allegations upheld. Not surprisingly, in 1987 Allison Morris drew attention to criminology's meagre and stereotypical treatment of rape, and criticised the way in which some researchers in the sociology of deviance were committed to understanding the offender's actions through his eyes only. She noted how, for example, one writer in his discussion of rape constantly placed quotation marks around the word victim, and referred to the rapist as an

uneducated, opportunistic, and basically goodhearted soul who takes his pleasure where he finds it. (Gibbons, 1977, quoted in Morris, 1987, p. 163)

Significantly, historical studies of sexuality tended to restrict themselves to anatomical observations and the mechanics of the sexual organs, with it being only comparatively recently that sexuality has come to be viewed as a social and historical construct (Bell, 1993; Foucault, 1981; Highwater, 1990; Smart, 1995). Rape has typically been viewed as an extension of the 'natural' sexual urge in men, and women advised to take all precautions necessary to keep men's sexual instincts in abeyance. Construing men as ruled by uncontrollable sexual urges has thus had clear social utility in shifting sexual responsibility onto women (Shapcott, 1988). Not surprisingly, women were blamed for bringing about their own rapes. When the sociologist Amir outlined factors that he believed indicated rapes to be victim-precipitated, he included amongst these victims 'who met their offender in a bar, picnic or party'; situations where alcohol was present, 'particularly in the victim'; and victims identified as having a 'bad' reputation

(Amir, 1967, p. 502). He asserts that:

> ... negligent and reckless behavior on the part of the victim ... does not make any offender innocent but allows us to consider some of these men, at least, less guilty and leads us to consider that the victim is perhaps also responsible for what happened to her. (ibid., p. 502)

The notion that, thereby, women 'ask to be raped' remains frighteningly popular. Studies of the acceptance of rape myths still reveal comparatively high levels of acceptance, especially amongst male participants (Hinck and Thomas, 1999; Lonsway and Fitzgerald, 1994). The belief that women are prone to making false rape accusations remains one of the most prevalent of these myths, and is examined further in the next section.

False rape allegations

The spectre of the vengeful, lying woman falsely accusing an innocent man of rape has become an almost iconic image in popular (mis)representations of sexual violence. This perception emerges from a fusing of the legacy of beliefs regarding women's inherent deceitfulness with men's denial of their responsibility for rape, with such views evident in the dominant discourse surrounding false allegations that emerged from the mid-nineteenth century onwards (Edwards, 1981). Medical and legal writers promulgated the notion of the impossibility of rape, alleging, for example, that non-consenting sex could be achieved only by 'stupefying' a woman (ibid., p. 126). Edwards maintains that the media helped in the construction of a moral panic concerning false rape allegations, utilising the phenomenon of 'the railway compartment complainant' to this end (ibid., p. 127). While the design of the nineteenth-century railway compartment may have provided men with both the opportunity and protective cover for rape, the 'gentleman' status of the accused was undoubtedly linked with acceptance of an alternative interpretation: that the complainants were lying. Allegations against men of class and substance were increasingly viewed as suspect, and the difficulties associated with successfully charging such men with rape are still apparent today.[16]

Throughout the twentieth century, legal and medical commentators displayed attitudes of profound disbelief regarding women's word in matters deemed to be sexual. For instance, writing in 1918, a doctor remarked to his colleagues:

> Considering the sense of shame which woman ordinarily manifests in all matters pertaining to sex the false accusation of rape would appear to be unusual. Practical experience, however, has shown that in no field of simulation has greater ingenuity been displayed by hysterical and revengeful women than in accusations of rape. (Bronson, 1918, p. 539)

Concerns about the possibility of false accusations were stressed, partly to remind doctors of the importance of their testimony regarding physical evidence of rape. The view was routinely expressed that substantial numbers of rape charges were unfounded, with one medical writer claiming that women made twelve false accusations for every one true charge (Mapes, 1906, p. 937).

A prevalent and particularly insidious myth derived from the notion that false rape allegations emanated from women's sexual fantasies (Edwards, 1981; Katz and Mazur, 1979; Taslitz, 1999; Torrey, 1991). Beliefs in female masochism reinforced the view that women often had a subconscious desire to be raped. For example, the neo-Freudian writer, Helene Deutsch, in her book, *The Psychology of Women*, maintained that girls were particularly prone to sexual fantasies in puberty, a developmental stage characterised by:

> ... ardent wishes to be desired, strong aspirations to egoistic possession, a normally completely passive attitude to the first attack, and a desire to be raped that asserts itself in dreams and fears. (Deutsch, 1944, p. 117)

In legal literature, the term 'pseudologia phantastica' became the authoritative label for the condition responsible for false rape allegations by women, and was described as a

> ... delusional state in which the complainant truly believes that she had been raped although no rape, and perhaps no sexual contact of any kind, had taken place. Since she firmly believes this non-fact, her story is unshakable. (Bessmer, 1984, quoted in Kanin, 1994; p. 82)

In his legal treatise, *On Evidence*, Wigmore warned of young girls and women

> contriving false charges of sexual offenses by men. The unchaste (let us call it) mentality finds incidental but direct expression in the narration of imaginary sex incidents of which the narrator is straightforward and convincing. The real victim, however, too often is the innocent man; for the respect and sympathy naturally felt by any tribunal for a wronged female helps to give easy credit to such a plausible tale. (Wigmore, quoted in Bourque, 1989, p. 105)

Bourque (1989) notes that the so-called 'ample psychiatric evidence' which Wigmore refers to consists of five case studies from a 1915 book involving rape charges made by women undergoing psychiatric treatment, three of which never went to trial, and the opinions of a handful of psychiatrists prior to 1933; yet this was the 'scientific' basis on which Wigmore concluded women had a propensity for falsifying charges of sexual offences (see also Tong, 1984, p. 101).

The argument that women are inclined to make excessive allegations of rape has obvious utility in helping to bolster men's protestations of their innocence. Taylor (1987), for example, suggests that men have planted responsibility for sexual aggressiveness on women by implying that women desire to be taken forcefully; when men dominate and overcome women, they are doing what women secretly want and desire. The use of force in sexual penetration can thus be justified on the basis that this is what women want. Lord Byron, for instance, reflected this view when he penned the following verse, subsequently adopted by legal writers such as Glanville Williams to provide 'evidence' of women's fickleness:

> A little still she strove, and much repented,
> And whispering 'I will ne'er consent' – consented.
> (Byron, quoted in Naffine, 1997, p. 106)

Women's concerns about appearing chaste were viewed as precluding easy acceptance of their sexual desires. Chastity and credibility came to be viewed virtually synonymously, as evidenced in comments made during a mid-nineteenth-century trial:

> [No] evil habitude of humanity so depraves the nature, so deadens the moral sense, and obliterates the distinction between right and wrong, as common, licentious indulgence. Particularly is this true of women, the citadel whose character is virtue; when that is lost, all is gone; her love of justice, sense of character, and regard for truth. (Camp v. State, 3 Ga. (1847), quoted in Tong, 1984, pp. 107–8)

Unchaste women were viewed not only as prone to lying, but prone to unconscious desires for sexual coercion to assuage the guilt of their sexual passion and indulgences. Thus an American legal journal in the 1950s stated that:

> [A] woman's need for sexual satisfaction may lead to the unconscious desire for forceful penetration, the coercion serving neatly to avoid guilt feelings which might arise after willing participation. (quoted in McSherry, 1998, p. 29)

The fact that, for centuries, the law specified that rape was acceptable in certain contexts, such as marriage, served to undermine and diminish the seriousness of sexual violation. If wives could be legally violated on a nightly basis, yet continue to cohabit, where was the harm?

The dominant factor affecting how women are treated stems from their lack of perceived credibility. Oppositional representations of male and female attributes have typically assigned 'positive' attributes to men and 'negative' to women. While reason and self-determination supposedly underlie men's actions, women's actions are seen as reactions, determined in large part by their mental weaknesses and emotional vulnerabilities. Instead of making objective decisions informed by reason, women are presented as being at the mercy of their emotions, sex hormones and physiological processes. Viewed in this light, false rape accusations emerge as consistent outcomes of women's own false natures – women's own minds lie to them.

The depiction of women not knowing their own minds has been evident in such pronouncements as 'when women say no, they mean yes' (Lees, 1997; Scutt, 1997; Taslitz, 1999). Women think they should resist men's sexual advances, initially at least, so as not to appear sluttish, when what they really want is, coincidentally and conveniently for men, what the man wants – sex. Thus his proceeding sexually does not violate what she wants, for he knows what she wants more than she does. Being male equates with science, knowledge and reason; being female is synonymous with art, imagination and fabrication. As recently as 1990, a male judge in Britain maintained that all the gentleman of a jury would understand that when women say no, they do not always mean no (Lees, 1997). Even more recently, in his summing-up to a rape trial, a New Zealand High Court judge, Justice Morris, said:

> If every man stopped the first time a woman said 'no', the world would be a much less exciting place to live. (*New Zealand Herald*, 5 June 1996)

It took the jury less than an hour to declare the 21-year old accused to be innocent.

To argue that women say no when they mean yes powerfully undermines the validity of women's word. If it is commonly believed and advanced in the courts that a woman says she does not want sex when she does, then the argument can easily be made that she will say she did not want sex when she did, and say she was raped when she was not. A man who gives you his word gives you his 'truth', but what weight does the word of a woman carry? Such a view obviously has

> · ... dangerous implications. If the female body has an existence of its own, totally out of control of its occupant, evidence of lack of consent is rendered irrelevant. Implicit in these ideas is that not only does a woman not know her own desires, but that she is responsible for the 'uncontrollability' of male desire once it is aroused. The defence counsel then puts arguments forward such as, 'Did she lead him on, prostitute herself, or consent and then change her mind at the last minute when the man was unable to control himself?' The idea that male sexuality once aroused is uncontrollable firmly shifts the blame onto the woman. Despite her own irrationality and lack of control, she is expected to exercise control on behalf of both of them. (Lees, 1997, p. 76)

The conception of sex underlying rape trials implies an active male predator encountering a passive female who may offer token resistance, be overcome and enjoys the 'sex' despite herself. Not only is the woman discredited for not knowing what she wants, but the man is credited both with knowing what she wants and ensuring that she gets it. As Sue Lees says:

> It reduces the whole issue of consent to absurdity, in which the woman is denied any subjectivity of knowledge of her own desire. (Lees, 1997, p. 77).

The woman does not know her own mind, nor does she have control over her own body. If a man accosts her sexually, her body betrays her. Any 'natural' lubrication of the vagina during forced sexual stimulation can be interpreted erroneously as evidence of consent, rather than merely evidence of stimulation. Defendants will sometimes argue in court that evidence of lubrication can be interpreted as signifying that 'she really wanted it'. Furthermore, Lees said she was 'horrified' to find that at least one police officer interviewed believed that forensic tests could be conducted on vaginal fluids to ascertain 'evidence' of consent (Lees, 1997, p. 77).

She says such discourses reflect 'hysterization' of women's bodies, which Foucault argues was one of the mechanisms of knowledge and power centring on sex (Foucault, 1981). In Lees's words:

> The woman is a sexual being, her rationality is therefore always debatable and her claim of rape always suspect. Men know best what her body really wants, and she is not more than her body. This is what renders women fickle and untrustworthy. (Lees, 1997, p. 78)

The social utility of such representations for men extends beyond women-blaming to advance a perspective within which male sexual desirability is assured. As Tony Jefferson has recently observed:

> The notion that 'no means yes' is a powerful, almost formulaic, masculinist fantasy within a certain discourse of sexuality. But note what it does: effectively, it transforms the fear of rejection ('no, I don't want it/you'), with all its attendant anxieties, into the positive 'come-on' of a 'yes, she wants it/me really'. (Jefferson, 1997, p. 291)

Obscured beneath the posturing of patriarchal power and control, masculine insecurities threaten to topple men from within. The suppression of their fears has been achieved in part by the oppression of others. Against such a backdrop, the words of men have fought to silence the testimony of women.

Conclusion

The response of the criminal justice system to rape complainants has been shaped by the beliefs outlined here: the first related to perceptions of the nature of rape and the second to perceptions of the nature of women. Both sets of assumptions have been challenged to some extent by significant shifts in thinking in the late twentieth century. Politically, developments in the areas of feminism and human rights have undermined men's traditional beliefs concerning their ownership of their wives and children. Traditional legal processes no longer have the authority and status they once commanded, and have been subject to stringent criticism regarding the need for extensive reform and for widespread education of key players, such as the judiciary (Gregory and Lees, 1999; Kennedy, 1992; Lees, 1996; Scutt, 1998; Thomas, 1994).

Against this backdrop, the traditional assumptions about rape and women are struggling to retain their grip. The anchor that secures them is the legacy of patriarchy, thousands of years of belief in the rights and superiority of men over women. Assumptions of the 'natural' supremacy of men, however, came under increasing attack during the latter years of the twentieth century. Feminists' analyses stressed the ways in which stereotypical and negative views of women have impacted on the criminal justice system's response to them, as both offenders and victims.

Despite such analyses and expositions, the historical and cultural legacy of mistrust of women remains manifest. Recent analyses of the media have highlighted the ways in which the 'new issue' of false rape allegations has been constructed to reinforce doubts regarding women's testimony (Gavey and Gow, 2001). Descriptions of allegations made and then retracted, along with rape trials resulting in not guilty verdicts, are uncritically presented as false complaints, with organisations representing men allegedly falsely accused of sexual abuse and rape gleefully amassing and republishing such cases to extend support for their claims.[17]

While greater societal acknowledgement of rape has been evident in recent law reforms and criminal justice system initiatives, these have brought mixed outcomes. One impact has been to encourage increased reporting by victims, particularly in relation to non-stranger sexual assaults (Harris and Grace, 1999; Sorenson and White, 1992). Given the predominance of rape allegations against men already known by the victim, however, it is the woman's credibility which has increasingly been put on trial. Discredit the woman and the allegation can be dismissed. It is salient to recall that men's 'right of access' to their wives has only very recently been challenged in law, and exists still as a site of disputation and conflict. Little surprise, then, that the sexual battleground remains a volatile and bloody scene. Not only is there a 'war against women' (French, 1992), but also a war *within* women. Women's lives, like those of trapeze artists, teeter on a highwire;

one foot wrong, and the fine balance between approval and approbation, commendation or condemnation, is lost.

Perceptions about the nature of rape combine with perceptions about the nature of women to create a cultural environment within which victims of rape will inevitably struggle to be believed. The extent to which complainants are viewed as credible plays a major role in how they will be treated by the police, whether their case proceeds to further investigation, and, if so, how it is likely to be assessed and adjudicated.

> For effective social change, it would be necessary to alter the cultural conception of woman as a sex object and completely change her economic position as an article of male property. Destroying the mythology surrounding the woman and her sexuality could perhaps remove part of the basis for her sexual exploitation. Without the old rationalizations, justifications, and ambiguities, rape could be defined by the woman, perceived by the man, and condemned by society as a violent and unjustified crime. Only then will it be possible to free the woman from the status of legitimate victim. (Weis and Borges, 1975, p. 141)

The chapters which follow contain the results of a series of studies examining women's experiences of reporting rape to the police, focussing in particular on issues of belief and credibility.

3

'Have you really been raped?' Criminal Justice System Responses

> The police were just wonderful to me. ... It gave me a lot of confidence in my belief of myself as a person of worth.

> The police are a big waste of time, and they haven't really got the complainant's interest and priority right. If only they knew how victims felt ...

> (Jordan, 1998a, p. 56)

Introduction

The responses of criminal justice system agencies to women rape complainants have reflected patriarchal legacies of thinking and representation. Legal discourse has reinforced views of women as inherently deceitful, their word as typically flawed. For a raped woman to have her allegation believed inevitably meant having her very person put on trial along with the offence. This chapter begins by reviewing legal and court initiatives before focussing on police responses to women rape victims. Relevant international literature is presented along with the results of a New Zealand study which sought to evaluate the impacts of recent reforms on women's experiences of reporting and trial processes.

Law reform initiatives

Law reform tends to be a frustrating exercise, given the difficulties associated with trying to achieve significant changes in a domain that has such conservative and patriarchal foundations. The questioning of a complainant's previous sexual history became an early platform for rape law reform. 'Rape shield' laws were introduced in many jurisdictions in an attempt to limit the impact of moral judgments about the complainant on trial outcomes (Allison and Wrightsman, 1993; Edwards and Heenan, 1994; Henning and Bronitt, 1998; New South Wales Department for Women, 1996; Taslitz, 1999; Temkin, 2002; Wiehe and Richards, 1995). In New Zealand, this resulted in changes to the Evidence Act prohibiting the questioning of any witness about the previous sexual experience of a complainant, unless the leave of the judge was obtained (Sullivan, 1986). This was extended in a 1985 amendment specifying that such questions could not be put 'directly or indirectly' (Sullivan, 1986, p. 45). In practice, however, defence lawyers still make insinuations and raise questions knowing the judge will intervene, while also knowing that it is the raising of the doubt in the jury's mind which is paramount (Adler, 1987; Lees, 1996; McDonald, 1997; New South Wales Department for Women, 1996; Taslitz, 1999). Thus, in some ways, raising such question marks over the woman's reputation can damage her credibility as much, if not more, as when she was expected to provide answers to such questions.

Simon Bronitt (1998) has observed similar potential dangers in relation to judicial direction concerning delays in reporting by rape victims. He suggests that recent law reforms aimed at encouraging judges to instruct juries that delays by victims in reporting may or may not be of import could, in fact, be counterproductive in their effects (Bronitt, 1998, p. 49). This outcome could eventuate because the jury may not know the legal rules underlying this direction, and may think it signals that the judge has question marks over the complainant's credibility (ibid.). In similar fashion, the abolition of judicial warnings regarding lack of corroboration in rape cases now leaves the situation entirely to the jury to assess, within the safe and secret confines of the jury room, beyond the reach of issues of transparency and accountability. Likewise, an unintended outcome of the promotion of gender neutrality may be that discrimination against women becomes more masked, with negative and stereotypical portrayals of women as unreliable complainants remaining pronounced but hidden and unable to be challenged (ibid., p. 43 footnote). Thus the spectre of the untrustworthy complainant who is dishonest, vengeful and prone to fantasy remains profoundly feminine.

Similar points could be raised with regard to testimony concerning the previous sexual history of the complainant. Historically, a major way to discredit a woman's allegation of rape was to discredit her sexual reputation (Adler, 1987; Estrich, 1987; Frohmann, 1995; Lees, 1996, 1997; New South Wales Department for Women, 1996; Scutt, 1997; Smart, 1990; Taslitz, 1999; Temkin, 2002). The dominant assumption, which defence lawyers often manipulated to the offender's advantage, was that an unmarried woman who agreed to consensual sex with any man was unlikely to be a genuine victim of rape. Women, it seemed, were completely lacking in discernment, and since, once their virginity was lost, they had nothing more to lose, wanton licentiousness followed! If such women ever said 'no', it could reasonably be interpreted as 'yes', and even more so if it was to a man with whom she had previously engaged in consensual sex. A woman's chastity, it seems, was like a locked door which, once either unlocked by her or kicked in by someone else, could never be locked again. Such thinking was particularly evident in relation to women working in the sex industry, who historically have been particularly vulnerable to sexual coercion yet denied 'legitimate' victim-status (Gilbert, 1993; O'Neill, 1997; Scutt, 1993). As Scutt puts it:

> Sex-for-money is one aspect of a woman's sex life which, in the assessment of the court, means she is 'used to sex' and therefore (by some sleight of hand, or perverse 'logic') will not be 'so upset' by rape. (Scutt, 1997, p. 46)

From the mid-1980s onwards, then, significant legal changes have been enacted in New Zealand, Australia, North America and the United Kingdom in response to feminist criticisms regarding rape injustices (New Zealand: Jordan, 1998a,b; Australia: Heath, 1998; Mason, 1995; New South Wales Department for Women, 1996; United States of America: Doerner and Lab, 1998; United Kingdom: Gregory and Lees, 1999; Temkin, 2002). However, writing within the Australian context, Simon Bronitt has commented that recent empirical studies in the Australian states of New South Wales and Victoria

> ... suggest that the criminal justice system's treatment of women who allege rape has not significantly improved, and in some respects may be worse than before the reforms were enacted! (Bronitt, 1998, p. 42)

Similar conclusions have been drawn with respect to the United Kingdom (Brown *et al.*, 1993a; Kelly, 2002; Lees, 1997), specifically in relation to the difficulties involved in significantly improving police responses to rape complainants (New Zealand: Jordan, 1998a; United Kingdom: Gregory and Lees, 1999; Temkin, 1997). Entrenched patriarchal thinking within legal and police cultures are often stressed as a significant factor underlying resistance to change (Brown and Heidensohn, 2000; Gregory and Lees, 1999). Bronitt (1998) argues that alongside these cultural explanations for the failure of rape law reform lie deeper structural explanations. He draws on the concept of 'counterproductive regulation', a term used by Peter Grabosky (1995) when describing the ways in which legal regulation can be resisted and subverted by individuals and organisations. This process of resistance can produce unintended consequences, in effect backfiring to produce a worsening of the situation which reforms were intended to remedy. Thus, argues Bronitt, the abolition of overtly discriminatory legal rules and definitions has been seen as progress in rape law reform,

> ... but often this substantive restructuring merely frees the trial judge and jury to apply discriminatory myths and misconceptions about female sexuality to the remodelled definitions of consent, relevance and credibility. (Bronitt, 1998, pp. 42–3)

Directing a jury to ignore a remark, for instance, can unintentionally reinforce judgmental attitudes already present within jury members' minds. More important than warnings, directions and evidential requirements is the context within which dominant rape narratives and discourses are constructed (Ehrlich, 2001; Matoesian, 1993; Taslitz, 1999). While adherence to traditional beliefs and attitudes persists, reforms will be limited in scope and effectiveness. In this sense, the most significant changes affecting rape laws are yet to be made.

Court and trial processes

Analyses of the criminal justice system's responses to female rape complainants have tended, for the most part, to focus on court and trial experiences. This is not surprising, given the relatively public nature of the courts and the extent of media coverage possible. Court trials provide a public spectacle, whereby legal rituals and authority symbols are utilised as devices for shaming and punishment. Feminist criticisms of rape trials have typically argued that it is the alleged victim, rather than the alleged offender, who experiences the most arduous assaults on her character and behaviour (Adler, 1987; Lees, 1996; New South Wales Department for Women, 1996; Smart, 1989; Taslitz, 1999; van de Zandt, 1998). Thus the rape trial has repeatedly been referred to as a second victimisation for rape victims, experienced as a brutal and degrading violation akin in nature to that of the rape itself (Adler, 1987; Hall, 1985; Kennedy, 1992; Lees, 1996; Madigan and Gamble, 1991; Matoesian, 1993; McDonald, 1997; Stanko, 1982). One writer argued, in fact, that:

> Rape continues to result in quadruple victimization, as the actual assault is followed by psychological assaults from police, medical personnel, and the judicial system. (Mills, 1982, p. 53)

Historically, as we saw earlier, the laws on rape reflected men's definitions of sexuality and their relationships with women. Women's experiences of sex or rape were not taken into account in the formulation of such laws (Easteal, 1998a; Lees, 1997; Smart, 1989; Young, 1998). The views which predominated depicted men as having a biological need and imperative for sex, which women as wives and nurturers had an obligation to fulfil. Against this backdrop, what women themselves want fades from view; it is simply not relevant. The quest for 'truth' and 'objectivity' in such a biased setting is destined to achieve neither. As Jocelynne Scutt has observed:

> It is a truism that objectivity is the name given to men's subjectivities. 'Objectivity' operates generally against women's interests. (Scutt, 1998, p. 166)

In the court setting, a woman's word is not enough to show a genuine lack of consent. Even where the perpetrator intimidates with threats of, or actual, force and violence, strong evidence of physical resistance may still be demanded on her part (Firth, 1975; Lees, 1997; Scutt, 1998). A lack of visible injuries may even be referred to in cases where the alleged offender and complainant know each other well, despite psychological evidence demonstrating that physical resistance may be even more unlikely in such relationship contexts (Wiehe and Richards, 1995).

A significant factor complicating judicial and court perceptions stems from the historic acceptance of violence within male–female relationships (Jackson, 1996; Kelly, 1988; Stanko, 1985; Walklate, 2001). This extends to sexual relationships, where the belief is still regularly advanced that at least some degree of coercion is the norm, prompting certain writers to refer to men being effectively granted 'a licence to rape' (Easteal, 1998b, p. 107; Stuart, 1993, p. 97). Such a view has been reflected in judicial pronouncements even comparatively recently. In a South Australian example from 1992, Justice Bollen asserted in his summing up:

> There is, of course, nothing wrong with a husband faced with his wife's initial refusal to engage in intercourse, in attempting, in an acceptable way, to persuade her to change her mind, and that may involve a measure of *rougher than usual handling*. It may be, in the end, that handling and persuasion will persuade the wife to agree. Sometimes it is a fine line between not agreeing, then changing of the mind, and consenting. (Bollen, quoted in Easteal, 1998b, p. 115) [My emphasis]

The cross-examination process in court has been uniformly described by complainants as savage and gruelling (Adler, 1987; Brown *et al.*, 1993a; Kennedy, 1992; Lees, 1997; McDonald, 1997; New South Wales Department for Women, 1996; Scutt, 1997; Stuart, 1993; Taslitz, 1999; Thomas, 1994). Women are routinely asked personal and invasive questions that have been designed to provoke, shame and compromise their integrity. Defence lawyers will focus in particular on aspects related to the woman's dress, behaviour, alcohol and drugs consumption and her relationship to the alleged offender (Adler, 1987; Brown *et al.*, 1993a; Ehrlich, 2001; Kennedy, 1992; Lees, 1997; Schuller and Stewart, 2000; Scutt, 1997; Shapcott, 1988; Temkin, 2002). Various international commentators have observed that although cross-examination of the complainant concerning her previous sexual history is now only admissible with the leave of the judge, inferences can be made, and questions can be posed which, even if overturned, nevertheless may plant doubts in the jury's mind regarding her sexual reputation or veracity (Lees, 1996; New South Wales Department for Women, 1996; Taslitz, 1999; Temkin, 2002). Anything that can be used to discredit her will be, in what has been described as a process akin to pornography (Smart,

1989). The witch trials of the fifteenth to the seventeenth centuries provided pornographic 'thrills' for repressed monks (Daly, 1979), in ways which bear strong parallels to the role played by modern day rape trials (Henning and Bronitt, 1998; Lees, 1997). According to Alison Young:

> In the law of rape is found the rape of law; that is, the events that constitute legal rape and – outside the frame – the events that follow when rape has been legalised. (Young, 1998, p. 161)

A major Australian study tracked 150 sexual assault cases progressing through the New South Wales courts in a one-year period (New South Wales Department for Women, 1996; van de Zandt, 1998). All of the complainants found it hard to answer repeated questions in court regarding the sex act, and involving descriptions of sexual organs. The study's author, Pia van de Zandt, notes that in 95 per cent of the trials studied, the complainant was asked questions about sexual organs. Complainants were asked on average 16 of these questions, although in one trial a woman with a psychiatric disability was asked 81 such sexual questions. Such questions forced women to talk about their bodies in sexualised ways, prompting van de Zandt to proclaim:

> A sexual assault trial is ritualised degradation dressed up as court process. (van de Zandt, 1998, p. 125)

Cross-examination of the complainant seems designed to 'uncover' the real villain in the trial, who may be portrayed as the whore, harridan, temptress or any one or more of the myths which protect men from allegations of sexual assault and hence from having to take responsibility for their own violence. As Lees describes this process:

> The myth of equal justice for all is no more blatantly exposed than in a rape trial. The whole procedure loads the dice against her. Not only her testimony, but her very life up to her complaint of rape and her motives in making that complaint are brought into question, and often aggressively or mockingly so ... It is a consolidation of heterosexual privilege; the privilege of men to decide when a woman says 'yes'; the right of men to have sex when, how and when (sic) they want; the right of men to control female sexuality and prevent female autonomy. (Lees, 1997, pp. 61–2, 88)

Obtaining a rape conviction is still a difficult undertaking. The attrition rate in cases of sexual assault is astonishingly high, and has also significantly increased in recent years (Gregory and Lees, 1999; Harris and Grace, 1999; Kelly, 2002; Temkin, 2002). While populist sentiment, fuelled by backlash reactions, claims that our prisons are full of the wrongfully convicted, for no other crime is a conviction apparently so difficult to secure. The require-ments of the court are often at odds with the reality of women's experience. For example, for evidence of a rape complaint to be admissible in court, it is preferred that the reporting of the alleged offence be made 'voluntarily, spontaneously and speedily' (van de Zandt, 1998, p. 134). This follows on from the historic belief cited earlier, which specified that the 'hue and cry' test be applied to victims' allegations of rape.

Today this practice continues in the expectation that genuine sexual assault complaints will be made by the victim at the first opportunity (Bronitt, 1998; McDonald, 1994; Temkin, 2002). In the New South Wales study, 55 per cent of the complainants told someone about the sexual assault within an hour of its occurrence; and another 28 per cent told someone within 12 hours; so, over-all, 83 per cent told someone within 12 hours (van de Zandt, 1998). In terms of reporting the assault to the police, half of the complainants told the police within five hours, 31 per cent within one hour; and 81 per cent reported it to the police within seven days (ibid.). Despite this, in 59 per cent of the trials studied, the defence raised the victim's delay in making the complaint as an issue during their cross-examination. Thus although women tended not to delay in telling others and police, they were nevertheless cross-examined over delaying and possible reasons for their hesitation (van de Zandt, 1998). Judges also on occasion reiterated this sentiment. One said, for example:

> A complaint is admissible if made at the earliest possible opportunity – if a man runs out of a house and doesn't tell anyone the house is burning until the night following, it is not consistent with him believing that the house was on fire when he ran out of it. (quoted in van de Zandt, 1998, p. 137)

Such pronouncements reveal more about judicial ignorance concerning the effects of rape than they do about the veracity of rape complainants. The desire to minimise or deny they have been raped is uppermost in many vic-tims' minds following the attack (Gavey, 1999; Kelly, 1988). Thus, if there is any substantive truth in the statement that 'women lie about rape', it is most likely to be in underestimating the severity of what has happened, conceal-ing the violation from those close to them, refusing to inform police of its occurrence and colluding to protect the identity of the offender. In other words, this is the complete opposite of what women are accused of doing, prompting one writer to proclaim:

> The myth is false claims of rape; the reality is severe underreporting of rape. (Torrey, 1991, pp. 1030–1)

In writing about the role of the judge in rape trials, Lees observed how, until recently, rape was the only crime where a warning was given to the jury concerning how easy it is to make rape allegations (Lees, 1997). No such similar warning is made regarding the likelihood of accused men lying to avoid conviction. As Temkin noted (1997), when women report other crimes, such as burglary, their word is not automatically doubted. There would be investigation of the woman's claim but not of her integrity or her whole life. Also glossed over are the difficulties women face in making complaints of rape, their fear and reluctance at doing so, and the fact that rape has one of the lowest reporting rates of any crime (Chambers and Millar, 1983; Feldman-Summers and Norris, 1984; Gilmore and Pittman, 1993; Kelly, 1988, 2002; Kilpatrick *et al.*, 1987; Koss *et al.*, 1988; Lees, 1997; Williams, 1984).

The assertion that women frequently lie about rape, however, continues to be one of the most influential rape myths. Doubts concerning the woman's credibility as a witness are routinely voiced, the underlying assumption being that she is prone to lying and fabrication. Such a perception outweighs, in many cases, evidence of resistance and visible injuries sustained by the victim, or even gross inconsistencies, changed stories and 'lies' in the defendant's account (Gregory and Lees, 1999; Mack, 1998). Writing within the Australian context, Annie Cossins has noted

> As the myths associated with lying, immoral women work to the disadvantage of the female complainant, they simultaneously work to the advantage of the male accused. The balance of justice in a sexual assault trial is clearly weighted against the complainant, since the mere allegation of sexual assault leaves a woman open to having 'her victimisation measured against the current rape mythologies'. (Cossins, 1998, p. 100)

The study of sexual assault trials conducted by van de Zandt revealed that the most common theme in cross-examination related to suggestions that a complainant had lied or made a false report, and to speculation concerning motivation (van de Zandt, 1998). Despite corroboration by others, or evidence of injuries, suggestions were frequently made by defence lawyers that complainants had ulterior motives in bringing cases to court. Of the complainants who were asked directly whether or not they were lying, each was on average asked seven questions (ibid.). In one case, the defence counsel accused the woman of trying to cover up her lies with tantrums; she was asked 178 questions regarding her general drug use, and it was put to her 70 times in court that she was lying or making the story up (ibid.). In over half the trials studied (54 per cent) the complainant was questioned about a possible motive which may underlie her making a false report to the police. A vast array of possible motives were suggested by the defence, including the possibilities of the complainant fabricating such an allegation out of guilt, anger, or to support claims for residency, child custody, or financial compensation (ibid.). Similar 'reasons' for women lying have been identified elsewhere, generally emphasising reputation, self-protection, revenge and self-gain (Chambers and Millar, 1983; Lees, 1997; Mack, 1998). Sometimes, the question of motive is completely glossed over, as if no motive is necessary when deception is regarded as a 'natural' character trait.

Research on rape trials conducted in Victoria, Australia, revealed the law and judiciary still operate with a profound suspicion of women and perceptions of their inherent deceitfulness (Edwards and Heenan, 1994). This mistrust extends, not surprisingly, to jurors in rape trials, in ways that demonstrate the dominance of prevailing cultural narratives (Frohmann, 1995; Kalven and Zeisel, 1966; Matoesian, 1993; Scutt, 1997). Whilst on a rational level, notions of women 'asking for it' may be rejected, the power of these narratives means that, if presented with a case involving a drunk, scantily clad woman who accuses her date of raping her, jurors may be disinclined to accept her account (Kalven and Zeisel, 1966; Kennedy, 1992; Matoesian, 1993; Scutt, 1997; Taslitz, 1999). In addressing the inadequacies of the current adversarial justice system for adducing rape cases, US Law Professor Andrew Taslitz has recently observed

> Our current adversarialism … is modeled after male 'ways of speaking' in everyday life. Just as those ways of speaking mute the female voice in business, education, and politics, so do they mute that voice at trials. The inability to engage with cultural narratives and macho adversarialism explains rape-law reform's failure. These primary mechanisms by which rape jurors determine credibility are unchanged. Consequently, unjustified acquittals mount. (Taslitz, 1999, pp. 154–5)

Similar sentiments have been echoed by Professor Mary Koss (2000) and in the New Zealand context by Justice Thomas (1994), who publicly voiced his reservations concerning the ability of the criminal justice system to deliver 'justice' to rape victims.

Clearly there are significant problems to be addressed in rape and sexual assault trials when key legal players in a variety of countries state they have such little confidence in the system that, if they or someone close to them, was sexually assaulted, they would advise them *against* reporting the offence and becoming a complainant in court (Dacre, 1996; van de Zandt, 1998). When those familiar with the court process want to see their loved ones protected from its rigours and injustices, what confidence can any victim of sexual assault have when deciding whether or not to report a rape?

Police investigative processes

Whilst there have been many studies conducted of rape complainants' experiences of legal, court and trial processes, considerably less has been written about their interactions with the police. Studies on the effectiveness of law reform initiatives have largely focussed on the prosecutorial level of the criminal justice system (Frohmann, 1998; Spohn and Horney, 1992), rather than on the possible impacts of these on law enforcement practices (Campbell and Johnson, 1997). Police processes are considerably harder to observe and document, yet the police's position as the gatekeepers to the criminal justice system makes their roles and responses critical (Adler, 1987; Gregory and Lees, 1999; Harris and Grace, 1999; Kelly, 2002; Kerstetter, 1990; LaFree, 1980; Radford, 1987). As Goodstein and Lutze observed

> Police response to rape may be the most crucial link in the chain to ensure fair treatment for rape victims. The police officer is the first representative of the criminal justice system the reporting victim encounters; the quality of her contact with the police officer may color her perception of the entire prosecution process. (Goodstein and Lutze, 1992, p. 169)

Reporting a rape is not a straightforward process. The decision to report is extremely difficult for many victims, and can raise issues of denial, safety, fear, shame and self-blame (Feldman-Summers and Norris, 1984; Gilmore and Pittman, 1993; Koss *et al.*, 1988; Williams, 1984). A reluctance to report the offence is further compounded in those situations where the rapist is someone known by the victim, possibly even a partner or family member (Easteal, 1998b; Gartner and Macmillan, 1995; Wiehe and Richards, 1995). The impact of reporting can also be fraught, depending on the reactions of those around the victim and also on the response of the police. The possibility always exists for reporting to result in secondary victimisation, with the police occupying a pivotal role as the first agency that, through its processes and attitudes, may revictimise the complainant (Campbell and Raja, 1999; Epstein and Langenbahn, 1994; Gilmore and Pittman, 1993; Stuart, 1993; Winkel *et al.*, 1991).

A negative police response can compound the trauma suffered by a rape victim, making it less likely that she will decide to proceed with legal action and a strong possibility that her experience will deter others from even making the initial police contact in similar circumstances (Gilmore and Pittman, 1993). If for no other reason, it is in the overall interests of law enforcement for the police to act in ways that are consistent with promoting the victim's emotional wellbeing (Burgess, 1999).

Irrespective of the kind of response received, reporting a rape is inevitably arduous. In the words of Gilmore and Pittman:

> The very personal nature of the crime, the intimate and sexual explicitness of its detail, means the process of step by step description of the assault is, for the victim, invariably harrowing. The prospect of relaying such detail to anyone is daunting; how much more so when such detail must be relayed to uniformed and armed strangers as is the case when

making a statement of formal complaint to the police. By virtue of their entry point function, these hitherto strangers have the power to decide whether or not to proceed with legal action. This is the power to formally invalidate the victim's experience or refer it to the courts in which reside the sole power to formally validate the woman's perception (and indeed her lived experience) that she has been the victim of a heinous crime. (Gilmore and Pittman, 1993, p. 9)

Police writers in the 1970s and 1980s referred to the skills needed for the 'interrogation' of rape victims (e.g., Firth, 1975; Wagstaff, 1982), while rape complainants graphically described feeling as if they were being interrogated (Chambers and Millar, 1983; Hall, 1985; Holmstrom and Burgess, 1978; Medea and Thompson, 1974; Toner, 1982). In England, the televising of a documentary in 1983 showed police interviewing a rape complainant (Adler, 1987; Dowdeswell, 1986; Gregory and Lees, 1999; Lees, 1997; Smith, 1989; Temkin, 2002). In a clear demonstration of the gulf which existed at that time between police officers and public sentiment, the police had expected reaction to the programme to be positive and to result in commendation of the officers' interviewing skills. Instead of applauding the detectives, however, their insensitive and brutal interrogation of a traumatised victim was soundly condemned in many quarters, such that to this day, Thames Valley Police still appear to be 'living this incident down' (Gregory and Lees, 1999, p. 4).[18]

Throughout the 1970s and 1980s, research on women who had been raped revealed inconsistencies in the ways in which sexual assault victims were treated by the police (Estrich, 1987; Holmstrom and Burgess, 1978; Medea and Thompson, 1974; O'Reilly, 1984; Smith, 1989). Many women negatively recounted their experiences of police investigations and reported feeling disbelieved and unsupported by the police (Chambers and Millar, 1983; Hall, 1985; Wright, 1984). It appeared that women's chances of receiving a sympathetic police response were most commonly linked to stranger attacks and increased in accordance with the extent of physical injuries suffered in the attack (Feldman-Summers and Norris, 1984; Koss *et al.*, 1988; Williams, 1984). Overall the reporting rate for rape was low (Adler, 1987; Hall, 1985; London Rape Crisis Centre, 1984).

In recent years, police departments around the world have attempted to improve their response to rape complainants. These efforts arose in part from criticisms of police practice, as well as from increasing concern over the extremely low reporting rates for rape and other sexual assault offences (Chambers and Millar, 1983; Gregory and Lees, 1999; Nixon, 1992). In the mid-1980s, Ian Blair (1985) visited the United States of America to see what could be learned from police practices there which might help to improve the situation in Britain. The basic difference he observed involved a preparedness in the United States of America to deal with the victim from the perspective of understanding how rape affects her and her interactions with the police; Blair advocated that this 'new approach' should also be adopted within the United Kingdom. Internationally, various measures have been introduced such as rape examination suites in England (Gregory and Lees, 1999; Walklate, 1995); specialised sex crimes units in the United States of America (Epstein and Langenbahn, 1994; LaFree, 1981) and England (Brown and Heidensohn, 2000); greater deployment of female police officers to sexual assault cases (Goodstein and Lutze, 1992; Pike, 1992); and training programmes designed to increase officers' sensitivity and awareness (Holmstrom and Burgess, 1978; Epstein and Langenbahn, 1994; Feild, 1978; National Center for Women and Policing, 2001; Nixon, 1992).

Despite such efforts, success, if taken to mean improved police understanding and increased victims' satisfaction, seems remote. Attrition rates in rape cases continue to be high, reporting rates remain low and beliefs regarding false complaints seem firmly entrenched. Such limited success reflects the limited potential for change in a context characterised at worst by masculinism and at best by ambivalence. As Jill Radford has observed

> On the one hand, the police are a paid full-time, professional agency, theoretically concerned with protecting citizens from violence and crime. Many women do turn to the police after being attacked and it is right that they should be treated with respect and sensitivity. Withholding protection from women adds to their humiliation, pain and insecurity. Further, the failure to condemn men's violence legitimates violence as an acceptable means of controlling women. On the other hand, the role of the police is to protect the status quo which, as one of the women interviewed pointed out, is 'white, male and middle-class'. The police failure to provide an adequate response to men's violence is perfectly consistent with this role. (Radford, 1987, p. 41)

Increasing effort has been made to ascertain the views of rape complainants themselves regarding their treatment by the police. One of the first such studies conducted in Britain involved a postal survey of 103 women aged 18 and over who had reported a rape or similar serious sexual offence to the Metropolitan Police between May 1990 and February 1991 (Adler, 1991). The results of this study appeared encouraging, with more than 80 per cent of the complainants stating that, in the first week following reporting of the offence, they found the police helpful and sensitive, and that this was irrespective of the victim's age, physical injuries or relationship to the assailant. Accordingly, Zsuzsanna Adler commented:

> Police attitudes were described in overwhelmingly positive terms, and most women indicated that they had found officers easy to talk to, supportive, patient, reassuring and considerate. (Adler, 1991, p. 1115)

The most commonly identified problem related to declining satisfaction levels over time, with 70 per cent of the women expressing concern that the police failed to keep them adequately informed about case progress and developments. On the basis of the generally positive results overall, however, Adler commented

> ... the conclusion must be that attitudes to victims of rape in the Met are now overwhelmingly caring and sympathetic. (ibid., p. 1115)

The results of Adler's study, however, seem not to have been supported by other research in this area. It is possible that the methodology she employed was at least partly responsible for the overall positive tone of the findings she obtained. Only women whose reports of rape were recorded as such by the police were contacted, meaning that no complainants were included whose cases had been 'no crimed' and which the police had decided to investigate no further. Moreover, postal surveys are not generally accepted as the most reliable of methodologies when it comes to sensitive subject areas such as rape, and it is interesting that subsequent studies based on interview procedures (Jordan, 1998a; Gregory and Lees, 1999; Temkin, 1997, 1999) have all produced significantly lower rates of complainants' satisfaction with police performance.

In the 1990s, Jennifer Temkin conducted two significant qualitative studies with rape complainants in England (Temkin, 1997, 1999). The first of these, conducted with women in Sussex, obtained in-depth information from 23 respondents. Some aspects of police procedures were greeted favourably by respondents; for example, all but one of the women was positive about the officers who took their statement and the way it was taken (Temkin, 1997, p. 514). Temkin also notes that all but two of the officers who took the statement were female, and links this to concerns about the victim's credibility. In two cases, she states, the victims were initially treated with suspicion and disbelief, but the police changed their attitude later – in one of these, no female officer was present, and in the other, the victim said she was upset that there was a male officer present with a female officer (Temkin, 1997, pp. 513–14). Temkin divided the 23 respondents into 3 categories based on their overall levels of satisfaction with the police. Those women who were described as 'Positive' (N = 13; 57 per cent) were wholly or mainly positive about their experience with the police; those in the 'Mixed' category (N = 7; 30 per cent) made comments which were fairly evenly balanced in terms of positives and negatives; and those referred to as 'Negative' (N = 3; 13 per cent) were wholly or mainly negative about their experience with the police. Positive evaluations, said Temkin, resulted particularly in situations where the women had not encountered disbelief from the police. Thus, she notes

> The experience of feeling believed was particularly vital ... Feeling believed was of significant assistance both in dealing with the criminal justice system and also in coping with the trauma of the rape itself. (ibid., p. 519)

One factor specified as important to complainants was the manner and attitude of the police. Since, as victims of rape, the women often had their own feelings of guilt and self-blame to manage, it was important for them not to feel judged by the police (Temkin, 1997).

Temkin also conducted qualitative research with 17 women in London whose cases were recorded as rape between 1993 and 1995, as well as interviewing 21 police officers, 8 of whom were involved in cases in the sample of victims (Temkin, 1999). This study was significant in finding that police guidelines provide a framework for a system of care for victims, but in practice these guidelines are not always followed. Of concern was the fact that disbelieving and stereotypical attitudes about women who report rape persist in the minds of many officers.

Attrition rates

High attrition rates in rape cases have long been noted, with concern expressed about the high proportion of reported cases of rape which are categorised by the police as 'no crimes' and not recorded (Chambers and Millar, 1983; Gregory and Lees, 1999; Harris and Grace, 1999; Kelly, 2002; Temkin, 2002). As Jeanne Gregory and Sue Lees commented

> It was clear from earlier research that the sexual assaults that are reported, whether to a rape crisis centre, a doctor or a police officer, are the mere tip of an iceberg of staggering proportions. It is all the more puzzling to discover that a large proportion of these reports fall away at later stages in the criminal justice process. (Gregory and Lees, 1999, p. 59)

An early pattern observed was that, at each stage in the criminal justice process, if some prior relationship existed between the complainant and the suspect, the more likely the case was to be dropped, or downgraded, than if it involved a 'stranger' attack (Adler, 1987; Bouffard, 2000; Gregory and Lees, 1996; Harris and Grace, 1999; Kelly, 2002). Studies in Scotland (Chambers and Millar, 1983) and England and Wales (Wright, 1984) found that approximately 25 per cent of reported rapes were 'no-crimed'. The argument was advanced that, to improve their performance record, the police 'lost' from their records many cases which they considered were unlikely to proceed to court or be cleared in some other way (Blair, 1985; Gregory and Lees, 1996). The impression thus given was that thousands of women made false allegations of rape and sexual assault. Of course, 'no criming' occurs in other offence categories also, such as robbery and burglary, but usually as a result of the offender not being apprehended (Polk, 1985). The overall rate of 'no criming', across all offences, has, in fact, been estimated at only 3 per cent

(Bottomley and Coleman, 1981). Gregory and Lees (1999) suggest that, in contrast, the high rates of 'no criming' for rape and sexual assault demonstrate the low priority attached by the police to these offences.

During his study tour of the United States of America, Blair (1985) noted that some police departments had three different categories for the equivalent of cases that were 'no crimed'. These were: 'inactive' (undetected); 'unfounded'; and 'victim withdraws allegation'. Contrary to the Scottish and English police forces, officers in San Francisco, for example, were not encouraged to seek a complainant's withdrawal of the allegation or to unfound the case. As Blair noted

> The attitude of both investigators and administrators is that in the majority of cases, classifying cases as unfounded or withdrawn is acting as judge and jury without the full facts. It is an unnecessary additional burden for the victim to bear. In order to protect the victim, therefore, doubtful cases are permitted to lie on file, often with little further investigation. (Blair, 1985, p. 58)

As a result, of 2485 cases of serious sexual assault investigated, only 2 per cent were classified as unfounded; in 14 per cent, the victims withdrew the allegation, and half were deemed inactive (Blair, 1985).

In response to mounting criticism, the Home Office introduced new guidelines stating that rape complaints should not be 'no crimed' unless the complainant herself retracted and admitted fabrication (Home Office Circulars 25/83 and 69/86, cited in Gregory and Lees, 1996, p. 4). This was further reinforced in Force Orders issued by the London Metropolitan Police, and the resulting fall in the 'no criming' rate from 61 per cent in 1984 to 38 per cent in 1986 was attributed to this directive (Smith, 1989). However, more recent research by Gregory and Lees (1996) highlighted the fact that, despite a supposed shift towards more sensitive treatment of victims, a high proportion of reported sexual assault cases are still 'no crimed' by the police. They studied two London police stations over a two-year period, examining the processing of all reported cases of rape, attempted rape and indecent assault. Their research revealed the 'no criming' rate to be still 38 per cent overall (116 of the 301 cases reported). When the rape and attempted rape cases were analysed separately, the 'no criming' rate rose to 43 per cent (47 of 109 cases) (ibid.). Gregory and Lees particularly wanted to include cases which were 'no crimed' within the first month, in contrast to other studies which sometimes excluded such cases. The reasons cited for 'no criming' included the complainant's failure to substantiate the allegation, and her withdrawing of the complaint (which was more likely when the perpetrator was known to her). In about one-third of the cases that were 'no crimed', the police said this was because there was insufficient evidence to substantiate the allegation. Police decisions in these cases were based on such factors as judgements made concerning the reliability of complainants as a source of evidence, and assessments of the extent to which they would be perceived as credible in court (ibid.).

A Home Office study (Harris and Grace, 1999) notes that there appears to have been a reduction in the 'no criming' rate from 45 per cent in 1985 to 25 per cent in 1999. Despite acknowledging that Home Office guidance advises police to 'no crime' a case if the complainant 'retracts completely and admits to fabrication' (Harris and Grace, 1999, p. xi), over one-third of cases were 'no crimed' because the complainant withdrew the allegation, and a further 15 per cent because of insufficient evidence. Analysis showed that the cases least likely to be 'no crimed' involved complainants aged under 13 or incidents where the use of physical violence in the assault was evident (ibid.). The researchers also noted that the reduction in the 'no criming' rate appeared to have been offset by an increase in the proportion of cases in which the police decided to take no further action against the suspects. They concluded that the cases that the police were most likely to proceed with involved

> ... complainants under 13 where violence was used during the attack and there had been no prior contact between complainant and suspect. (Harris and Grace, 1999, p. xi)

High levels of 'no criming', however, have been confused with the issue of false allegations, as if the one signified the other (Gregory and Lees, 1999; Stace, 1983). Although this is a clearly erroneous equation, it has helped to reinforce an attitude of police disbelief and suspiciousness towards rape complainants.

Police, rape and false allegations

A central strand running through police involvement in rape investigations links the societal legacy of beliefs about the nature of women with the attributes of police occupational culture. Writing in 1975, Peters made the following observation.

> If a woman alleges assault other than rape, she is generally believed, examined medically and treated if necessary. Police and court response is direct and usually according to law. However, if the assault is sexual, that is, if she is alleging rape, the response may be quite different. No one wants to believe her. (Peters, 1975, p. 34)

A core of disbelief towards women reporting sexual assaults appears to lie at the heart of the police culture. The basis for this view lies in the legacy of attitudes towards women already identified in this chapter, which is further reinforced by the cynicism and masculine ethos of the police occupational culture. Whilst acknowledging that 'police culture' is not a distinct, homogeneous entity (Chan, 1996), nevertheless, common attributes identified have included traits of suspiciousness, conservatism, authoritarianism and machismo (Reiner, 1994). Police officers are trained to be suspicious, alert for signs of discomfort, inconsistencies and concealment (Chambers and Millar, 1983). Such traits can be both highly useful and potentially counterproductive. For instance, in writing about a particular psychological, attentional type, Goleman termed it 'The Detective' because of obvious similarities with a Sherlock Holmes-style approach (Goleman, 1985). Of the kind of 'driven search' characteristic of these investigators, Goleman warns of a

> … distinctive distortion in The Detective's perception. He looks so keenly that he does not quite see; he hears so astutely that he fails to listen. In other words, his deficit is not in his attentional powers, which are often brilliantly attuned. His attention is off because it is guided by a lack of interest in the obvious. The surface of things is for him far from the truth of the matter; he seeks to pierce through plain facts to the hidden reality. He listens and looks not to gather what is apparent, but what it *signifies*.
>
> Looking so hard for the telling clue to a hidden meaning is like peering into a microscope. The Detective is apt to search so intently that he loses sight of the context that gives meaning to what he sees. That, of course, fits well with his basic stance toward it anyhow: its *seeming* context is the merely apparent, which is for him a false reality. He grasps at a small detail that fits his schema, while ignoring its actual context. The net effect is that he loses a sense of the fact's real significance, replacing it with a special interpretation.
>
> While built upon factual details, such a subjective world can be totally askew in the meaning given those details. (Goleman, 1985, p. 138) [Emphasis in original]

Research on factors affecting police officers' perceptions exemplifies this well. Mulder and Winkel (1996) conducted studies in which the participants were shown reconstructions of an interview with a rape victim, with the sound removed. The results showed that the same scenario was interpreted completely differently based on the dominant perspective adopted by those viewing it. Those operating with a victim focussed approach tried to appreciate the effects of trauma on how the victim might appear, and interpreted, for example, the complainant's nervousness as indicative of trauma. Conversely, those who viewed the scenario from a 'police' or truth focussed perspective thought the victim appeared deceptive and concealing. The authors concluded that the study clearly revealed the need to train police officers more fully in interpreting non-verbal behaviour in victims of crime and in appreciating the destructive potential for police attitudes to cause secondary victimisation in rape complainants (Mulder and Winkel, 1996, p. 318).

One dominant and destructive characteristic underpinning police participation in rape investigations arises from exaggerated beliefs in the prevalence of false rape allegations. Concern has been expressed internationally regarding the high proportions of sexual assault complaints that are believed to be false (Blair, 1985; Chambers and Millar, 1983; Fairstein, 1993; Feldman-Summers and Palmer, 1980; Gilmore and Pittman, 1993; Gregory and Lees, 1999; Jordan, 2004; Kanin, 1994; Kelly, 2002; London Rape Crisis Centre, 1984; Mintz, 1973; National Center for Women and Policing, 2001; O'Reilly, 1984; Scutt, 1997; Temkin, 2002). One early study conducted in the United States of America, for instance, revealed that the police officers who participated in the research believed approximately three out of every five rape complaints to be either false or mistaken (Feldman-Summers and Palmer, 1980). Factors identified as relating to the perceived 'truthfulness' of an allegation were noted:

> Specifically, a rape complainant who displays physical injuries, is consistent in her account of rape, is willing to take a lie detector test, doesn't wait 48 hours before reporting, does not engage in premarital or extramarital relations, has not had social contact with the assailant previously, and does not reach the location of the rape voluntarily is seen by others as having been raped. Given what information is currently available about rape complaints, most women who report being raped will not fare well under these criteria. (Feldman-Summers and Palmer, 1980, p. 16)

Likewise, in Chambers and Millar's (1983) Scottish study, many detectives estimated false complaints to be very common, with one saying he believed only 1:20 were 'real rapes' (Chambers and Millar, 1983, p. 85 footnote). Junior detectives would typically say that, although they had dealt with few false ones themselves, nevertheless they 'knew' false rape complaints were common (ibid.).

In New Zealand, considerable media attention has been given to this issue in recent years (see, for example, articles headlined as 'False rape claims "prevalent", say police' (*The Press*, 3 March 2001) and 'Cops warn on false rape claims' (*The Evening Standard*, 29 November 2000)). A recent headline proclaimed, 'Rise in false rape complaints' and began by asserting: 'A rash of false rape and sexual abuse accusations by young teenage girls is jeopardising genuine complaints' (*The Daily News*, 13 October 2003). Earlier, similar comments were published by Lower Hutt police who said they were concerned about the number of young women who 'get drunk' and then make false sexual assault and rape complaints (*The New Zealand Herald*, 22 October 1998). In another article, police in Hamilton claimed that one quarter of all sex complaints made to them were false.

These are not all the cases the police decide are unfounded; these are the ones proved false. *(COSA*[19] *Newsletter,* 6 (2), March/April 1999)

This estimate tallies with that found by Jennifer Temkin (1997) when interviewing police in Sussex, half of whom considered a quarter of all rapes reported to be false. She provided the following extreme example:

One CID officer, DC X, considered that there were 'few cases of genuine, very genuine rape'. Genuine rapes he described as 'off the street, didn't know the victim at all' rapes which he contrasted with 'we went out for the evening sort of rapes'. (Temkin, 1997, p. 516)

Other detectives, however, believe the proportion of false complaints to be closer to one-half (for e.g., Lees, 1997, p. 184), with Ian Blair noting

...there is considerable evidence that investigators...seem prepared to give serious consideration to the proposition that between 50 per cent and 70 per cent of all allegations of rape are false. (Blair, 1985, pp. 53–4)

This was exemplified in an informal survey conducted with police in Denver, Colorado, where detectives' estimates of the proportion of false rape complaints ranged from 5 per cent to 65 per cent (cited in National Center for Women and Policing, 2001, p. 5). One cynical detective even maintained:

After six years on the force, I don't believe any of them. (quoted in Burgess, 1999, p. 9)

In an Australian study, police officers were asked directly whether, at the time of the initial rape complaint, its possible falsity was uppermost in their mind: nearly two-thirds (64 per cent) said 'yes' to this proposition (Wilson, 1978).

The motives said to provoke false rape complaints tend often to be based on notions of vengeful and fickle women, or on the women's protection of their sexual reputation (Burgess, 1999; Kanin, 1994). The latter explanation has often been proffered in relation to women needing to find an alibi or excuse for behaviour likely to be deemed 'immoral'. Writing on these matters, psychiatrist John Macdonald has maintained:

Pregnancy in an unmarried girl, in a woman who is divorced or separated from her husband, or in a married woman whose husband has had a vasectomy, was overseas, confined in a penitentiary or otherwise away from home at the time of conception is an awkward situation for which some explanation is desirable. A false claim of rape does much to maintain family harmony. (Macdonald, 1995, p. 88)

In a similar vein, officers in an Australian holiday resort commented that they turned 'droves' of young girls away over the Christmas period for wasting their time with false rape complaints, telling them simply to 'go home and forget about it' (Wilson, 1978, p. 73). Such scepticism permeates the criminal justice system, with both public and police cynicism being reinforced by comments from judges, such as:

> It is well known that women in particular, and small boys, are liable to be untruthful and invent stories. (Judge Sutcliffe, 1976, quoted in Chambers and Millar, 1983, p. 83)

Senior detectives have, at times, encouraged such scepticism to shape and inform police interviewing practices with sexual assault complainants. One such detective, for example, noted that:

> Women and children complainants in sexual matters are notorious for embroidery or complete fabrication of complaints. (Firth, 1975, p. 1507)

He went on to comment:

> It should be borne in mind that except in the case of a very young child, the offence of rape is extremely unlikely to have been committed against a woman who does not immediately show signs of extreme violence.
>
> If a woman walks into a police station and complains of rape with no such signs of violence, she must be closely interrogated. Allow her to make her statement to a Policewoman and then drive a horse and cart through it. It is always advisable if there is any doubt of the truthfulness of her allegations to call her an outright liar. It is very difficult for a person to put on genuine indignation who has been called a liar to her face. It should be possible to tell from the reaction received to such an accusation if in fact the complainant is a liar. If she is lying then she can clear up the crime she has alleged by retracting it.
>
> Watch out for the girl who is pregnant or late getting home one night; such persons are notorious for alleging rape or indecent assault. Do not give her sympathy. If she is not lying, after the interrogator has upset her by accusing her of it, then at least the truth is verified and the genuine complaint made by her can be properly investigated. The good interrogator is very rarely loved by his subject. (ibid.)

Considerable empirical evidence exists which demonstrates that police beliefs in false complaints have generally been greatly overstated. The New York Sex Crimes Unit, for example, noted only 2 per cent of reported rapes to be false (Chappell and Singer, 1977; London Rape Crisis Centre, 1984). Similarly, when the police in Portland, Oregon, examined 431 complaints of attempted or completed sexual assault lodged in 1990, 1.6 per cent were determined to be false. This was in comparison to a rate of 2.6 per cent for false reports of stolen vehicles (Hecht-Schafran, 1993, cited in National Center for Women and Policing, 2001, p. 9). Likewise, writing within the British context, Temkin maintains that there is no evidence that allegations are more frequently fabricated in rape cases than in other crimes (Temkin, 2002). The exception to these findings is a study of false rape allegations conducted in a small metropolitan police agency in the mid-west of the United States of America (Kanin, 1994). On the basis of complainants recanting their initial allegation, Kanin maintained that false allegations constituted 41 per cent of the total forcible rape cases (N = 109) reported over a nine-year period from 1978 to 1987 (Kanin, 1994). The author maintains, however, that it would be highly problematic to generalise from the results of this research, and notes the widespread variation in police agency policies on rape.

> ... variations so diverse, in fact, that some police agencies cannot find a single rape complaint with merit, while others cannot find a single rape complaint without merit. (Kanin, 1994, p. 89)

Kanin's study produced results that were described by some commentators as 'unusual' (Macdonald, 1995, p. 87), and the findings have not been replicated elsewhere. More recent research has continued to demonstrate high levels of scepticism in police officers, and adherence to traditional beliefs regarding 'lying women' (Gregory and Lees, 1999).

Why, then, is the belief in false complaints so high? One major reason identified pertains to the false picture which has been created by police recording practices. In the United States of America, for example, the percentage of unfounded cases has sometimes been mistakenly interpreted as equating to false complaints (Estrich, 1987; National Center for Women and Policing, 2001). Cases that are 'unfounded', however, can include those for which there is insufficient evidence to prosecute or which the complainant withdraws. Neither of these outcomes means that the initial allegation was false. Aiken *et al.* have noted:

> Prosecutors and investigators find the term 'false allegation' of little use unless the claimant says in some way that the account is untrue. It is more common to use general terms such as unfounded, refusal to prosecute, and the like. These categories allow law enforcement to close cases without completing the investigations. Cases of false allegations are included in these categories. Some jurisdictions have reported that 35 to 40% of all cases are relegated to this disposition. This is one way in which rates of false allegation have been inflated and misrepresented. It may be reported that false allegations of rape occur at the rate of 30%, for example, when

what is really meant is that 30% of cases are 'unfounded'. (Aiken *et al.*, 1999, pp. 223–4)

A similarly confusing picture has been identified in the United Kingdom through the use of 'no criming' (Gregory and Lees, 1999), and in New Zealand through the 'no offence disclosed' category (Stace, 1983; Young, 1983). Thus, in examining the overuse of the latter category, Stace remarked:

> The police acknowledge that the 'no offence disclosed' category is a broad one and is used a little bit like a dust-bin category for the disposition of offences which do not fit in anywhere else – for example, if the woman withdraws the complaint. (Stace, 1983, p. 5)

The distorted perceptions that can arise from the misuse of this category are damning in their effects. This was wonderfully illustrated in an account penned by a former sex crimes investigator with the New York Police Department, who asked:

> Do we really have women running around making false accusations against innocent men? Does this happen? Are there false reports? Of course there are, and we must always be on the alert and be aware that victims may be telling a lie. Some women do lie, of course, but the number of women who make false reports is negligible in comparison with the number of valid complainants. In a six-month period in New York City there were around 2000 reported rapes, of which about 250 were unfounded reports. But 'unfounded' does not mean lying. Let's see what this means: 200 of the 250 were simple administrative errors. They should never have been called rapes in the first place; for example, a woman phones the station and yells rape. The police car goes out and there's no one home. The next day a detective goes to follow the incident up and the woman says 'Oh yes, my boyfriend and I had a fight last night and I yelled "rape"'. 'Why did you yell rape?' 'Because if I had yelled disorderly conduct, nobody is going to come, but if I yell rape I know damn sure that a cop is going to come in a hurry.' That kind of thing is not a false rape charge, but a mild inconvenience to the police.
>   We are therefore left with potentially 50 liars out of a total of 2000 complainants. Of that 50, perhaps 20 cases of false report were made as some kind of attempt by the woman to protect herself against a tyrannical father or husband because she had violated some family rule, usually a time curfew, and she has to account for why she is late. Rarely in these cases, however, does she accuse a specific person; rather, she claims that some mysterious figure in the night pulled her into a car and did this awful thing to her and caused her to be two hours late in coming home. Other times we have women who have psychological problems,

loneliness being the main one, and they know if they say 'rape' the offi-cer will come and talk with them awhile. These women have lied, of course, but no more maliciously than has the woman with the tyranni-cal husband/father.

After analyzing all the 'unfounded' reports, we found that there were actually only five cases of women maliciously telling lies and deliberately falsely accusing men of rapes that had never been committed. In these cases the women are arrested for making false accusations – false charges are crimes which must be punished. The bottom line, then is that out of 2000 charges of rape, there were five proven liars. That is good enough evidence for me to conclude that most victims are telling the truth! (O'Reilly, 1984, pp. 96–7)

Whilst efforts have been made in many jurisdictions to respond to criticisms and reduce the use of these categories (Blair, 1985), levels of police disbelief appear to have decreased little. The complexities surrounding corroborative evidence in sexual assault cases appear to have persuaded many police to assume the role of 'judge and jury' during the investigative process. In discussing police attitudes regarding the prior sexual behaviour of rape complainants, for example, Warren Young observed:

Some police officers seemed to use the evidential difficulties which might arise from such factors as a way of judging the genuineness of the complaint itself. They were thus inclined to assess the veracity of the complainant according to their view of possible jury attitudes and the likely outcome of a prosecution in court. Consequently, the amount of evidence required to convince them that a rape had occurred might have been higher than that needed to establish a prima facie case. (Young, 1983, p. 50)

Numerous rape researchers have pointed out that there appears to be little rational basis for such beliefs about the high number of false complaints (Blair, 1985; Gregory and Lees, 1999; Jordan, 2004; Kelly, 2002; Lees, 1997; National Center for Women and Policing, 2001; Nixon, 1992; Shapcott, 1988; Temkin, 2002; Vogelman, 1990). As Blair says:

The embarrassment and discomfort of investigation, medical examina-tion and trial make it most unlikely that considerable numbers of women will make false reports where consensual sex has occurred. If the above arguments are accepted, then there can be no credible basis for the sug-gestion that 70 per cent, 50 per cent or even 20 per cent of allegations of sexual assault are false, in the sense of untrue. (Blair, 1985, p. 54)

Fundamental to police decision-making regarding the 'truth' or otherwise of rape allegations is the extent to which officers themselves accept that what happened was a serious criminal offence. The tendency to view 'real' rapes predominantly as violent, stranger attacks means that the majority of rape complaints, since they involve mostly known perpetrators and few visible injuries, may automatically have a shadow of suspicion hanging over them. An American training manual published by the National Center for Women and Policing (2001) notes that there is evidence from many jurisdictions of premature dismissal of reported rapes if they do not conform to 'real' rape stereotypes. This has resulted in cases where, even though victims have sustained bruises, black eyes, cigarette burns and bitten nipples, officers have declared such complaints unfounded if there was evidence of a previous sexual relationship between the parties (Hecht-Schrafan, 1993, cited in National Center for Women and Policing, 2001, p. 7).

Writing within the Australian policing context, Christine Nixon suggested:

> The hidden issue may well be that police see little harm in most rapes. Statements such as 'she had no physical injuries' to describe someone violated by unwanted sexual intercourse confirms such suspicions. This view allows police to define many rapes as 'false complaints' and underplay the effect on the victims. In this sense, police culture has merely reflected the attitudes of a wider society, which also relies on mythology as the basis for understanding rape and sexual assault. (Nixon, 1992, p. 42)

Moreover, knowledge of the prevalence of such beliefs amongst the police can impact detrimentally on complainants (Feldman-Summers and Palmer, 1980; Gilmore and Pittman, 1993). Fearing disbelief and judgment, victims of rape may try to embellish their accounts, or conceal wrongdoing, in order to make themselves appear more 'believable' to the police. From their interviews with complainants whose cases had been 'no crimed', Chambers and Millar remarked:

> Some women told us that they knew that in order for the story to be well received they would have to appear to have been engaging in 'respectable' and 'acceptable' behaviour. Consequently women 'told lies' about the amount of alcohol consumed, for example, or 'invented' stories which they thought would make the circumstances seem to the police less compromising. Such 'inventions' were invariably spotted by detectives, and as a result, the credibility of the whole complaint was undermined. [Thus] police scepticism promoted the narration of the very inaccuracies which, in turn, consolidated the police view that women fabricate complaints and make false allegations. (Chambers and Millar, 1983, pp. 86–7)

Perceptions of falseness, however, do not only emanate from complainants anticipating particular police responses. Many police themselves expect 'real' victims to look and behave in very specific ways, adhering to a victim 'script' which they believe should be followed. It has therefore been observed by Aiken *et al.* that:

> Credibility for victims is elusive. Women who are unemotional may also be conveying that they were not disturbed by the 'alleged' event, hence the absence of harm. Women who are overwrought come across as emotionally unstable, and thus not credible. (Aiken *et al.*, 1999, p. 222)

Rape complainants may be regarded suspiciously if they act in what investigators consider a bizarre fashion in relation to the offender who has supposedly just raped them. In a recent New Zealand case, for example, the complainant held the rapist's hand after the assault, in a manner which 'threw' the investigating officers and nearly resulted in the complaint being rejected (Male detective, pers. comm., 2000). Freckelton's comments regarding rape trials are also relevant with respect to police interviews:

> What the cross-examiner seeks to invoke is the idealised attribution of the 'real victim'. The trouble is that such a victim is mythical, and the fact that a complainant behaved differently after a trauma does not necessarily mean that the complainant is not telling the truth about what happened to them. It may simply be that they have accommodated or adapted to an abnormal situation as best they could – a reasonable response in unreasonable circumstances. (Freckelton, 1998, p. 147)

In some ways, therefore, it appears that as long as a rape complainant's appearance and behaviour correspond to that of a 'real victim', then she stands at least some chance of having her complaint believed. Her case may be helped by the presence of such factors as the assailant being a stranger, her having told the police immediately and her having visible injuries resulting from her active resistance (Harris and Grace, 1999; Temkin, 2002). As we have seen, however, none of these factors is common or typical. Most women know the offender, find it difficult to name, let alone report, what happened to them as rape and do not have visible injuries (Gregory and Lees, 1999; Kelly, 1988). To not act like a 'real' victim may result in being viewed as a non-victim. More sinisterly, it may promote the redefinition of the victim as the offender, as one who falsely maligns and impugns the reputations of men.

Within the current debate over false complaints, a balance is needed between the binary opposition of 'women always lie' and 'women never lie'. Issues of belief, 'truth', and credibility occupy highly contested territory, and reflect the tensions and ambiguities surrounding women's sexuality and men's violence. As Liz Kelly has rightly observed:

> ...belief has become a more nuanced and complex matter. (Kelly, 1996, p. 45)

Women surviving violence will not always choose or feel able to tell the 'truth' about their experience. Sensing that their behaviour as the victim is also on trial, some may try to conceal aspects that they think may result in judgment and blame and that could detract attention from the offender. Examples of cases drawn from police files that reflect this scenario are contained in Chapter 4 of this book.

The last decade of the twentieth century saw many police departments around the world responding to pressure from feminists and victims' advocates to improve their service delivery to complainants of rape and sexual assault. As the community policing philosophy came to be more fully embraced in some quarters, even if only ideologically, police managers have been increasingly challenged to improve the quality of policing in their districts. The need to increase levels of citizen satisfaction with police performance has been noted, particularly in relation to those crimes for which the police have borne the brunt of public and media criticism (Gregory and Lees, 1999; Temkin, 1997). This shift within policing ideology has been accompanied by challenges for criminal justice system agencies to become increasingly victim-centred in their approach, particularly in relation to crimes involving sexual violence (Kelly, 2002; Lees and Gregory, 1997; Mawby and Walklate, 1994; Shapland and Cohen, 1987; White and Perrone, 1997).

Such challenges were voiced within the New Zealand context also, prompting research and initiatives which are summarised throughout the remainder of this chapter, and form the platform on which the subsequent studies are presented.

New Zealand research

In New Zealand, feminists began expressing concern about rape in the early 1970s and in 1973 the Wellington Women's Workshop was the first in the country to establish a telephone service for victims of rape, a move prompted in part by the realisation that such victims were not deemed eligible to use existing emergency services (Dann, 1985). In 1976, a staff reporter with *The New Zealand Herald*, Ann Lloyd, interviewed victims, offenders, criminal justice system professionals and rape crisis workers for a publication aimed at increasing awareness and understanding of the crime of rape (Lloyd, 1976). The first New Zealand 'Reclaim the Night' march was held in 1979, the same year as self-defence courses, combining martial arts with feminist principles, were begun by Sue Lytollis in Auckland (Dann, 1985).

Christine Dann, in her history of women's liberation in New Zealand, notes how it quickly became evident to feminist activists that information on sexual violence was lacking, and in 1979 Miriam Jackson (Saphira) undertook a survey on rape through the magazine, the *New Zealand Woman's Weekly*. The responses received helped to shatter some of the commonly held myths and showed rape to be more prevalent than was often assumed. The survey also indicated reporting rates to be low, and generally helped to establish rape as an issue of concern.

The first permanent rape crisis centre was established in Auckland in 1978, followed soon after in Wellington and other cities (Dann, 1985). In 1982, a national meeting of workers from rape crisis centres was held to conduct initial discussions regarding whether an umbrella agency should be formed, a move acted upon after three years of discussion (ibid.). The 1982 gathering also discussed existing rape laws, and rape crisis workers later contributed to a Rape Symposium organised by the Justice Department and other agencies concerned with rape law reform (ibid.). In 1983, feminists seeking law reform were amongst those who made submissions to the parliamentary committee considering changes to rape laws, and also participated in a Young Women's Christian Association (YWCA) conference that year on 'Rape and Sexual Violence to Women and Children' (ibid.).

New Zealand *Rape Study* 1983

Prompted by rising public concern over the incidence and treatment of rape victims, the Minister of Justice directed the Department of Justice and the Institute of Criminology at Victoria University of Wellington to undertake a study on rape (Young, 1983). Since very little information was available, several preliminary research studies were needed to establish a baseline of information (these Research Reports were published in *Rape Study*, Volume 2). The result was the first comprehensive examination of rape law and procedure in New Zealand (Young, 1983).

Significant findings from this study established that, contrary to popular beliefs about stranger rape, the victim and assailant were generally known to each other (Young, 1983), and almost half of all rapes occurred in either the victim's or assailant's home (Stone *et al.*, 1983). Included in this project was an interview-based study documenting the concerns and experiences of women who had been victims of rape. The findings reinforced what many women working in this area had long observed: namely, that the existing system was experienced by many complainants as a repeat violation, similar in its effects to the original rape incident (e.g., Holmstrom and Burgess, 1978; Medea and Thompson, 1974). Concern was also expressed in the 1983 study that police officers involved in sexual assault investigations generally lacked an adequate understanding of the effects of rape on victims, particularly in relation to the immediate impacts on demeanour and behaviour (Stace, 1983).

Mounting criticism of the criminal justice system's response to rape victims prompted the introduction of the Rape Law Reform Bill, passed on 12 December 1985, and effective from 1 February 1986. Ginette Sullivan asserted at the time that this legislation went a considerable way towards acknowledging feminist perspectives on rape (Sullivan, 1986). The substantial reforms introduced included:

- broadening the definition of rape to include other sexual violation offences, thereby acknowledging the severity of non-consenting anal and digital penetration, and violation by the use of a foreign object such as a bottle or broomstick;
- abolishing spousal immunity, thereby making it possible for sexual violation of a wife by her husband to be regarded in law as a criminal offence;
- enabling the complainant, as principal witness, to give evidence in writing at the hearing of depositions, rather than requiring this to be presented in person; and
- allowing for the court to be closed to the public while the complainant presents oral evidence. (Sullivan, 1986, p. 11)

Significant changes were also made at this time in relation to police training, the conducting of post-rape medical examinations, and the provision of crisis support counselling.

Ten years after these reforms were introduced, the Institute of Criminology and the Faculty of Law at Victoria University of Wellington began a research project to assess, from the woman's perspective, how she experienced in the 1990s both the reporting of the offence to the police and any subsequent trial processes (Jordan, 1998a). The data-gathering phase of the study was funded by the Foundation for Research, Science and Technology (FRST). A summary of the methodology and key findings from this study follow.

Rape study 1998

The overall aim of the research project was to evaluate how rape and sexual assault victims' complaints to the police were responded to and dealt with by the various agencies involved. In-depth, qualitative interviews were conducted with 48 women who had approached the police between 1990 and 1994 with a complaint of rape/sexual violation or the attempt thereof.[20] The study aimed to obtain accounts of the women's dealings with the police, doctors and support agencies (Jordan, 1998a, p. 128) as well as their experiences in court and during the trial (McDonald, 1997).

Of the 50 incidents reported to the police, less than one-third involved an offender who was a stranger. In 35 of the incidents (70 per cent), the rape/sexual assault was perpetrated by someone previously known to the victim. This figure included spouses and ex-spouses, boyfriends, family members (including a brother-in-law and a future father-in-law), neighbours, acquaintances (including friends of friends or of partners, co-residents or fellow party guests), and those with whom the woman may have had a professional relationship (such as a doctor, teacher, counsellor or masseuse). In one case, two perpetrators were involved in the assault, one known and one a stranger, and another case involved two known perpetrators.

One major limitation, with implications for international research, arose from the difficulties encountered in recruiting indigenous and ethnic minority women to participate in the study. Despite extensive efforts in this regard, the results primarily reflect the experiences of New Zealand European/ European women. This outcome was undoubtedly associated with the methodology, which relied largely on participants being approached through support agencies, and was restricted to women who had reported an incident of sexual violation to the police. Māori women, and women from ethnic minority groups generally, may be less likely to report sexual victimisation to the police, or approach external agencies for assistance. A recent national victimisation survey, however, revealed higher overall sexual victimisation rates for Māori than New Zealand European/European women, and particularly high levels of multiple victimisation (Morris and Reilly, 2003). Issues pertaining to the additional barriers women of minority group status face in terms of accessing justice are undoubtedly significant and have been noted internationally (Bell, 1991; LaFree, 1989; Thomas, 1993; Wriggins, 1998). Within New Zealand, research on Māori interactions with the police identified the very low confidence levels Māori place in the police as a traditionally monocultural institution (Te Whaiti and Roguski, 1998), as well as police distrust generally of Māori people (Maxwell and Smith, 1998). The particular ways in which these general attitudes are translated into the context of sexual violence have yet to be adequately researched.

The study overall provided the most extensive information obtained on women's experiences of reporting rape to the police in New Zealand. Summaries of the results regarding initial contact and statement-taking are presented below, followed by a comparative analysis of the 1983 and 1998 rape studies.

Initial contact and reporting

As regards initial contact, one significant finding was that in only six of the cases in the research sample were the police the first people the woman told about the incident. The women were, in fact, three times more likely to tell a friend about what had happened to them (36 per cent; N = 18) rather than call the police in the first instance. Others disclosed what had happened initially to family members, their partner, a colleague, a neighbour or a counsellor, before deciding to approach the police.

Although it may not have been the police whom the woman told first about the incident, nevertheless in over half the situations (54 per cent; N = 27), she was the person who informed them of the incident. On seven occasions it was a friend who told the police, and less frequently it was either other people she knew (such as her partner or other family members), or those she approached for assistance directly after the rape/assault.

In those instances where the complainant herself reported the rape/sexual assault to the police, she was asked what factors influenced her decision to do so. One-third of the women simply said 'I felt I should'; a further 30 per cent said 'to protect others'; more than a quarter (26 per cent) said 'they didn't want him getting away with it'; and almost a quarter (22 per cent) said they reported the rape because 'they were scared of a repeat attack'. Other factors present in their decision included being persuaded to report by others or feeling pressured to report the rape.

Of the 50 incidents, well over half (62 per cent) were reported to the police either immediately after the rape/sexual assault or on the same day. There were delays in reporting the rape/sexual assault in just under two-fifths of cases (38 per cent). While half of these were reported within a fortnight of the incident's occurrence, the remainder took considerably longer to be brought to police attention and, in three cases, it took more than ten years. There were a number of reasons for delays in reporting. Some said they needed time to accept what had happened to them, or to acknowledge their need for assistance. At least two of the women said they held back because they felt confused about the incident and whether it constituted rape. Sometimes the reason given for delayed reporting seems to have been fear based, arising from the woman's concern over how the offender, the police or family and friends would respond. In one case, the offender's death threats against the woman and her relatives kept her 'silent', she said, for ten years before contacting the police.

Nearly two-thirds (64 per cent) of the women felt either satisfied (40 per cent; N = 20) or very satisfied (24 per cent; N = 12) with the treatment they received from the police during the initial reporting phase. Thirty-two per cent, however, were either dissatisfied (20 per cent; N = 10) or very dissatisfied (12 per cent; N = 6). The remainder (4 per cent; N = 2) said they felt neutral. The women who rated the police highly cited the importance of being believed, being taken seriously and feeling cared for and supported. Even small gestures of friendliness counted for a lot when the women were feeling so vulnerable – for instance, the police officer getting the woman a cup of coffee, allowing her a smoke or letting her stop and have a break when she got upset. Some women felt they needed clear information at this stage about the procedures to be followed and appreciated being provided with this and given some choice over whether and how to proceed.

The women who were dissatisfied with the initial police response identified particular behaviours and attitudes which they found distressing. Several commented on the lack of empathy they felt they encountered at a time when they desperately needed some caring and validation. Feeling as if the police did not believe them and that they were judging them was also mentioned by several of the women at the reporting stage. One young woman expressed this forcefully:

> They asked me so many questions *I* felt like the bad person. They really made me feel so stink. I just wanted to cry. They should be more sensitive. He was like a pig to me (you know how they call police pigs? – he even looked like a pig, he reminded me of a pig.) They should be more direct and up front, and say they have to sort out the truth for court. It made me very angry. (Jordan, 1998a, p. 23)

A further source of dissatisfaction for some women arose from their feeling that their complaint was unimportant to the police. This could be conveyed in various ways, including a cold and dismissive attitude or by indicating that other jobs had greater priority.

The initial reporting experience emerged from this study as a critical determinant of whether complainants will be able to develop sufficient trust in the police to feel able to proceed with an investigation. It occurs at a time when the woman is feeling highly vulnerable, with heightened needs for safety and reassurance. Overall, the comments made by the women reflected their desire for the entire reporting process to become more victim-centred and cognisant of their needs rather than being oriented exclusively around police operational requirements.

Police statement-taking and interviewing

Following the reporting of a rape/sexual assault, the complainant will usually be referred for the forensic medical examination and put in contact with a support agency before returning to the police to provide a full statement.[21] Subsequent police interviews may also eventuate as details are checked and the court case prepared.

In approximately three-quarters (73 per cent; N = 35) of cases, the woman's statement was taken in a police station. Nearly half (49 per cent; N = 21) of the 43 women who commented on the atmosphere during interviewing and statement-taking considered it to be warm and supportive. Other women experienced the interviewing atmosphere in less positive ways. Nearly a quarter (23 per cent; N = 10) described it as a cold, clinical environment, and the remainder (28 per cent; N = 12) used a range of other descriptions, such as unreal, grotty or overwhelming. One woman, for example, said it was hard to feel comfortable being interviewed in a room full of police riot gear. Others were distressed at the number of interruptions while they gave their statement, with some feeling on show as the latest 'rape'. Overall, what the women said they valued the most was being in a comfortable and relaxed environment where they were treated in a friendly, caring manner and could be guaranteed privacy.

Half of the women (51 per cent; N = 25) were interviewed by male officers; most of the remainder were interviewed by female officers (41 per cent; N = 20), although a small number of women (8 per cent; N = 4) were interviewed by officers of both genders. In general, a preference for female officers being involved was apparent. Given the sensitive nature of the incident, and the intimate questions which needed to be asked, some of the women found it very difficult to be questioned by a male. Several said categorically it had to be a woman, especially if the interview was conducted in their own home. Disclosing explicit, sexual details about the incident to male officers could compound the woman's sense of vulnerability: 'It's like you're sitting there with your legs open, you might as well be' (Jordan, 1998a, p. 28). Some women also commented about the lack of sensitivity and awareness displayed by male detectives towards them as rape victims.

Maleness per se, however, did not appear to determine the quality of an officer's response to sexual assault victims. While some women found it traumatic being interviewed by a man, others felt this was not nearly as important as the officer's attitude. Several of the women interviewed, in fact, said they had requested a woman officer only to end up feeling disappointed with the outcome. Some of the women expressed surprise when the women officers they saw displayed hostile, disbelieving attitudes. Since policewomen operate within the same organisational culture as policemen, and may struggle even harder for acceptance within it, such outcomes should probably not be totally unexpected. These could be conveyed non-verbally at times and were sometimes reflected in the tone of the general interviewing environment. For instance, one woman felt uncomfortable being asked intimate details about her rape in a room in which pictures of semi-naked women were displayed on the wall calendar. Likewise, another felt the detective interviewing her was being reasonable until she overheard his male colleagues telling a sexist, anti-woman joke in the next room, which went unacknowledged by him.[22]

The women were asked to provide an overall rating as to how they felt their complaint was responded to and dealt with by the police. There was virtually a 50:50 split between those who expressed overall satisfaction or dissatisfaction with the police. A total of 20 women (40 per cent) said they were either satisfied/very satisfied compared with 19 (38 per cent) who said they were dissatisfied/very dissatisfied. At the two extremes within these categories, 11 women were very satisfied and 13 were very dissatisfied. Generally, therefore, the women's responses were quite polarised. In addition, a small number (6) felt unable to summarise their overall satisfaction level because, while they were pleased with some aspects of the police response, this was compromised by their dissatisfaction with other aspects. A further two women could not provide an overall satisfaction rating, stating that the negative police attitude expressed when they made their initial complaint deterred them from proceeding any further with it.

It is, therefore, clear that while a significant number of the women felt very positive about the response they received from the police, an equally significant number were highly dissatisfied. Precisely why such a polarisation exists is difficult to determine. It may be related in part to the nature of rape itself, and the fact that it is such an overwhelmingly traumatic experience for the woman to experience, combined with the undoubtedly strong views held by many police officers on its occurrence. Because rape is such an intense and sensitive area, when the police act with professional caring and demonstrate their respect for the victim, this is noticeable and greatly appreciated. When such qualities are lacking, however, their absence is also very noticeable. Either way, this results in heightened emotional responses and polarised views.

Overall, the characteristics the women said they appreciated in the police can be summarised as those reflecting a caring professionalism underpinned by respect for and belief in the victim/survivor. These results appear consistent with those found in an earlier New Zealand study by Anstiss (1995). Although her small sample of complainants expressed divided views concerning their treatment by the police, questionnaires completed by police officers yielded interesting results. Approximately half of the officers surveyed felt that women 'provoked' rape through their dress or behaviour (ibid., p. 63), while one in four officers considered with suspicion allegations of rape made by women working as bar girls, dance hostesses or prostitutes (ibid., p. 64). Regarding false rape allegations, one in six officers felt that many women who reported rape were lying and wanted revenge, while roughly one in three agreed that both guilt about engaging in premarital sex, and protection of a woman's reputation, were reasons for falsely alleging rape (ibid., p. 64). Anstiss further notes that:

> Of the officers that volunteered estimations of false rape allegations the figures given were, or in excess of, 60%. (ibid., p. 65)

Comparison of the 1983 and 1998 rape studies

One aim of the 1998 research project was to provide material which could be compared with the 1983 *Rape Study*, in order to ascertain the extent to which women's experiences of the reporting process may have changed.

The 1983 *Rape Study* states that the women's descriptions of how the police treated them varied considerably,

> ...ranging from glowing praise to severe criticism. Overall, their positive and negative responses were fairly evenly balanced. In fact, only two women had predominantly negative perceptions of the police. Most felt that they had generally received 'a good deal', as one woman put it, and that at least some of the police officers they had encountered had been helpful and sympathetic. (Young, 1983, p. 46)

What the women interviewed in 1983 said they most appreciated was having their complaint dealt with by understanding and supportive detectives who displayed a degree of kindness as well as professionalism. Such qualities continued to be highlighted as important by the women who participated in the 1998 study. Both studies, in fact, indicated the same, common themes within the women's responses.

These themes can be summarised as:

- the need to be believed;
- the need to be treated with respect and understanding;
- the need to be allowed to retain some degree of control over proceedings; and
- the need to be provided with adequate information.[23]

The results of the 1998 study suggested that, despite changes in the law and police training since 1983, little had altered in terms of women's experiences of the reporting process. Analysis of the content of the women's concerns, as revealed in their stories and comments, confirmed that, as Temkin (1997) also found in the Sussex study, little of substance had changed. Despite apparent improvements in police processes, women reporting rape/sexual assaults to the police were likely to encounter similar police attitudes and behaviours to those experienced by women in the early 1980s. While it was clear that some individual police officers may respond supportively to rape complainants, it was equally apparent that such a response could not be guaranteed. This lack of consistency runs counter to increasing expectations of acceptable professional conduct in the 1990s. As one of the women in the 1998 study commented:

> Individual cops are really, really good and deal with these situations really, really well, and probably now there are more individual cops who are good than there were, but it shouldn't be an individual thing. They're paid by us and they need to be able to respond to things appropriately and it's not good enough when it's just left up to individuals. It shouldn't be a case of just who you happen to get. (Jordan, 1998a, p. 62)

One of the recurrent themes within both studies, and which provoked some of the strongest utterances, related to issues of belief and complainant credibility. Comments and examples from the 1998 study are presented below to illustrate the influence and potency of police scepticism on rape complainants' feelings and experiences.

Belief and complainants' credibility

Rape complaints have always posed difficulties for the police because so often, in the absence of other evidence, they essentially become the victim's word against that of the offender. At least 18 women in the 1998 study (one-third of the total sample) considered belief had been an issue at some stage during the reporting process. They felt the police regarded their complaint with scepticism and spoke of feeling as if it was up to them to persuade the police of the genuineness of their allegation before an investigation would proceed.

Examples provided by the women suggest an initial range of factors that appear to be correlated with police distrust. These included:

- presumed desire for self-gain;
- perceived motivation of revenge or malice;
- reluctance to accept accounts implicating partners/husbands as the perpetrator;
- expectation that rape victims will present in a particular emotional manner;
- perceived credibility of the victim; and
- perceived credibility of the alleged offender.

Each of these is explored briefly below, using relevant examples from the research.

Desire for self-gain

Some women expressed strong resentment at police officers' presumptions that they were manipulating the system for financial purposes. In the case which follows, the detective appeared to waste no time before directly accusing the complainant of such behaviour.

After years of therapy, Hannah decided she wished to lay charges against the man who had raped her years previously. On phoning the police, she asked initially to speak with a female detective but was told none was available. After a prolonged rigmarole (see Jordan, 1998a, p. 18), Hannah was finally interviewed by a male detective in a police station where she felt very uncomfortable. Rather than finding this detective understanding about her tentativeness in coming forward, he asked if she was making the complaint just to get an ACC (Accident Compensation Corporation) lump sum payment, explaining that: 'You wouldn't believe how many women make statements to the police in order to get lump sum payouts from ACC' (Jordan, 1998a, p. 18). Hannah's response reflects her anger and frustration: 'The bastards, eh? For goodness sake, lump sum payments finished in 1992!' (Jordan, 1998a, p. 18). (It was 1994 when she contacted the police.) At the time of being interviewed, as far as Hannah knew, the alleged offender still had not been spoken to by the police.

Perceived motivation of revenge or malice

A classic stereotype exists of women making rape complaints out of revenge or malice. Only two women mentioned this explicitly, however, saying they had been accused of being malicious by the police officer dealing with them. In Melissa's case, for instance, she alleged having been raped on a date and was later accused by the police of trying to get back at the guy concerned. The police accused her of being a liar and told her she was lucky not to be charged with wasting police time.

Reluctance to accept accounts implicating partners/husbands as the perpetrator

Women who were sexually assaulted by men they knew, or had known, intimately recounted how difficult it was to have their accusations believed and taken seriously. In Lydia's case, for example, her husband had attempted to rape her and threatened to kill her very early one morning. She had pretended she was going to work and driven straight to the nearest place open, a petrol station, where the attendant phoned the police. She had no visible injuries and felt the police played the attack down, despite her husband having previously received diversion on an assault charge against her. She felt the officer minimised the seriousness of the incident and attributed blame to her, implying that if her husband was so terrible she should have left the relationship long ago. Finally, the police persuaded Lydia not to go ahead with the charges because of her apparent lack of injuries and because, they said, marital rape was very hard to prove.

Expectation that rape victims will present in a particular emotional manner

Women commented that at times they felt the police were looking for them to behave or act in a particular way, as if there was a typical mode of expression or behaviour that would be exhibited by genuine rape victims. Emma, for example, believed her lack of visible distress was a factor in the police expressing disbelief that she had been raped:

> I think that was something that they really couldn't understand, that I was so calm. There were no tears, there was no hysteria, there was nothing, and I think they couldn't accept that I wasn't dissolving. (Jordan, 1998a, p. 23)

Perceived credibility of the victim

Many of the women felt that the police were judgmental of them and doubted their veracity. As one woman said:

> I went seeking help but then it turned and I was accused of false allegations. (Jordan, 1998a, p. 23)

In several cases, diminished credibility appeared to be associated with the complainant being young and intoxicated. In Jane's case, for example, she was raped at her twenty-first birthday party. She found the police aggressive and blaming.

> It was disgusting. No wonder they are working with dogs – something to yell at and boss around. It felt like, 'Look, she's pissed so she asked for it.' I felt like they came up with their own decision on the spot. (Jordan, 1998a, p. 17)

The factors associated with whether or not the women were likely to be believed did not always appear clearcut. In some cases (e.g., see Beth's story, Jordan, 1998a, pp. 35–6) the women felt, like Jane, that the officers' responses were influenced by rape myths regarding good and bad victims.[24] When the police saw Beth, for example, she feels they saw a young woman who had been drinking at a party, had sex with an acquaintance, then regretted it, and accused the man of rape. Other women, however, expressed surprise when their fears that the police would judge them according to such moral beliefs proved to be unfounded (e.g., see Harriet's story, Jordan, 1998a, p. 44).

Perceived credibility of the alleged offender

In some cases, the women felt that the police perceived the alleged offender as more respectable and credible than they were. This made it difficult to secure police cooperation and commitment to their case. One woman, Sarah, said she felt it was hard to convince the police that the man who raped her, a well known local businessman, had in fact done this to her. She felt that the detective was continually trying to catch her out and saw her as having less credibility than the man who raped and subsequently threatened her. Sarah commented:

> Right from the very beginning the detective in charge of my case said to me that fifty percent of the cases who come forth with rape complaints are false, and I thought, 'Oh, gosh, no wonder they are like they are, if they (police) have to suss people out like that'. I don't know if it's true or not, but that's just what he told me. He said women get themselves in situations, like if a married woman gets caught by her husband with another man she's going to cry rape to save her marriage – or that's how he explained it to me. (Jordan, 1998a, p. 45)

Another complainant, Peggy, was convinced that police hostility and disbelief towards her was directly related to the status of her suspected attackers. In her case, she was accused by a detective of fabricating the entire incident, despite the presence of multiple fractures and bruising.

Effects of police attitudes of disbelief

The effects of a disbelieving attitude on the part of the police can be destructive and counterproductive. For instance, at least four of the women said the police's apparent disbelief prevented them from saying all they wanted to during the interview. As one woman said:

> I did (give my account), but I felt very uneasy towards the end, as if I wasn't being believed or they were playing down the crime. I felt like I couldn't convince the detective – he just thought I was wasting his time. (Jordan, 1998a, p. 32)

It was difficult in such an environment for the women to be forthcoming and provide full disclosure to the police. In two cases, the women said categorically that the negative and disbelieving attitudes expressed by the police were the reason they decided to withdraw their complaint. In other cases, the investigation did not proceed because the police decided not to continue with it after concluding the complainant was lying. Sometimes this decision appeared to be based on perceived inconsistencies in the complainant's account of events. At times, however, the women said the circumstances in which the police obtained their statement directly contributed to such inconsistencies being present. Such a situation often arose when the women felt that the police neglected the victim's needs in favour of adherence to investigation procedures. This resulted in women sometimes being required to make their formal statement whilst in a state of physical and emotional exhaustion.

> I suppose some of my reactions came from the tiredness and the thought of having to focus on detail when I was just barely managing to not walk out the door. I think it was counter-productive for me in the long term that they insisted on getting details from me when I wasn't really capable of giving them what they needed. (Jordan, 1998a, p. 32)

In Kylie's case also, she felt it was the police's insistence on continuing to obtain details from her when she was 'past it' that began what she termed 'the slippery slope'. When the police subsequently re-questioned her, they became upset at apparent inconsistencies and gaps in her memory. She said:

> It was a little bit like what you laugh at in the movies with the good guy and the bad guy. That interview that morning began with a detective constable, female, saying to me, 'We need to go back over your statement, there are holes, there are inconsistencies.' In the middle of the afternoon she left and he (her 'boss') walked in the room and he accused me of

making a false statement, just completely out of the blue, and I was on my own, there wasn't even another police officer, just me and him. (Jordan, 1998a, p. 34)

Kylie describes being interviewed 'for hours and hours and hours' on end, with the re-questioning culminating in the police cautioning Kylie three times and threatening to charge her with making a false allegation.

Other women expressed strong feelings over the way they felt the police kept trying to catch them out, to see if they were lying. Emma, for example, said:

What really worried me was that after two hours of sitting there going through all this the gentleman said to me, '(Emma), have you *really* been raped?' I just about exploded. When he said, 'Were you really raped?', I said, 'Ha ha, of course not! I wake up at 4 o'clock every morning and I think, What am I going to talk about this morning at morning tea? And this morning I thought I'd say, Oh, yes, I've been raped!' I was just spitting. I was so angry (that's why) I just said, 'Yes, I've made the whole thing up!' (Jordan, 1998a, p. 35)

Encountering such attitudes clearly does not make for a positive police–client relationship, yet it is of vital importance to the police that they establish a supportive relationship with complainants. The possibility of a case reaching court depends on a cooperative complainant, and to alienate her on first contact jeopardises the prospects of this happening.

Conclusion

While being believed was experienced as extremely validating by the women in the study, *not* being believed was also hugely significant in its impact, having the potential to compound the devastating effects of the rape.

Several of the women recounted how the detectives investigating their case kept emphasising the high numbers of false rape complaints received by the police, with some putting the figure at 50 per cent or higher. Sometimes, as in the examples listed above, the police gave the women reasons for their disbelief; thus one woman was accused of making it up as an attention seeking device; another was told she seemed too calm to have been raped; and a third was asked on two separate occasions if she was making it up out of malice or revenge. At least three of the women interviewed said the police had threatened to charge them with laying a false complaint.

In both New Zealand studies, the respondents identified belief as both critical in importance to them and invariably problematic to the police. This finding has been also repeatedly evident in overseas research (Chambers and Millar, 1983; Gilmore and Pittman, 1993; Gregory and Lees, 1999; Hall, 1985; Temkin, 1997). Despite its importance, little research appears to have been done which has focussed specifically on the issue of belief. Key questions for researchers, however, are: What makes a rape complainant credible? How are the police influenced in their assessment of complaints? What factors do they attach central significance to when deciding whether or not to proceed with a rape investigation? What do police officers believe about false complaints, their frequency and the motives underlying them?

The 1998 study of sexual complainants' experiences with the police provided the impetus for my subsequent research. Identification of the centrality of the issue of belief and victims' credibility prompted a research design that incorporated three diverse but related studies to enhance understanding of police perceptions of victims' credibility. These three studies, each of which provides a different lens on the issue of credibility, are presented in subsequent chapters of this book. Considered together, the results of these three studies provide greatly enhanced understanding of police responses to women rape complainants, and enable the construction of an explanatory model in relation to police processes and decision-making.

4
Beyond Belief: Police Files on Rape

> In practice, the average policeman exercises greater judicial discretion over cases than does a judge.
>
> (Blumberg and Niederhoffer, 1973, quoted in LeDoux and Hazelwood, 1999, p. 13)

> Female victims are a special category in the police world. Viewed as helpless and/or unpredictable, women are usually more trouble for a police officer.
>
> (Pike, 1992, p. 265)

Introduction

In the year 2000, many of the New Zealand public were outraged at publicity that a historic charge of rape had been made against then Cabinet Minister Dover Samuels. Others were sceptical, and believed their perspective was supported by the police's decision that there was insufficient evidence to prosecute the accused, who was loudly proclaiming his innocence. Samuels admitted that he had been sexually involved with a teenage girl in his care, and helped her to obtain an abortion, but disputed that he had raped her. In a speech made to his Parliamentary colleagues, Samuels proclaimed:

> I find the offence of rape or sexual abuse of women and children abhorrent and repugnant. There is only one offence more abhorrent, repugnant or contemptible, and that is for a person or persons to fabricate the allegation of rape knowing that the person being accused is completely innocent. (Quoted in *The Dominion*, 26 July 2000)

According to this view, and consistent with the material outlined in previous chapters, a woman lying is perceived as more reprehensible than a man raping. Subsequent media reports alleged that Samuels had been 'cleared' of wrongdoing, and the strong impression given portrayed the politician as an innocent man who had been wrongfully accused (e.g., *The Age*, 8 August 2000).

This recent example illustrates the widespread public confusion surrounding police terminology. The police decision not to proceed with a prosecution may or may not mean there was no wrongdoing on the part of the alleged offender. All we can deduce with any certainty is that the police felt it would be a difficult case *to prove*. While this decision may indicate the suspect's innocence, it could equally indicate culpability, accompanied by insufficient evidence to support this conclusion in a court case. A lack of proof can in no way be seen to correlate automatically with a lack of guilt.

The Dover Samuels case raised questions regarding issues of proof, evidence and complainants' credibility. Chapter 4 attempts to shed light on the reasons underlying police decision-making in rape and sexual assault cases and to identify factors that emerge as key determinants of police judgments and actions.

Reporting rates

The offences of rape and sexual violation have notoriously low reporting rates (Du Mont *et al.*, 2003; Epstein and Langenbahn, 1994; Gilmore and Pittman, 1993; Gregory and Lees, 1999; Kelly, 2002; Kemmer, 1977; Kilpatrick *et al.*, 1987; Koss *et al.*, 1987; Mack, 1998; National Victim Center, 1992; Schultz, 1975). Few victims approach the police of their own accord, and even fewer cases proceed to the point of prosecution (Gregory and Lees, 1996; Harris and Grace, 1999; Holmstrom and Burgess, 1991; Kelly, 2002). Many studies have been conducted of rape cases which resulted in prosecution, examining in particular the progress of such cases through the court system, and the ways in which victims of rape experience trial procedures (e.g., Adler, 1987; Lees, 1997; McDonald, 1994; van de Zandt, 1998). This chapter presents the results of a study primarily focussed on rape and sexual violation cases that did *not* proceed to trial.

A high proportion of reported sexual assault offences are cleared by the police as 'no offence disclosed', the equivalent of the English category of 'no criming'. The use of this clearance code, however, is highly ambiguous. 'No offence disclosed' may be intended to convey the non-disclosure of a criminal offence, with the emphasis being on the absence not of a crime but of evidence of that crime – in other words, an offence may have been committed but there is insufficient evidence, including testimony by the complainant and any witnesses, to support the claim. The other way in which 'no offence disclosed' can be interpreted is to emphasise the 'no offence' part of the phrase, implying that investigation reveals there to have been no crime actually committed. In the latter option, the inference is that the complainant may have attempted to mislead the police into believing sexual violation occurred when it did not – either because the complainant was a consenting partner to sexual intercourse with the accused, or because there was no sexual intercourse at all.

In the 1983 *Rape Study*, the 'no offence disclosed' category was roundly criticised for its overuse and, in particular, for the misleading impression it gave that there was no actual offence (Stace, 1983; Young, 1983). Stace (1983) noted that,

> It may well be that some of the concern about the police processing of rape complaints comes from a literal reading of what is, in fact, a statistical artefact. At the least it would seem that a separate category of 'insufficient evidence to proceed' should be created. (Stace, 1983, p. 14)

A police circular in December 1982 instructed officers not to clear rape complaints as 'no offence disclosed' when there was insufficient evidence, but instead to file such cases as 'uncleared'. Stace notes that, if adopted, this practice would result in a larger number of uncleared files in the future. However, the 'no offence disclosed' category continued to be sizeable and throughout the 1990s, approximately 30 per cent of rape complaints have been cleared as 'no offence disclosed' (Newbold, 2000, p. 139). As the following 1997 analysis of cases shows, 15 years after the concerns expressed in the 1983 *Rape Study*, this category was still being applied to a wide range of cases, including those where there was insufficient evidence.[25] Statistics provided by the New Zealand Police for the year ended 30 June 1997 show that of 520 reported offences of Male Rapes Female, 198 (38 per cent) were cleared as 'no offence disclosed' (refer Table 4.1).

Also of concern is the fact that very recently, academic commentators were still erroneously equating a police determination of 'no offence disclosed' with false complaints (e.g., Newbold, 2000).

Table 4.1: Selected sexual violation offences, reported, cleared and cleared by 'no offence disclosed' (NOD) for the year ended 30 June 1997

Offence	Total reported	Total cleared	% cleared	Cleared by NOD	% cleared by NOD
Male rapes female over 16 years	520	393	6	198	38
Husband rapes wife	22	19	86	7	32
Unlawful sexual connection female over 16 years	135	88	65	24	18
Total sexual violation[26]	772	533	71	252	33

The overall aim of the current study was to acquire greater understanding of the factors affecting police decision-making processes in relation to rape and sexual assault investigations, focussing in particular on cases where the investigation was terminated prior to the arrest and prosecution of an offender. The research objectives were:

- to analyse police procedures from the initial report of an incident through to the decision as to whether or not to proceed with a prosecution;
- to identify the factors affecting police decision-making concerning whether or not to proceed with an investigation; and
- to examine the circumstances surrounding cases in which complainants decide to withdraw the complaint.

Data gathering involved the analysis of a sample of police investigation files on rape and sexual assault. Central themes were identified and the relevant cases were grouped together for further examination.

Sampling and methodology

Negotiating access to police files proved to be a protracted and difficult undertaking. Limited precedent existed for permitting non-police personnel access to such files, and the significant confidentiality issues involved necessitated extensive consideration of access, storage and publication protocols. It took eight months for a contract to eventually be signed, with some of this delay due to this particular study being used to establish more generalised research agreements between the New Zealand Police and Victoria University of Wellington. Permission was obtained from the New Zealand Police to obtain and review police rape and sexual assault files for the year 1997 from three major cities – Auckland, Wellington and Christchurch.[27] The files requested were those where the complaint was cleared as 'no offence disclosed', known elsewhere as unfounded complaints, and those which the police classified as a reported offence but ceased investigating, either because there was insufficient evidence or because the complainant withdrew the allegation.

Of the 164 files examined, three quarters involved rape allegations and the remainder involved other sexual violation offences.[28] Eleven cases involved multiple offenders and/or victims, resulting in a total sample size of 181 offenders and 166 victims. The majority of the complainants were young, with 60 per cent aged 25 and under; in terms of ethnicity, nearly 40 per cent were described as Caucasian; and in 84 per cent of cases, the victim and the alleged perpetrator were previously acquainted in some way.

The files were divided into four main categories, determined largely by police perceptions of the legitimacy of the complaint. The categories identified were as follows.

Genuine cases: N = 34 (21 per cent)

Cases categorised as genuine represent those about which the police gave clear indications on the file concerning their legitimacy. For example, prosecution action may have been commenced against the alleged offender, a warning may have been issued, or comments may have been made which indicated the complainant's account was believed by police.

Within this category, four small but distinct subgroups emerged:

(i) Cases clearly perceived as genuine, for which an offender was detected, and prosecution action was commenced (N = 13; 38 per cent of genuine cases overall);

(ii) Cases clearly perceived as genuine, for which no offender was detected (N = 5; 15 per cent of genuine cases overall);

(iii) Cases clearly perceived as genuine and for which an offender was detected, but where the police made the decision not to prosecute (N = 3; 9 per cent of genuine cases overall); and

(iv) Cases where the police clearly believed the complaint was genuine but the complainant insisted on withdrawing the complaint (N = 13; 38 per cent of genuine cases overall).

Possibly true/possibly false cases: N = 62 (38 per cent)

The second category comprised cases which fell into a grey area. The police seemed unsure, from their file comments, whether or not to treat these complaints as genuine. Remarks were often made suggesting that, from the evidence available, it was impossible to determine if the complainant was telling the truth, or whether the incident reported constituted a criminal offence. Frequently the phrase 'insufficient evidence' was used in relation to these cases. Cases were also included in this category where the police noted some irregularities or discrepancies in the complainant's testimony but refrained from declaring the complaint false. Those cases which the complainant withdrew, and about which the police also expressed some misgivings, were included as part of this grouping.

In practice, it was difficult to identify fundamental differences in the criteria which the police used to decide that a complaint was dubious, and separate these from those evident in the 'police said false' category. This is not surprising, given that the factors seen as giving rise to doubts over a case's legitimacy are likely to be similar in all these cases. The main reason determining why cases were included in the 'possibly true/possibly false' category rather than the 'police said false' category revolves around what the police said on the file concerning the complainant's legitimacy. In situations where the police discussed the evidence available as being insufficient for them to make a definitive judgement, cases were included in the 'possibly true/possibly false' category. If the police stated outright that a complaint was false, and/or speculated as to what they believed were the motives underlying the complainant's actions, then the case was included in the 'police said false' category.

Cases which the police said were false: N = 55 (33 per cent)

Cases were included in this third category when comments on the file clearly stated that the police considered the complaint to be false. This included cases which the police decided to halt investigating, as well as those suspected of being false for which the complainant withdrew the charge. Officers sometimes tried to identify motives underlying the complaint – for example, 'cried rape to avoid a hiding', and 'a woman scorned'. In other cases, the police maintained it likely that sex had occurred but was consensual, and that for some reason the complainant wanted to conceal this fact. A suspicion of falsehood was not enough for a case to be placed in this category; if the police seemed at all equivocal, the case was categorised as 'possibly true/possibly false'.

Cases which the complainant said were false: N = 13 (8 per cent)

The final category is the smallest. It comprised those reports of sexual assault which the complainant decided to withdraw after having stated that the allegations were false, in that sex had been consensual, or that there had been no sex and the report of a sexual attack had been fabricated for personal reasons.

Cases involving complainant withdrawal

Within each of the above categories were cases which resulted in the complainant withdrawing the allegation, for reasons which were not always apparent. Complainant withdrawal was in fact the most common reason for why the police investigation of cases was halted. Of rape and sexual violation complaints that did not proceed, nearly half (47 per cent; N = 77) were because the complainant withdrew the allegation. This is discussed separately here because this figure suggests cause for concern.

One major assumption by the police is that a complainant's withdrawal of an allegation should be viewed as a retraction; a denial that any offence occurred. It was clear from the files studied that numerous other reasons existed and warrant consideration. These include the fact that some complainants withdrew the charge because they never wanted their case to involve the police in the first place, a point which becomes more evident later in the file analysis. Others did not want to see the offender prosecuted and were satisfied if their reporting of the incident gave him the message that his behaviour was violating and unacceptable. It is also possible that, in some cases, the initial police response to the complainant influenced her to withdraw the complaint. This could be because she felt disbelieved by the police, or because they told her that she would lack credibility in court.

More than three quarters of cases where the complainant withdrew the allegation involved acquaintances and partners. Cases involving sexual assaults perpetrated by acquaintances or partners of the complainant may have high withdrawal rates for a variety of factors. Police doubts concerning the chances of successful prosecution in such cases may be communicated in some way to complainants, thereby dissuading them from continuing with the process. Moreover, the complexities involved in taking someone known to you to court will undoubtedly deter many complainants from proceeding. In some cases, this will be because of fear-related issues; in others, it will arise from a desire to see the offender warned but not necessarily prosecuted; and in still others, it will be because factors of self-blame and recrimination may be linked to case withdrawal.

Complainant withdrawal, then, may signify many different things. It could signal, as the police often assume, a false complaint; equally, however, it could denote a withdrawal of the complainant's confidence in the police. What is withdrawn in such cases is not simply a complaint, but a sense of trust. This can be evident in various ways. If the complainant feels the police have no trust in her, she is likely to withdraw her trust in them and remove her case from them. If the police feel they have trusted her in the past, and been let down, then they may appraise any fresh complaint as being beyond belief. Who believes who is vital.

What can complicate this in many rape cases are the effects of sexual violation itself. The experience of being raped undermines a sense of self-trust and self-belief (Frazier and Seales, 1997; Kelly, 1988). Women often describe themselves as 'feeling all over the place' as they struggle to understand and move on from the attack. The effects of rape are, in fact, likely to produce unconvincing complainants.

Throughout the following analysis, cases within the complainant withdrawal category are considered jointly with cases where the investigation was terminated by the police. This decision was made because my principal interest lies in understanding what gives a complainant credibility from a police perspective. In trying to ascertain the significance placed by the police on different factors and cues, the issue of whose decision causes the investigation to be halted becomes a secondary consideration.

Victim attributions

File analysis yielded information on additional factors concerning complainants' characteristics. These included noting the relative frequencies of inclusion on police files of information concerning the state of the complainant – for example, comments concerning perceptions of alcohol and drug use, intellectual impairment and psychiatric conditions. Reference was also made on police files concerning whether or not the complainant had experienced previous rape or sexual abuse. There is, however, no way of knowing how consistently such information was either obtained or recorded.

Key factors were identified that police officers noted on the files and used in their assessments of a complainant's credibility. These factors are listed in Table 4.2, which shows the proportion of cases affected by each factor, and

Table 4.2   Victim attributions (N = 166)

Factors indentified in file analysis	Genuine N = 34	Possibly true/ possibly false N = 62	Police said false N = 57	Complainant said false N = 13
Drunk/drugged N = 85 51%	17 20%	33 39%	28 33%	7 8%
Delayed reporting N = 37 22%	5 14%	19 51%	13 35%	0
Previous consensual sex with accused N = 36 22%	6 17%	17 47%	13 36%	0
Previous rape or abuse N = 31 19%	4 13%	13 42%	13 42%	1 3%
Psychiatric disturbance N = 30 18%	3 10%	8 27%	18 60%	1 3%
Perceived immorality N = 25 15%	3 12%	13 52%	8 32%	1 4%
Intellectually impaired N = 16 10%	3 19%	5 31%	7 44%	1 6%
Previous false rape complaint N = 11 7%	0	4 36%	7 64%	0
Concealment N = 10 6%	0	4 40%	6 60%	0

the extent to which its presence could be correlated with determinations of case credibility.

Table 4.2 provides an initial window into characteristics of the complainants which appeared to influence police perceptions and responses. In relation to alcohol and drug use, for instance, it is clear that approximately half of all the files analysed involved complainants whom the police described as drunk, intoxicated or high/stoned. While one-fifth of cases involving drunk complainants were perceived as genuine complaints, nearly three quarters (72 per cent) were regarded by the police as false or possibly true/false. This suggests that drunkenness is correlated with doubts about complainants' credibility.

While drunkenness was the most commonly recorded factor, other victim attributions were also noted by police. Delayed reporting was a feature of 22 per cent of the files studied, with similar numbers of cases involving complainants who had previously engaged in consensual sex with the accused. Both these factors appeared to be linked to credibility concerns, with 86 per cent of complainants who had delayed reporting being viewed suspiciously, along with 83 per cent of those who had a prior sexual relationship with the accused.

Over one-quarter of the files studied involved complainants who were described as either intellectually impaired[29] or psychiatrically disturbed[30] in some way. As Table 4.2 shows, the largest proportions of cases involving either intellectual impairment or psychiatric disturbance were regarded by the police as false complaints. Of cases involving complainants with some degree of psychiatric disturbance or disorder, 87 per cent were viewed by the police as false or possibly true/false. Similarly, three quarters of the cases involving victims with intellectual disability were viewed as suspicious. Of all complaints made by intellectually impaired or psychiatrically disturbed persons, only 13 per cent were regarded as genuine by the police.

In 31 of the files studied (19 per cent), reference was made to the complainant having been the victim of prior sexual victimisation, either as a child or adult. This means that nearly one in every five sexual assault complainants had experienced some form of sexual victimisation prior to the latest incident reported. However, notations on the file suggesting prior sexual assault also appear to be strongly linked to police doubts about the veracity of the current incident. As Table 4.2 shows, in 84 per cent of cases involving complainants with previous known rape or abuse victimisation, the police perceived their current complaint with scepticism. Half of these complainants (N = 15) withdrew their most recent complaint, thereby deciding to end police involvement and investigation of their case. Some provided reasons for this decision, such as wanting to put the incident behind them or not wanting to go to court, but from the files alone, it is difficult to assess the impact on complainants of feeling that the police viewed them disbelievingly.

Subjective assessments of the complainant's morality also appeared significant, with 15 per cent of cases being characterised by file comments indicating the police perceived her as 'sluttish' or promiscuous. Also worth noting are two factors which, when they were evident, were always associated with police doubts and the decision to discontinue an investigation. The first of these involved situations where the current complainant had previously made a complaint of rape which was perceived as false (7 per cent of cases, N = 11). The perception that the previous complaint was false was often based simply on the fact that the charge was not proven, and the investigation ceased, but this fact clearly triggered strongly suspicious cues if a subsequent rape was reported by the same complainant. Similar reactions were evident if it became apparent in the course of an investigation that the complainant had deliberately concealed aspects of her behaviour which may be viewed as incriminating, such as excessive drinking. In all cases where this was commented upon (6 per cent of the total, N = 10), the police discontinued the investigation because they considered the current complaint false or likely to be false.

Each of the factors identified in this study is briefly outlined below in the context of international research into police rape investigations.

Drunk/drugged

If a woman presents as having been drunk or drugged at the time of the alleged rape, police may see that as contributing to her sexual violation, rather than condemning the way in which the perpetrator exploited her vulnerability and diminished competency. Numerous research studies have demonstrated an association between rape and alcohol consumption (Abbey *et al.*, 2001; Amir, 1971; Crowell and Burgess, 1996; Harrington and Leitenberg, 1994; Russell, 1984; Ullman *et al.*, 1999; Warshaw, 1988). In one of the most extensive studies conducted on date and acquaintance rape, 75 per cent of the men who had committed sexual assault had consumed alcohol or drugs prior to the assault (Warshaw, 1988). Within the criminal justice system, as in society at large, alcohol consumption by the victim has long been regarded as a discrediting factor – but only for the victim (Kelly, 2002; Schuller and Stewart, 2000). Naomi Wolf describes how,

> In Rome two millennia ago, a woman's drinking more than a little wine could be punishable by law since such behavior suggested sexual looseness. We still take for granted that 'loose' behavior by women will provoke punishment. (Wolf, 1997, p. 86)

Today, as Wolf says, 'Rome still lives in us' (ibid.). Alcohol is still blamed for loosening a woman's inhibitions, and the fact of her intoxication interpreted as evidence of overall moral turpitude (Abbey *et al.*, 2001; Etorre, 1992; Lees, 1997). By comparison, drunkenness in the offender appears to receive little condemnation. This may be related to the double standard which considers a drunken woman more reprehensible than a drunken man (Etorre, 1992; Otto, 1981). Against this backdrop, a woman who is drunk is more likely to be seen as 'asking for it' than he is for 'taking it' (Abbey et al., 2001; Baker, 1999; Shapcott, 1988; van de Zandt, 1998; Wiehe and Richards, 1995). A drunk woman tends to be viewed as responsible for what happens to her, while a drunk man may be absolved of responsibility for what he does while 'under the influence'.

Recently, however, exceptions to such thinking have been evident in cases of suspected 'drug rape'. The deliberate administering of a drug to an intended rape victim has prompted expressions of police concern and fuelled investigations of serial drug rapists in particular. Perceptions of the predatory nature of such offenders have tended to lessen judgments regarding those whom they target, yet, as a Detective Chief Inspector with the Metropolitan Police has observed, similar consideration is still withheld from victims of the oldest and most common drug used in rapes – alcohol (Sturman, 2000).

Delayed reporting

The police see a delay in reporting sexual assault offences as abnormal and as a factor which reduces the victim's credibility (Bronitt, 1998; Brownmiller, 1975; Freckelton, 1998; Temkin, 2002; Thomas, 1994; Torrey, 1991; Wolfthal, 1999). It is likely that less physical and forensic evidence is available and it is believed that victims will have more time to construct a fabricated account of events. Conversely, a rape victim will typically tend to hesitate before involving the police, and may feel scared, shamed and - self-blaming in the aftermath of rape (New South Wales Department for Women, 1996). Often the victim has to reach a stage where she feels as if she has the right to report the offender, and feels relatively safe and secure in doing so, before she can approach the police. Besides, the majority of reports that are reported promptly result from a third party contacting the police, not the victim herself (Holmstrom and Burgess, 1974; Burgess and Hazelwood, 1999; Jordan, 1998a).

Previous consensual sex with the alleged offender

This factor dates from the days when men claimed virtual ownership of women through sexual conquest (Brownmiller, 1975; Gordon and Riger, 1991). From a police perspective, the fact of a previous sexual relationship can raise suspicions that the complainant is acting out of scorn or revenge. For the victim, however, the person whom she may be most at risk of being sexually assaulted by could be her partner or ex-partner, or someone whom she had sex with once who considers that consent one day means 'yes' for all time. The fact that wife rape was not recognised as a crime until very recently suggests that remnants are likely to still be evident of attitudes endorsing men's sense of entitlement to unlimited access to a woman's sexuality (Brownmiller, 1975). Given many men's expectations that a woman who has had sex with them once will have sex with them repeatedly (Johnson, 1997), it seems highly likely that women face considerable risks of being forced to have sex if, on subsequent occasions, they either appear less willing, or their consent is deemed irrelevant.

Previous complaint of rape

A complainant whom police discovered, or believed, had made a previous complaint of rape which had not been proven seemed likely to be perceived as highly dubious. The inference was that a woman is unlikely to be raped more than once, and that a woman who has already had a rape complaint not proven is particularly suspicious if she subsequently alleges having experienced another incident of sexual violation. Such deductions fly in the face of an accumulating body of research evidence which documents high incidences of repeat rape victimisation (Doerner and Lab, 1998; Morris, 1997). For many women, an earlier sexual assault is followed by multiple episodes of sexual victimisation, either from the same or different perpetrators.

Psychiatric disturbance and intellectual impairment

It has been well documented that persons perceived as having diminished competency are likely to have enhanced vulnerability to sexual victimisation, arising from a combination of factors including impaired judgment, difficulties in communication, lack of knowledge regarding sexual matters, ignorance of their rights within the law and the likelihood of their living and working in high risk environments within easy access of both opportunists and sexual predators (Hayes, 1993; Luckasson, 1992; Wilson *et al.*, 1996). A recent Canadian study estimated that 83 per cent of women with disabilities will be sexually assaulted during their lifetime (Roehar Institute, 1995, cited in Brook, 1997, p. 16). Research conducted in Australia by the National Police Research Unit and Flinders University also found that persons with intellectual disability were ten times more likely to be sexually assaulted than non-disabled people (Brook, 1997, p. 16–17). These findings have serious and far reaching implications for organisations such as the police, and draw attention to the need for greater understanding of the power, control and dependency dimensions associated with disability. A tendency in the police to view intellectual or psychiatric impairment as factors which reduce the 'truth' value of the complainant's testimony can unwittingly benefit sexual predators. Indeed, statements from convicted rapists have revealed some perpetrators to be adept at selecting victims whom they know will be perceived as less believable and who are viewed as 'easy pickings' (Luckasson, 1992; McCarthy, 1996). In England, the sexual assault and murder of a woman with Down's syndrome prompted the Dorset Police

Superintendent in charge of the case to state:

> During this enquiry my officers have been surprised and sickened by the number of men who are prepared to prey on mentally disabled females. We have identified people who have committed very serious offences against these vulnerable people. Police have taken steps to remind persons responsible for the mentally handicapped of their vulnerability in this type of crime. (Quoted in McCarthy, 1996, p. 126)

Increasing recognition of the ways in which abuses of power are perpetrated against vulnerable sectors in our communities will hopefully contribute to an environment within which intellectually impaired rape complainants will be appraised more sensitively. Otherwise, the police may unwittingly be playing right into the offender's lap by dismissing the complainant's testimony in such cases.

Perceived immorality of the complainant

Perceptions of dubious morality can diminish a victim's credibility in the eyes of the police and affect their assessments of the likely responsiveness of a jury to her complaint (Lees, 1997; New South Wales Department for Women, 1996; Scutt, 1997; Shapcott, 1988). What is generally not questioned are the ways in which the same cues the police see as indicating the complainant is a 'slut' may be the very factors that make her vulnerable to rape. For example, the fact that a young woman had consensual sex with a man she met at a party may mean that his mate assumes she will also 'come across' for him. It is even possible that, rather than lose face, the first man may have said he and she had sex when they did not. Either way, the expectation is created that she is 'easy' and may contribute to a social context in which any protestation from her will be ignored and negated, first by the offender and second by the police. A slut is someone who is perceived by others as *wanting* sex; by definition, rape is *unwanted* sex.

Previous false complaint

Once a woman has a record of making an allegation that was not substantiated, she runs the risk of having any subsequent allegations dismissed prematurely. She is perceived as likely to be a person who makes false complaints, rather than the possibility being countenanced that she is a person who is vulnerable and prone to repeat victimisation.

If a complainant withdraws or retracts a rape allegation, the police tend to interpret this as evidence that the allegation was fabricated (Aiken *et al.*, 1999). The possibility must also be acknowledged, however, that the victim was too afraid to proceed, or decided that the likely costs of pursuing the complaint might outweigh the advantages. The latter conclusion could be reached as a result of encountering hostile reactions from the perpetrator, negative responses from family or friends, disbelieving or judgmental police perceptions, or from her own fears, doubts and self-blaming processes. Case retractions or withdrawals can therefore signify many different things, but a woman who retracts once may find it difficult to have any subsequent rape allegation seen as credible. It is important for the police to try to ascertain what it signifies for the victim rather than stamp their own interpretation on her actions.

Concealment

When a complainant attempts to conceal factors, such as the extent of her drinking on the night in question, most police will see a liar (Chambers and Millar, 1983). If she denies having danced with the suspect, or shared a joint with him, the police are likely to conclude that she is not trustworthy and dismiss her allegation. The woman who is doing the concealing, however, knows that her behaviour may be viewed as having compromised her credibility and is trying to find ways of bolstering it. Paradoxically, her efforts to do so may diminish her credibility more than if she had told the police the truth, no matter how possibly damning, from the outset.

Two additional factors need to be mentioned because they have been identified elsewhere as linked to perceptions of a rape victim's credibility, even though they emerged as less significant in this particular study. First, serious, physical, visible injuries are often taken by the police as proof that a rape occurred and are viewed as a necessary corroborative factor (Du Mont *et al.*, 2003; Edwards and Heenan, 1994; Harris and Grace, 1999; Kelly, 2002; Kennedy, 1992). In fact, many rape victims do not feel able to physically resist an attacker, and may go into a state of immobility (Burgess and Hazelwood, 1999; Galliano *et al.*, 1993; Smart, 1976). Active, physical resistance may be even more difficult for women who know the person attacking them, because they fear hurting this person or find it difficult to accept that this man, whom they thought loved them, is intent on violating them and will not stop (Wiehe and Richards, 1995). For most victims, the most serious injuries they sustain are the invisible ones, imperceptible to police scrutiny. In this study, the police files noted visible injuries in only nine of the cases recorded, with most being bruises or scratches.

The second factor involves assessments made on the basis of a complainant's demeanour. In seven cases, remarks made by police officers indicated that they had clear views as to how a victim of rape would look and act. Such beliefs, if fixed, have the potential to seriously impact on police judgments of complainants (Aiken *et al.*, 1999; Freckelton, 1998). Victims' reactions may not always seem consistent with how others expect they should be; some women try to deal with rape by being angry, others may withdraw and close down, some will cry and look vulnerable, others may laugh and try to shrug it off. In terms of behaviour, some women manage the effects of rape by taking time out from their work and life while they come to terms with what has happened; others may throw themselves into activities in an attempt to ward off the pain (Burgess and Hazelwood, 1999; Freckelton, 1998). Thus, demeanour alone can be a highly misleading factor in determining a complainant's credibility, and tells us more about the preconceptions of the officers concerned than it does about the complainant's veracity. Given its significance in other research, it is likely that this factor may have been more influential than in the few files which made explicit mention of aspects of demeanour.

Overall, the file analysis is useful in clearly identifying the cues and triggers which appear to influence police officers in their assessments of rape complainants' credibility. The ways in which these factors assume significance become even more apparent when considered in the context of specific cases, examples of which are presented next.

Qualitative analysis

The aim of the qualitative case analysis was to determine what police 'see' and to understand what informs *their* interpretation of its significance. In reality, of course, this classification relied on my interpretation of police comments recorded on file. Thus the subjectivities of both the police and myself inevitably underlie these categories. Given that one might expect police files to reflect only what officers feel is acceptable to commit themselves to in writing, however, biases in interpretation are more likely to show the police in a positive than a negative light. In other words, comments actually recorded on files may have been 'censored' and reveal simply the tip of an iceberg of police attitudes and judgments.

Examples for each of the major categories identified are presented to illustrate the ways in which factors perceived as denoting credibility affect and influence police decision-making processes.

Genuine cases

Cases clearly perceived as genuine, for which an offender was detected and prosecution action commenced

Cases resulting in police prosecution of an offender were rare, in part due to the method of case selection which omitted all offences cleared by immediate arrest. Of the 13 cases in this category, half involved attacks by acquaintances/friends (N = 7), two involved attacks by strangers, two arose in the context of work relationships, one involved a family member and one involved a partner.

Of these cases, five resulted in conviction, mostly from the offender pleading guilty. Only one case that went to trial by jury resulted in conviction (Case 122); this case involved a young Pacific Island schizophrenic who raped a Caucasian woman in her 60s in her home one morning. She reported the attack immediately, sustained physical injury and there was clear evidence linking the offender to the crime scene. In five of the cases prosecuted, the defendant was found not guilty at jury trial – in three of these cases the complainant had met the defendant while out drinking, and the other two involved situations where young women said they awoke to find a visiting male violating them.

A further three cases did not proceed. In the first, this was because the charges were withdrawn because the complainant was not a competent witness (Case 92); in the second, it was because the complainant withdrew the charge and the defendant was committed as a psychiatric patient (Case 128); in the third, the offender was discharged halfway through the trial after the judge expressed concerns about the reliability and consistency of the evidence being presented (this case involved the alleged kidnapping and sexual violation of an escort, whose manager raised doubts concerning her veracity) (Case 142).

The police cannot, of course, determine court outcomes, but do control the access gates to criminal trial processes. It is, therefore, of interest to attempt to understand which factors influenced them in deciding to proceed with these cases. The complainant being drunk, for instance, did not automatically exclude their case from advancing through the process, although, as we will see when discussing the other categories, drunkenness can certainly place a question mark over a complainant's credibility as a witness. Closer examination of some cases helps to elucidate the reasoning processes involved in police decision-making.

Case 7, for instance, involved a young Caucasian woman who was in a highly intoxicated state when friends, including an off-duty police officer, put her in a taxi. She began drifting in and out of consciousness and vomited over the cab. The driver informed her that an additional $50 to the fare would be needed and she asked him to stop at a cashflow machine. She fell over on the footpath and said she was too drunk to get the money, so gave the driver her pin number and asked him to withdraw $60, which bank records show he did. This was despite the advice of other taxi drivers driving by, and the taxi base, telling him that in such circumstances he should not use her cashflow card, for his own protection, but instead drive her to the police station. No one knew where he went when he drove off with her in the back of his cab. She says she came to in a closed garage at the taxi driver's home, to find him sucking her nipple and rubbing her vagina. She leapt out of the cab and demanded to be taken home, which he agreed to do. When they arrived she jumped out quickly, leaving her wallet behind. Later that day the driver handed the wallet into the police. He subsequently admitted to the police that she had spent three hours in his cab but denied assaulting her. The fact that he had handed her wallet in was, he said, 'proof' that he had done nothing.

It is clear from the file notes that the police did not believe that the driver's action in handing in the wallet proved his innocence. What made them suspicious was the fact that he had, by his own admission, kept the young woman in his car for three hours, when the journey to her address should have taken less than ten minutes. Moreover, the taxi driver agreed that he had driven her instead to his home address. This had been simply so he could change his clothes, he said. The police were not convinced, and he was charged with Unlawful Sexual Connection. It is possible that the police were influenced by the driver being nearly 30 years older than his female passenger, and by his being from a culture in which women have low status. In court, the defence lawyer emphasised the bad circumstances currently surrounding the driver – a bitter custody dispute, a recent burglary, imminent bankruptcy – and the young woman's account was rejected by the jury, who found in the driver's favour. On the police file, it states that the driver's taxi licence had been suspended pending the outcome of the prosecution and the sergeant was emphatic in declaring this man to be unsuitable for this line of work and advised him strongly against updating his licence. Thus, in this case, the police interpreted the woman's drunkenness as rendering her vulnerable and saw the taxi driver as abusing her dependency on him to transport her safely home.

As with drunkenness, it was also clear that, at times, delayed reporting of a rape' did not automatically preclude it from further investigation and police action.

In Case 93, a Māori woman in her early twenties waited three weeks before approaching the police. She said she had woken one night to find her boyfriend's mate sodomising her, and screamed. Her boyfriend was in the bathroom at the time, and when he came into the room and found her crying and his mate out on the verandah, he was not sympathetic. Instead, he began abusing and threatening her. The complainant tried to explain to the police why she found it hard to speak about the attack and felt the need to tell her partner about it first. Yet she was in a bind, because she feared his reaction:

> I couldn't tell [partner] what had happened. I was too scared. I couldn't tell my partner someone had sex with me. We started arguing and in the end I had the Police come and remove [partner] from my home. I was angry and upset and wanted [partner] out of my house. I told the Police that he might kill me because [he] is possessive of me and if he knew what had happened I was afraid he might kill me .... I told [him] about three weeks after the attack what had happened. Before then I hadn't spoken to anybody else about this. I kept it to myself because I felt yuck, disgusted and ashamed of myself. I went and spoke to [partner] once I felt strong enough to deal with it myself.

In this case, the police seemed to consider several factors when assessing the genuineness of the complaint. The victim had delayed reporting, but explained reasons for her hesitancy, reasons which in her case the police knew to be valid. Her partner and his mate, the offender, had been in prison together and often met up in the early hours of the morning to commit burglaries. The latter had multiple previous convictions, including two convictions for Male Assaults Female, had gang associates, and had his application for bail opposed by the police because they felt concerned for the victim's safety. Meanwhile, she had sought medical assistance for the injuries sustained to her anus and vagina and seen counselling services who validated the serious impact of the offence on her life. The police probably hoped this was one way to get a known repeat offender behind bars for a while, so seemed prepared to overlook delayed reporting and the questionable circumstances of the incident and proceed with the case. In other words, the alleged offender's lack of credibility was also considered to be relevant. At the High Court trial, however, the jury returned a verdict of Not Guilty against the defendant.

There were other cases which the police regarded as genuine but which did not proceed to prosecution. These included cases where no offender was detected (N = 5; 3 per cent), cases where an offender was detected but not prosecuted (N = 3; 2 per cent), and cases which the complainant decided to withdraw (N = 13).

Cases clearly perceived as genuine, for which no offender was detected

Four of the five cases which the police perceived as genuine and for which no offender was detected involved stranger attacks, all on women aged between 16 and 29, two of whom were Māori and two Caucasian. One of the stranger attacks occurred in the complainant's home – this case was referred to the Offender Profiling Squad for further investigation. The remainder occurred in street settings. Two of these incidents were recorded as Unlawful Sexual Connection, one as Attempted Rape, and one as Inducing Unlawful Sexual Connection. The police appeared to accept the complainants' accounts of these incidents as genuine, in part because most of these could be substantiated by recent complaint witnesses.

The complainant in Case 39 was a 17-year old who had been drinking at a house with friends. She said she was attacked while walking home and indecently assaulted before she was able to kick herself free. She ran to a service station, where the attendant said she sat, crying and shaking, while he called a taxi. Both he and the taxi driver asked if she wanted to go to the police station, or have the police called, but she insisted that she be taken home. Both men confirmed her account of these conversations. Shortly after she arrived home, her boyfriend and his friends arrived and they rang the police. With no other evidence being retrievable, the police recorded the incident as an Attempted Rape and filed it.

In this case, the victim's demeanour seemed consistent with how the police expected a sexual assault victim to present. This factor was mentioned in another similar case in this category.

In Case 55, a woman said she had an argument with her boyfriend late one night while they were travelling home in a taxi. She left the vehicle to walk home alone, and was attacked and sexually assaulted by a man with his jersey pulled over his face. She went immediately to the police station to report the incident. The police interviewed her boyfriend, who denied any involvement in the assault and she also was adamant that he was not the attacker. He said in relation to her that he believed she had been attacked, adding: 'she's not the type to lie'. Examination by a police doctor revealed bruising, torn clothing and evidence of the use of force and finger grip marks on her upper arms. What the police also noted was that her demeanour seemed 'consistent with the offences as described'.

The fifth case in this category involved the rape of a 17-year old intellectually disabled woman by a family member, in circumstances where the fact of her abuse was clearly evident, but it was impossible for the police to determine who in the family was responsible. Hence this case was filed as 'no offender detected'.

Cases clearly perceived as genuine and for which an offender was detected, but where the police made the decision not to prosecute

A small number of cases in the study sample involved situations which the police determined to be genuine offences and which had been committed by an identifiable offender, but for which no prosecution resulted. The cases included here all depended on the police deciding not to charge the alleged offender, even when they considered him to have committed a criminal offence. It is the fact of police decision-making which distinguishes these cases from other cases, perceived as genuine, which did not proceed because the complainant withdrew the allegation.

Two of these cases involved Male Rapes Female offences while the third was recorded as Other Sexual Violation. Two involved sexual assaults perpetrated by acquaintances and one occurred in a work context. The workplace incident involved the rape of a young naval woman by naval officers overseas; in this case (Case 43) the police referred the incident to the navy for further investigation.

In another case, the police chose to give the offender a warning rather than prosecute. This case, Case 119, involved a young Caucasian woman who met a good friend of her boyfriend while she was in a bar. He told her she was welcome to 'crash' the night at his parents' inner city apartment. She said she woke to find him raping her. He denied the offence. The police made it clear that they believed her but decided not to charge him. Instead, the detective noted that the offender was:

> ... brought in with his lawyer, and warned of the consequences of any similar behaviour in the future. He was told that I believed [complainant],

however would not arrest him in this instance because of the effect that a jury trial would have on the complainant in these circumstances.

The police said they explained to the complainant and her mother how the situation would look if the case went to court and they were happy to accept the offender being let off with a warning.

The third case, Case 167, involved the only situation in which the alleged offender was female. Staff at a rest home feared that a 92-year-old woman had sexually assaulted a woman co-resident, a situation further complicated by the fact that the victim had dementia. The victim's son was notified and mention was made on the file that he was aware the police would not prosecute a 92-year old.

There are insufficient cases here from which to draw definite conclusions. What these cases suggest, however, is that the police decision to prosecute appears not only to be affected by available evidence but also, at times, by factors such as the victim's competency or willingness to proceed, the offender's age and the context in which a rape or sexual assault occurs.

Cases where the police clearly believed the complaint was genuine but the complainant insisted on withdrawing the complaint

This category included cases where, despite the police clearly believing that the report of a sexual assault occurring was genuine, the complainant insisted on withdrawing the allegation. All but one of these cases was cleared by the police as 'no offence disclosed', despite evidence of victimisation being obvious. If the complainant would not disclose details of the offence, or wished to withdraw an allegation made earlier, then from a police point of view there was no offence to investigate. This is different from police policies regarding family violence, which, in theory at least, no longer have to depend on the victim's willingness to make a complaint for the police to charge an assailant. In cases of family violence, however, the victims are more likely to bear visible evidence of physical injuries which can be used against the defendant; most sexual assaults lack such visible evidence. The impact of psychological shock and trauma on the victim, however, often effectively silences her. Since the assailant is, as in family violence disputes, most likely to be already known to her, she is faced with having to decide whether to make a police report against someone she loves, or fears, or both.

There was little information recorded on the files studied concerning the reasons for these victims withdrawing the complaint. In five cases, it appears that the victim and perpetrator were either partners or ex-partners, and the complainant wanted them warned but not charged. These cases may, therefore, parallel quite closely cases of physical family violence in which the complainant voices a desire for the violence to stop but not necessarily for the relationship to end, or where she is too scared of the perpetrator's reaction to press charges. In two further cases, at least, the complainant also appeared to want the police to give the offender a warning and desired no further action. Two complainants, whose offences were reported without their full agreement, declined police involvement on the basis that they wanted to forget about the attack and 'get on with life'. There were also several cases where it seems, from what is recorded on file, that although the police believed the sexual assault allegation was genuine, they had strong doubts concerning how credible the complainant would appear if the case went to court.

Police comments on the file indicated that they believed the complainant was telling the truth in these 13 cases, despite the fact that she decided to withdraw the complaint. In at least three cases, the level of physical injury sustained appeared to be a factor in convincing the police that the complaint of sexual violation was genuine.

Case 26, for example, involved a young prostitute who, while drunk, was violated by a client. The victim showed clearly visible signs of physical attack, and was found curled up and hysterical, in the street by a passing taxi driver and his passenger. The victim had not wanted the police called and was insistent that 'she just wanted to forget the whole incident and go to bed'. Concern was expressed by the sexual assault counsellor who was called that the complainant had injuries to her wrists from a recent suicide attempt and the 'Psych' team[31] were notified.

The above case involved a victim who was drunk, a prostitute and perceived as mentally unstable. The report of her rape was accepted as valid by the police, however, partly because the obvious physical injuries provided corroborative evidence. The fact that the complainant had not called the police herself may also have bolstered her claim – she was not alleging rape but had, in effect, two recent complaint witnesses (the taxi driver and his passenger) whose testimony supported her account of her attack.

In some cases, the victim's complaint was substantiated not only by the injuries she received but also by police knowledge that the offender had a previous record of violence, and his own incriminating remarks.

Case 126, for instance, involved a teenager who, by her own admission, had a heavy night of parties, alcohol and drugs. She felt cold and exhausted when a guy asked her to have sex with him, and said she told him: 'I don't care, because I'm freezing cold.' Later, the pair climbed into a bed already occupied by a man in his thirties. The latter woke up and forced her to give him and the first guy oral sex, then raped and sodomised her. She escaped when he let her go to the toilet, left most of her belongings in the house and told her friends and the police what had happened. When interviewed, the offender admitted to having been rough with her, and to forcing her head down on his penis repeatedly, but said it was all 'part of the game. Being forceful'. A woman detective spoke with the complainant, after which the latter decided not to proceed with the complaint.

In several cases, police awareness of previous family violence incidents involving the offender appeared to substantiate the victim's allegation; however, her knowledge of the same facts sometimes clearly dissuaded her from continuing with the complaint.

Overall, it appears that many of the cases in this category were treated by the police as genuine because there was clear evidence of physical injury and/or of previous violence by the alleged offender. These factors, however, should not be interpreted as sufficient and consistent indicators – analysis of some of the incidents deemed by police to be false complaints showed these factors to be present in some of these cases also. Police assessment of a complaint is also affected by who reports it and when, and by the perceived credibility of the complainant compared with the alleged assailant.

The principal focus in this piece of research is to identify what factors affect whether or not a rape complaint proceeds beyond first base? What sends a complainant's credibility plummeting, and how do the police decide whose version of events to believe?

These questions are considered further in analysis of the other major file categories.

Possibly true/possibly false complaint

Thirty-seven sexual violation cases were categorised by the police as falling into the grey area where the latter seemed unsure whether or not to treat the complaint as genuine. Three quarters of these were Male Rapes Female cases, plus there was one Husband Rapes Wife case. The remainder constituted cases of Unlawful Sexual Connection (N = 7), and one case that was recorded as Other Sexual Violation. Also included in this category are 25 cases which the complainant withdrew and which the police had regarded as possibly true or possibly false. Most of these were Male Rapes Female charges (N = 22), plus two of Unlawful Sexual Connection, and one of Other Sexual Violation. In total, therefore, this category comprises 62 cases, making it the largest single grouping.

As in the cases perceived as genuine, the highest proportions of complainants in this category were young (with 63 per cent being 25 years and under), and Caucasian (45 per cent). In terms of the relationship between the victim and the offender, the overall profile was similar, but there was a slightly higher proportion of Possibly True/Possibly False complaints involving acquaintances (60 per cent involved acquaintances, compared with 47 per cent where the complaints were viewed as genuine) and slightly fewer involved stranger attacks (10 per cent compared with 18 per cent where the complaints were viewed as genuine).

The majority of the cases in this category arose from complaints involving acquaintances, followed by partner attacks and incidents involving persons connected through workplace relationships. There were also six accounts of stranger attacks and two arising within the family that had doubts raised regarding their legitimacy.

Of all the cases in this category, in 37 the police decided to halt the investigation, while in the remaining 25 cases it was the complainant who decided to withdraw the allegation.

Cases withdrawn by the complainant

In at least half of the Possibly True/Possibly False cases withdrawn by the complainant (N = 14), it was clear from the files that the complainant had not wanted the police involved from the outset. Someone else had reported the incident on the complainant's behalf, often against her wishes. Case 50, for instance, demonstrates this. It involved a schoolgirl who sought medical examination following a rape and the clinic advised the police about the incident.

The girl had been drinking and smoking marijuana with friends, one of whom raped her when he was supposed to be driving her home. She was very reluctant to proceed with a complaint, citing as a major reason her knowledge that the offender had already influenced others to accept his version of events and she feared the consequences of taking the case further. Her mother tried to persuade her to change her mind but she was adamant that she wanted the complaint withdrawn. The police recommended counselling and gave her referral information to a support agency. The report was cleared as 'no offence disclosed'.

In other cases where the police felt corroborative evidence was lacking, the complainant's fear of the repercussions of reporting seems to be a factor in the complaint being withdrawn.

Case 106, for example, involved a young Māori woman who accepted a ride home from a nightclub. The man drove her to a house where he detained and raped her. Initial police investigations yielded some corroborative evidence from a witness next door and they were willing to take the case further. The complainant, however, refused to make a formal complaint and was reluctant to provide any details. The police note on the file:

> [Victim] is very concerned that the offender and his associates are all gang members and she fears for her safety should this complaint be made. Her hesitation in making the complaint is solely her fear of any retribution.

Also noted was the fact that the complainant had apparently made a previous rape allegation, for which the offender was convicted but served only a minimal sentence.

> She stated that she had no faith in the justice system and feared that if she pursued a complaint again, that the offender prior to the trial would

be given bail and that if he was convicted there would only be a short period of incarceration.

She was extremely fearful of gang retaliation and wished now, she said, simply 'to get on with things'.

The remaining discussion of the Possibly True/Possibly False category considers those 37 cases where the police decided there was insufficient evidence to proceed.

Cases where the police decided to proceed no further

The criteria evident in many of the apparently 'grey' and dubious cases in this category echo the findings of international research identifying factors that diminish the credibility of rape complainants (Adler, 1987; Burgess, 1999; Estrich, 1987; Gregory and Lees, 1999; Harris and Grace, 1999; Kelly, 2002; Lees, 1997; Scutt, 1997; Taslitz, 1999). For example, a delay in reporting a rape by the victim is often interpreted as questionable; the assumption is that the first thing any genuine victim would do is to contact the police (Bronitt, 1998; Kelly, 2002; Torrey, 1991). While evidentially there may be advantages in early reporting, the belief that this factor indicates genuineness may be misplaced, with many victims taking significantly longer periods of time in making the difficult decision to approach the police.

Case 23, for example, was labelled as an 'historic rape' although the time lapse between the incident's occurrence and its reporting was less than three weeks. A woman student, who had recently broken up with her boyfriend, reported drinking and smoking cannabis with another male friend. She alleged that she became very intoxicated and, while lapsing in and out of consciousness, was raped by this man. Police clearly viewed with some suspicion the fact that she then left the house, told no one else about the incident for several days and did not inform the police for more than a fortnight. The complainant claims that, when she came to and found him on top of her, she insisted he stop and tried to fight him off. He told a male friend, however, that it was she who had 'jumped on him' and had sex with him. When spoken to again by a detective, the file noted that she admitted she had only made the complaint at the insistence of her ex-boyfriend, with whom she wished to be reconciled. The detective also noted:

> She told me she did not believe she had been raped. She was just annoyed that [alleged offender] had not stopped having sex with her when she said no.

Conversely, prompt reporting by a complainant may be interpreted positively by police. In Case 140, for example, while weighing up the credibility of a case, the detective specified that one of the factors in support of her allegation was that the complainant reported within 24 hours of the alleged rape.

Earlier New Zealand research (Jordan, 1998a) showed that rapes are typically reported by persons other than the victim. The decision to report a rape is not a straightforward one (Chambers and Millar, 1983; Epstein and Langenbahn, 1994; Feldman-Summers and Norris, 1984; Gilmore and Pittman, 1993; Kelly, 1988). Whereas victims of burglary may feel an immediate sense of anger and injustice at returning to find the sanctity of their home violated in their absence, the victim of rape's physical presence during the offence both heightens the effects and complicates the response. Choosing to expose one's self to police scrutiny is a complex, painful and often terrifying decision. Victims of rape know only too well that it is not just the offender's actions that will be scrutinised, nor simply the victim's actions either, but her character, morality and integrity (Estrich, 1987; Kennedy, 1992; Lees, 1997; Scutt, 1997). This is illustrated in the following case.

Case 89 involved a woman in her thirties who went tenpin bowling with her neighbour, where they met up with friends and all went on to a nightclub together. Considerable amounts of alcohol were consumed and the women danced with men they met at the club. At about 1.30am the neighbour decided to go home, leaving the complainant at the club. She was, by her own admission, quite intoxicated and about 3am told the people she was with that she was going to catch a taxi home. One of the men she had been dancing with offered to walk outside with her, there were no taxis outside and he said he would walk her to a taxi stand. En route she said he knocked her to the ground and tried to sexually violate her but she struggled violently and he ran off. She walked home, distressed, called her ex-de facto and he encouraged her to contact the police, which she agreed to do. The police were not in fact notified until a few days later when her former partner took her into a police station. The detective admitted to having considerable doubts about the validity of the complaint, some of which involved judgments made about the complainant's actions on the night:

> When I spoke to the complainant she was crying, shaking and very distressed.
>
> I have concerns about this complaint, in that she remained at a nightclub, after her friend left when she claimed not to know anyone she was drinking with. She walked home after the assault, rather than calling Police or catching a taxi. She lied to her ex boyfriend about making a complaint to Police. The scene is not where she said it was (It was further along [—] Road); the circumstances of her recent break-up with her boyfriend, and that she seeks reconciliation with him, (it is possible that the complaint (sic) is attention seeking from him).
>
> I developed rapport with the complainant, and did question her about the validity of her complaint (but didn't force/push the issue

what-so-ever.) She maintained that she was telling the truth. She also had the scratches to her chest.

One way in which credibility became problematic arose in situations where the complainant had initially concealed factors associated with the incident, or subsequently changed her/his 'story'. In Case 11, for example, a young woman initially alleged abduction and rape from a suburban party. When challenged concerning aspects of this incident, she admitted the incident had occurred in the context of a prostitute–client relationship. She maintained she had been abducted and raped, but in a different context to that initially alleged. The original story had been quickly concocted to conceal her identity as a sex worker and to protect her manager – understandable concerns on her part – but the fact of concealment damaged her reputation in the eyes of the police more, it seems, than the fact that she worked in the sex industry.

Thus some of the cases in this category became suspicious to the police once it emerged that the complainant had attempted to conceal parts of the story or lie about certain aspects associated with it. In some cases, such concealment arose from efforts by the complainant to minimise the amount she had been drinking or to obscure the fact that she had taken drugs.

The drunkenness of the complainant was noted as a factor in nearly half of the cases in this category (46 per cent) and has been identified previously as contributing towards police scepticism (Kelly, 2002; Torrey, 1991; Wiehe and Richards, 1995). Drunkenness per se did not appear to be a significant determinant of police suspicion, however, and this is evidenced in part by its high occurrence in all the categories discussed in this chapter. One major difficulty posed by high alcohol use is the poor recall usually associated with it. This makes it difficult for the police to obtain clear and consistent accounts. However, these seem to be interpreted more often as raising doubts concerning the complainant's testimony than the alleged offender's. In part, this may be influenced by the legal safeguards accorded to accused persons, safeguards which are necessary to prevent wrongful convictions.

In Case 131, a Pacific Island student went on a drinking binge with a female friend, met up with some guys they knew and later that night one of them allegedly forced her to perform oral sex on him. She approached a counselling agency in some distress and the police were informed. The detective reviewed the circumstances and concluded:

> In all fairness, the defences in this matter were numerous and unfortunately there were a large number we could not refute.
> – Drunkenness
> – her drinking is a regular occurrence at [—]
> – Consent – or lack of

– bruising possibly self inflicted (Victim states her friend told her she was falling over a lot and admits she was wasted).

Investigation was ceased and the file cleared as 'no offence disclosed'.

It is important not to attach too much significance to any individual factor when, in reality, most cases incorporate a range of influential variables. Case 159 demonstrates this well. The complainant was 17 and alleged that she had been raped following her abduction from this party by an old school friend and his mates. She was heavily intoxicated at the time and police had to wait for the effects of alcohol to lessen before they could obtain a statement from her. The detective noted that earlier in the evening she had engaged in consensual oral sex with another male at the same party, stating that her behaviour was clearly affected by alcohol 'because she is not normally inclined to sexual activity with virtual strangers (her flatmates refer to her as the "nun" of their group)'. Later that night this guy encouraged her to get into a vehicle, which was full of other males including the former schoolmate whom, she says, raped her. Friends described seeing her struggling to get away as the car sped off from the party and assumed she had been abducted.

A medical examination revealed a number of recent injuries on the complainant's body, especially around the genital area. The detective said:

After interviewing the complainant, it is difficult to believe she is lying and her demeanour is entirely consistent with other rape victims I have interviewed. Having said that, however, there were a number of inconsistencies both in her behaviour and according to witnesses which would undoubtedly be taken advantage of under cross-examination.

This detective goes on to note that:

Although it has no legal relevance to the issue of consent to any sexual activity with [accused], the complainant did admit to engaging in oral sex in a toilet with a person she had only met that night at the party ... . The implication is that she was intoxicated to the point where her normal inhibitions were almost completely absent.

Additional factors mentioned that could be used against the complainant included the fact that she seemed reluctant to discuss intimate details associated with the rape:

While this reticence could simply be a result of acute embarrassment, it could also be seen as an attempt to play down her behaviour that night.

It was also noted that she appeared to have made no effort to run away:

> Even allowing for her to have acquiesced out of fear, there was no mention in her statement of any force being used or threats being made.

The detective noted in conclusion:

> This is unfortunately a situation where a young woman who is not accustomed to drinking large quantities of alcohol has become intoxicated at a party, and as a result, has engaged in sexual activity which she later regretted. She presents as a genuine victim of sexual violation, but it is my view that with the combination of generous portions of self-recrimination and regret, together with some over-zealous [intervention] from her piers (sic), [the complainant] is trapped in a lie or even actually believes that she was raped.
>
> Although one must be sober to consent to sexual activity of course, there is no evidence that any of the youths concerned (and especially [the accused]) believed that [she] was anything but willing to go along with them...
>
> [The complainant] has had these matters explained to her and although she maintains her position, she realises that a conviction would be unlikely in the circumstances. She does not wish to have to give evidence anyway.

No further action by police indicated – for filing.

This case clearly illustrates the way in which different factors may combine to reduce the apparent credibility of sexual assault complainants. Intoxication, the suggestion of promiscuity, seemingly compliant behaviour by the victim, embarrassment and probable shame – all these combine to place a question mark over the allegation. Sometimes detectives seemed to disagree as to which way the evidence was weighted; in Case 159, however, the battle seems to rage within an individual detective as he attempts to assess the complainant's credibility in what was perceived as a borderline case.

One additional factor that appears to be correlated with police closure of an investigation is that of diminished competency in the victim. This may be seen as resulting from intellectual disability or psychiatric illness. Complainants in such cases undoubtedly pose difficulties for the police, ranging from possibly poor or confused recall through to concerns about their competency in the witness box. Of particular concern to police will be apprehension over the vulnerability of such victims to defence lawyers' tactics and intimidation. Whilst not disputing the legitimacy of police concerns, the result may unwittingly be that victims with intellectual or psychiatric disabilities have diminished access to justice. Case 88 illustrates some of these difficulties.

The report form outlines how the complainant phoned the police for assistance ten days after an alleged rape, when the offender rang to say he was coming to pay her another visit. Detectives were at the house when the offender arrived and questioned both parties about the alleged rape.

The accounts differed somewhat in that, although both said they had met when she was dating his brother, she denied previous consensual sex with the accused whilst he claimed it had occurred infrequently between them. He referred to her 'kissing like a chicken, being a lousy screw', and said 'I'd never rape her – I'm not that desperate'. Despite these insults and utterances, however, he admitted that he rang her that night because he wanted 'to see her, for a fuck, or whatever you want to call it'.

The detective clearly had some doubts about the complainant's account and noted:

> [Complainant] was quite happy talking to me concerning the background information about her relationship between the [brothers], but as soon as questions were asked of her concerning the events of the morning in question, she would start crying, withdraw into herself and refuse to answer questions. She refused to read the statement and sign it, and would not say anything more.

The police said that, whilst being questioned, the complainant 'changed her story' and claimed not to have seen the accused for two years prior to the rape. She was also inconsistent in her recall of some events and the order in which they occurred – for example, whether or not she had made other phone calls that night, and when. When the police challenged her about an error in her recall, the file notes:

> [Complainant] then started crying and blubbering and saying that everything is just a lie and everyone's calling her a liar and no one believes her.

The interview was stopped and the services of a Victim Support worker were obtained to explain why the truth was important. Four pages into the report form, mention is made for the first time of the complainant's intellectual disability. The complainant's situation was discussed with a manager for the IHC (Intellectually Handicapped Children's Society) who stated that, given the level of disability, the complainant may suffer memory loss in relation to events such as the one alleged.

Despite police concerns over the complainant's reliability, some evidence seemed to support her account. One of the major discrepancies noted was between the accounts of the complainant and the accused concerning the timing of his phone calls and his subsequent arrival at her flat. She alleged he rang her about 3am to invite himself over; he claimed it was only about 10.30pm; a police check of phone records later showed her account to be the more accurate. Other evidence emerged when the doctor who examined the complainant noted that 'the findings were consistent with upper body restraint and a struggle'.

Police re-questioned the accused, who was now in prison on an unrelated matter, but clearly still held concerns about the complainant's veracity. What seemed to raise further doubts in the minds of police was the discovery of a rape complaint made four years previously by the same complainant. In the midst of conflicting accounts, the fact of this earlier rape complaint had pivotal significance attached to it. The detective decided to make the latest complaint an associated file of the former case:

> This is in case [complainant] makes any further allegations against other people for similar offences. In light of the afore-mentioned discrepancies and the unreliability of [complainant] as a witness, I recommend that the matter be filed and of course, the [complainant's] family informed accordingly.

The assumption in Case 88 seemed to be that if the complainant had made a previous complaint which had not been proven, any subsequent complaint was also likely to be false. The complainant's intellectual disability and the ways in which this might make her vulnerable, first, to sexual assault and, second, to not being viewed as a credible witness, did not appear to be acknowledged by the police involved with this case.

What is it, then, that makes cases grey as opposed to black and white? Since similar factors seem to underlie both the grey and the black/white categories, what tips the scales one way or the other? The scales of justice analogy may well be useful here, since in practice it does often seem to be a question of balance. Do the factors interpreted as adding plausibility to a complaint outweigh those seen as undermining it? Seldom does one individual factor seem to tip the balance; rather, clusters of variables emerge that, considered together, are interpreted as indicators of a complainant's credibility.

Hence while factors such as drunkenness might not be sufficient individually to provoke suspicion, if the victim was drunk, had delayed reporting the incident and had also engaged in previous consensual sex with the accused, such a combination of factors would impact very negatively on police perceptions of her credibility. Similar clustering of variables was evident in the next category also, which involves cases determined by the police to be not simply of dubious credibility but actually false.

Police said the complaint was false

Cases deemed to be false included those where the police halted the investigation as well as some cases which were perceived as false by the police but were withdrawn by the complainant.

There were 29 cases (17.7 per cent of the total sample) which the police ceased to investigate because they concluded the complaint to be false. Most of these were Male Rapes Female cases (N = 24, including one Attempted Rape), but this category also includes three Other Sexual Violation offences and two offences of Unlawful Sexual Connection.

In addition, in 26 cases withdrawn by the complainant, police file notes made it clear that they suspected the complaint to be false. Of these, 19 were Male Rapes Female cases, three were Other Sexual Violation offences, three involved Unlawful Sexual Connection and one was recorded as Husband Rapes Wife.[32]

As in the previous categories, the largest numbers of complainants were young and Caucasian, the majority of incidents involving acquaintances, followed by partner attacks and stranger attacks. The remaining three incidents arose in the context of family relationships.

When assessing cases as false, officers sometimes tried to identify motives underlying the complaint – for example, 'cried rape to avoid a hiding', and 'a woman scorned'. In other cases, the police maintained it likely that sex had occurred but was consensual, and that for some reason the complainant wanted to conceal this fact. A suspicion of falsehood was not enough for a case to be placed in this category; if the police seemed at all equivocal, the case was categorised as Possibly True/Possibly False. Hence the incidents in this category were perceived by the police as being more black and white than the grey terrain of the previous category. Many of the same factors were evident, such as delayed reporting, and contributed to police doubts in similar ways to those already identified. So what made the police so sure that the cases in this category were false?

It is possible that some of the difference in emphasis was simply the result of variability amongst detectives, or even within the same detective responding to different complainants. However, what is worth noting in this category is that, overall, the cases provide even clearer indications of the factors identified by police as detracting from complainants' credibility. It should be noted that my examination of these cases is not intended to imply that I believe the police necessarily to be mistaken in their conclusion that the complaint was false; my focus is not on the 'truth' or otherwise of particular cases, but on understanding the processes used by police in *their* assessments of a complainant's veracity.

Concealment of particular aspects associated with the incident often produced sceptical police reactions. Women under 20 sometimes lied about having been in a bar,[33] minimised the amount they had drunk, or denied cannabis use. The women's motives for doing so are understandable, in that they feared they would be blamed for what happened to them or even prosecuted themselves for law violation. From a police perspective, however, the fact of their lying about what seemed to be a small detail opened a window of doubt over their whole testimony. Case 151 illustrates this issue.

A young woman made a delayed report of rape following a drinking session she and her friends had with a male neighbour in his fifties. While she was in the toilet, he allegedly made remarks considered 'unsavoury' by her friends and they left. She claims he detained and raped her; he alleges sex was consensual. The complainant lost credibility with the police when she told her friend to say she had drunk only three beers instead of the large quantity of mixed drinks and spirits that had been consumed. In outlining on the file why the investigation was halted and the incident cleared as 'no offence disclosed', the detective said:

> The offence was reported some 2 1/2 weeks after occurring, and subsequent investigations revealed inconsistencies in the complainant's version of events, and an apparent attempt on her behalf to influence the testimony of one of the witnesses.
>
> There is no medical or forensic evidence, and while it is clear that sex took place, there is only the seemingly unreliable testimony of the complainant, coupled with an equally unreliable recent complaint witness, to support the allegations...
>
> I therefore recommend that the complaint be taken no further, and that some action be taken against [complainant] and her flatmate in relation to wasting Police time.

In this case, the police uncovered that the alleged offender had question marks over his credibility also, in that he had previous convictions for assault and possessing indecent documents for sale; the complainant's efforts to conceal how much she had drunk, however, caused greater concern.

What influenced the police to regard Case 151 as a definite false complaint, rather than a possible false complaint, appeared to derive from the fact that they believed the complainant had deliberately lied to them. The fact of her lying, added to other doubt generating factors, pushed this case into the realm of non-believability.

Over half of the cases in the 'police believed complaint to be false' category involved persons perceived as intellectually disabled or psychiatrically disturbed (55 per cent). Examples of police thinking and decision-making in such cases are provided in the following case examples.

Cases 4 and 179 involve two separate rape allegations made by the same woman against her de facto, with whom police said on the file she had been 'in a rocky relationship for two years'. During this time she is said to have made repeated complaints against her partner for assault and sexual violation. Police noted on her file:

> The suspect for these complaints is allways (sic) her boyfriend....[She] is extremely erratic and suffers from severe mood swings. When police

investigate her complaints [complainant's] statements are repetitive of former complaints and do not stand up to cross examination. Complaints stem from domestic disputes between [complainant] and [partner]. When prosecution is considered [she] withdraws initial complaint. [Her partner] is a well known drug user and suffers from a mental disorder of soughts (sic).

Comments were also made regarding how the complainant appeared to the police attending the rape complaints:

[She] presents as mentally disturbed, intoxicated and irrational.

The interior of [her house] can only be described as a mess. Property is piled up in all rooms leaving only a minimal amount of space for living in. [She] is abusive toward us and obstructive.

The complainant later criticised the police for their failure to act on the information she provided them, to which the police replied:

This woman can only be described as a habitual complainant who suffers from delusions and paranoia. ... On every occasion she has complained about alleged offences committed mainly by her ex-partner [—]. The offences have ranged from very minor to very serious. To my knowledge none of these has been proved. [Local police] do not give any credence to her complaints.

Her living conditions resemble that of a rubbish dump. By her own admission she has a psychiatric history.

Police officers also appeared to find it difficult to view complainants with intellectual disabilities as credible. Case 172 involved a young woman assessed as having the mental age of a 10–12-year-old child.

A male police constable was visiting the educational facility she attended when she approached him and said, 'quite boldly', he remarked, that she had been raped. He sent a female officer to talk with her, and the complainant alleged that she had been visiting a girlfriend when two teenage boys came to visit. All four young people went for a walk into a disused factory site, where she found herself alone with one of the boys. She says he asked her if she had ever slept with a boy, to which she said 'no' but that she had been raped by an older man the previous year. The boy asked if she became pregnant then, to which she said 'no', then he asked if she wanted to get pregnant, to which also she replied in the negative. He asked her to lie down and began touching her breasts and genital area; when she tried to pull away, he said he would never speak to her again if she did not do what he wanted. He touched her some more and asked if it felt good; she said she did not want to do it any more; then, she says, he penetrated her.

The officer wrote:

> [Complainant] stated that [offender] had raped her. She said it was the same as the 45yr old man. I said to [her] that married people make love or have sexual intercourse and she was happy with this. I then asked her what it was called when unmarried people do this and she had no answer. I asked her to tell me what rape meant and she said it was like being murdered by another person.

The complainant's teacher said that, a week before the police visit, the complainant had spoken to her and was distressed that the boy in question kept ringing and pestering her. She spoke about having been with her girlfriend and these boys, and how she had been left with [offender] and felt uncomfortable, 'like it had been "arranged" '. Significance was attached, both by the teacher and the police, to the fact that this conversation had included no mention of the rape incident. Additional comments made by the teacher in relation to the complainant described her as 'attention seeking', tending to 'dramatise', and having a reputation from her former school of being 'promiscuous'.

The other teenagers were all interviewed and, it was noted, came across as 'credible' to the police. None of them said they had seen anything sexual involving the complainant, nor seen her distressed. The alleged offender was interviewed in the presence of his mother and a lawyer and denied the allegation; the detective commented:

> I have no reason to doubt this, apart from the obvious conflict from [complainant's] allegation.

The complainant's mother was rung, and the detective says:

> I told her that an investigation into an alleged rape against her daughter had taken a slight turn and that at this stage, it looked as if the original complaint made by [complainant] was false. I advised [mother] that this was a serious situation, if in fact it was a false complaint. I explained to her that in the worst case scenario for such a serious situation, [her daughter] could possibly end up being charged. We then arranged to have a meeting with [mother], myself and [daughter] to discuss the matter.

The file notes that the complainant's mother was difficult to deal with at times and questioned the need for ongoing investigation by the police. Finally the mother agreed to a joint meeting in the presence of a solicitor.

> Unfortunately [mother] refused to bring [daughter] to the meeting. She stated that this brutalised the situation and didn't want to subject her

daughter to such a traumatic meeting. [Mother] was clearly being obstructive and had no intention of giving me an opportunity to speak to [daughter] in the presence of her mother. This was contrary to what we had arranged and the sole reason of me arranging the meeting. [Mother] stated very clearly that she believed her daughter had had a sexual experience on the evening in question. She further stated that she believed [her daughter] would probably be subjected to several 'rapes' in her life and that unless [her daughter] suffered serious physical harm as a result of one of these attacks, then she would avoid bringing these attacks to the attention of the Police. She felt that she could handle these situations and deal with them 'in house'.

The complainant was removed to a specialist facility where the police spoke with her again.

I explained to [complainant] what the witnesses had said and that despite her claims, I couldn't find any proof that a rape or sexual violation had occurred. [She] still maintained that she was 'raped' although I have my doubts about her interpretation and understanding of the meaning of this word.

In conclusion, I believe [complainant] did not experience rape and I believe [she] has falsely stated she was raped, however, I have a small element of doubt in my mind.

Cases involving complainants with psychiatric histories or intellectual disabilities seemed to be doubly difficult for the police to assess as credible. Initial doubts regarding the possibilities of a woman lying about rape may therefore be enhanced by additional concerns they hold regarding her competency as a witness.

In more than a third of the cases that the police said were false, officers tended to ascribe motives to women whom they suspected of having made a false complaint. It is virtually impossible to tell from the file evidence available whether or not such scepticism is well founded in reality or simply emanates from a police occupational trait of general suspiciousness (Reiner, 1994). What is significant, however, is the identification of suspicious cues by police. These are sometimes triggered in situations where it seems the complainant stands to gain personally from a rape allegation. In Case 64, for example, the complainant, a Pacific Island woman in her late twenties, reported a stranger rape ten days after its alleged occurrence. The delay was noted, along with a description of her stating that she

... suffers from some degree of mental impairment and her complaint of Rape is possibly a false one. ... [She is] a IM who appears to have made a complaint with the sole purpose of making a claim through ACC.

Lump sum compensation for rape victims through the ACC ended five years before this complaint was made, yet the suspicion that this was what motivated women to allege rape remained.

In some cases, the motives which detectives attributed to complainants reflect stereotypical beliefs and assumptions concerning the nature of women. The image of the scorned and vengeful woman is one such belief and is reflected in the following example.

Case 34 involved a rape complaint made by a woman in her thirties against a man of similar age. She lived overseas and had corresponded with him as a penpal for two years, after answering an advertisement he placed in a foreign newspaper. He offered to pay her airfare over to see him, inviting her to stay at his island home. She arrived and made her own way by boat to his place, where he was joined also by a male friend and beers were consumed. When the visitor left, the alleged offender asked her to sleep in his bed. She was reluctant to do so but was tired and jet-lagged, so kept a tee shirt and underwear on, and climbed into the bed, there being no other. He talked about having sex with her, she said he kept pressuring her to agree until finally she said there could be no sex without a condom. According to the file:

> [Offender] then attempted to have intercourse with the victim but was told that she now did not want to. Intercourse then took place.

The complainant said she went to the bathroom and cleaned herself, had a drink of water and felt exhausted. The detective notes:

> She then returned to the offender's bed where she went to sleep for the night. Slightly unusual behaviour for a female if she has just been violated.

The next morning her host informed her

> ...that she was not what he expected and that it was not going to work out.

She went out for a walk and when she returned, found her bags packed on the doorstep. The offender's friend, whom she had met the night before, turned up; she told him the offender had forced himself on her and thrown her out; he told her she could stay at his place. Several days later she went to the doctor, and a week after the alleged rape she went to the local police. There she was informed she would need to go to the mainland to report the incident. More than a month had lapsed since the alleged rape by the time she made a statement, during which time she had become romantically involved with the man who took her in. The constable she spoke with identified key issues that he was concerned about in her account, including the fact that she had:

- visited a male penpal in another country en route to New Zealand;
- slept in the same bed as the alleged offender;
- stated she did not want sex but demanded he was to wear a condom if he wanted sex with her;
- did not resist when he took her panties down;
- moved in next day with a man she'd known 3 hours; and
- took 4 days to see a doctor and a further 4 days to report to Police.

The constable concluded:

[Complainant] appears to have got a raw deal from [alleged offender] in fact that she has been invited over to New Zealand to stay with him and then told that she was not what he had expected and has been kicked out the next morning.

It appears that [she] has been a woman scorned. She feels that [he] has used her and she wants him punished for this. When I told her that there was no offence in New Zealand for being treated badly she came back to the fact that she had said no before sex and therefore she had been raped.

A detective took over the case at this point, and notes that it became hard to get hold of the complainant, who now had employment on the island, and to arrange for her to speak with him:

It was at this stage that my difficulties began with my very uncooperative victim.

From what is recorded on file, it appears that she and this detective were not communicating well, and continued to have trouble liaising over a time suitable for them both to meet. The following month the complainant rang the constable she had given her statement to, inquiring as to case progress. When the constable advised her that the detective she had been speaking with was the investigating officer, she pretended that she had not yet been contacted by the police. The constable informed the detective of this exchange, who in turn rang and asked her why she had said that, to which she replied that she had forgotten he had rung her a fortnight ago.

The detective says he tried to make a time with her; she said she was leaving the country but agreed to a meeting, which she did not turn up for. He managed to track her down after she had left the country to inform her that there was to be no further police investigation. He notes on the file that, when he spoke with her, it was clear she was in the same bed as the man who answered the phone.

I then advised [complainant] that due to her dodging my enquiries whilst she was in New Zealand, her allegation of Sexual Violation will be filed at my recommendation.

[She] advised me that she was not happy with my course of action and that she would be complaining to the Police Complaints Authority about my total lack of enthusiasm. I advised her that she was most welcome to make a complaint over the issue but I would still be recommending that this matter be filed.

The detective summarised his decision to terminate the investigation and file the complaint on the following grounds:

1. The complainant simply is not a credible witness. She refused to meet with me and has basically obstructed my enquiries when I have attempted to find suitable dates and times to meet and discuss a plan of action.
2. Due to the current workload in the Combined Investigative Unit Office, I am simply too busy with other serious matters to waste time and resources into this matter.
3. As the complainant has left the country, she obviously does not deem this matter important, hence my recommendation to file.

The comments recorded on this case file suggest high levels of annoyance and frustration in the detective involved, which the complainant would undoubtedly have perceived also. Some of the factors that were assumed to demonstrate her lack of credibility reflect sexist judgments and highly stereotypical beliefs regarding victim demeanour. From what is recorded on the file, it seems that the complainant was desperately trying to find a way of following up the case while minimising contact with a detective who, from his written comments, was probably abrasive and confrontational in his approach. Whatever happened, he did not believe her, and she lost faith in him.

Rape complainants also appeared to be regarded with considerable suspicion if they were on record for having made previous rape complaints that did not result in prosecution. This was the case in Case 27, involving an intellectually impaired Māori woman in her twenties who made a complaint against a man, also Māori, in his twenties, and a sickness beneficiary.

She alleged that this male friend of hers had come to visit when her parents were out, kissed her and made her touch him sexually before inserting his hand into her vagina. When spoken to by police, the alleged offender said it was she who had approached him sexually, and he had inserted only one finger. A man working nearby told police he had seen this man visit before, and police noted that he

... states that from his observations that there appeared to be no animosity (sic) between the two, [she] even coming to the front door to wave [offender] good-bye when he left, hardly the actions of a woman who has just been violated.

The detective investigating the case concluded:

> It is my belief that there was contact between [complainant] and [offender] of a sexual nature, but that it was consensual. [She] appears to live in a fantasy world and tells all and sundry about her sexual experiences, some of these people then inform the Police and she then thrives on all the attention she receives from the resulting investigation.

An IHC adviser commented that the complainant had a limited understanding about society's 'rules' regarding the appropriateness of public and private behaviour, and she may find it hard to make good decisions concerning what is appropriate to do or to talk about. However, her disability may also make her more vulnerable to sexual assault. The adviser recommended that this case be investigated in same manner as all such investigations, although a skilled child interviewer may be useful. It appears this advice was not followed.

The previous two cases also raise issues concerning the ways in which perceptions of promiscuity or immorality on the part of the victim may detrimentally affect her credibility as a rape complainant. What is evident from analysis of police files is that it is often the combination of particular variables that underlies doubts about complainants' credibility. For the complainants whose cases fell into this category, that combination was sufficient for police to believe their complaint to be false. At times that conclusion seems, on the basis of the evidence presented, to be justified, especially when there is evidence corroborating the suspect's testimony and refuting that of the complainant. However, there is also the possibility that some of the cases dismissed as false are genuine, and that the reasons for their dismissal are associated more with police beliefs and attitudes than with evidential realities. Some cases perceived by the police as arising from false complaints did in fact appear very likely to be fabrications. What is also important to acknowledge, however, are the reasons and emotional states which can prompt such allegations. Case 112, for instance, illustrates well, and sadly, how previous abuse may sometimes underlie subsequent false allegations.

The complainant, a woman in her late forties, reported that her teenage son had raped her. She was highly intoxicated at the time, and in pain, and the boy had phoned for a doctor. The police were immediately sceptical, stating:

> The Police are not willing to accept that a seemingly well adjusted 15 year old son would rape his drunken mother immediately after having phoned for a doctor to attend his mother's plight of severe abdominal pain. Equally the police do not believe the mother who claims to have been in

control of herself, would allow her son to undertake such a task with no resistance.

The file goes on to note that she was given a thorough interview by three detectives,

> ... the outcome of which has added weight to Police assessment that the offence did not occur.

An interview with her ex-husband revealed that in the past his wife had suffered bad dreams after drinking, during which she would call out, 'No, don't do that'. One detective was also able to establish that

> ... as a 16 year old the complainant was allegedly raped at a beach in Christchurch. The Police declined to investigate the matter and on being taken home she was subsequently placed in the bath by her father and scrubbed raw.
>
> It has been suggested to [complainant] that she has been reliving this distress for some years and that her consumption of alcohol contributes to these memories coming to the fore. Her reply whilst pensive, was also in agreement. She accepts the police version of events but cannot bring herself to withdraw her complaint.

The police referred her for counselling and the case was resulted as 'no offence disclosed'. In this case, the police involved were open to considering the emotional factors underlying the woman's allegation and responded accordingly.

While false complaints do occur, approximately three quarters of the incidents concluded by the police to be false appeared to have been judged to some extent at least on the basis of stereotypes regarding the complainant's behaviour, attitude, demeanour or possible motive. Suspicious file comments were made by detectives regarding a woman who laughed whilst being interviewed, others who were seen as 'attention seeking', and some who were said to be 'crying rape' for revenge or guilt motives. In one case, for example, a medical examination confirmed extensive injuries consistent with the victim's account, and she appeared traumatised, yet the police felt her

> ... morality (or lack of it) would come under intense scrutiny should this matter ever come to a trial situation,

and were relieved when the complainant decided not to proceed.

In cases such as this, where it was clear that the police were dubious and the complainant then withdrew the complaint, detectives often interpreted this as 'proof' that it was false. As noted earlier, however, complainant withdrawal may signify many different things. In some cases ending in the withdrawal of the complaint, for instance, the complainant may always have been a reluctant complainant. This situation can arise when a third party either pressures the victim to contact the police or decides independently to notify police about the incident. The complainant may or may not concur with such action, a factor with significant effects for subsequent cooperation with the police.

In Case 133 a woman in her twenties rang her girlfriend requesting a routine piece of information. The girlfriend thought she sounded unusually quiet and phoned back to ask what was the matter. Eventually the woman disclosed that she had been raped by an intruder. The girlfriend immediately came round with her boyfriend, and the boyfriend phoned the police against the complainant's wishes. The girlfriend told the detective that the complainant said she had been attacked by a man with a knife while she was in the shower, received some cuts in the attack, then lay there without resisting while he raped her. The attending police raised doubts concerning the complaint's validity. Although the victim had cuts to her face and chest, there was no blood in the bathroom. A constable commented that while the detective was speaking with the girlfriend, her boyfriend and the complainant were talking and joking:

> [Complainant] was laughing, and they talked about movies with heads being blown off.

This occurrence also had significance attributed to it by the detective, who wrote in the report:

> [Complainant] claimed she had been raped 10 years ago and had had a bad experience with the Police on that occasion and this is why she refused to make a complaint on this occasian (sic), yet she appeared to be suffering very little 'trauma' and was openly joking and laughing with [girlfriend's boyfriend] while I was speaking with [girlfriend].

The detective noted that the matter could proceed no further because she would not continue with the complaint; stated that its validity 'may be in question', but submitted the file in case the complainant changed her mind or other rapes were reported in the area with a similar MO (modus operandi).

Doubts about the complainant's veracity in this case seemed to rest largely on police interpretations of the complainant's behaviour. Her reluctance to involve the police, combined with her lack of conformity to stereotypes of how rape victims 'should' behave, raised considerable doubts in the minds of the police. Clear expectations seemed to be held as to how trauma victims should present, and there appeared to be no police option for interpreting this complainant's responses as indicative of a different, yet equally valid, way of responding to trauma. From the information recorded on file, it is possible that the victim was managing the rape by dissociating, going into a state of denial, and even becoming quite hysterical and over the top in her responses (Herman, 1992). Insufficient information is recorded here to be certain one way or the other; what is disturbing is the lack of allowance by police for alternative interpretations of her behaviour to be possible. Moreover, even if the police interpretation was the right one, this case raises further questions about necessary and appropriate responses. For instance, if the complaint was false, and the cuts were self-inflicted, then this would suggest this complainant to be in need of professional support and counselling, possibly to help her to come to terms with the previous unresolved rape experience. No such suggestion or referral appears to have been made.

In summary, then, it is possible that this complaint was genuine but was not interpreted as such because of police beliefs concerning how rape victims should behave, in which case this victim received a harsh, insensitive response; or it is possible that the complaint was false, in which case the complainant was signalling that she was having significant personal difficulties and needed positive assistance. However, a third scenario is also possible; it could be that something abusive and violating happened to the complainant that night but, for whatever reason, she did not want the police involved. From a police perspective, cases such as this are fraught with difficulty and frustration. It is understandable that some officers resort to 'pigeon-holing' complainants and making quick assessments based on stereotypes and police folklore. From a complainant's perspective, however, this is not acceptable behaviour. Police are in danger of taking a couple of pieces of a puzzle and, because these pieces seem familiar, assume they know what picture they form. Puzzles can have trick pieces in them; most puzzle compilers need the picture on the box to guide them; puzzles, by definition, puzzle. Because of the nature of their job and professional training, however, the police are in danger of thinking they can see the picture on the box when all they have is a couple of pieces which could fit one of several diverse, and even contradictory, images.

The final category involved cases which the complainant, rather than the police, claimed to be false.

Complainant said allegation was false or not rape

There were 13 cases which involved complainants who stated either that their rape allegation had been completely fictitious, or that intercourse had occurred but was not rape. Nearly 70 per cent of these (N = 9) involved complainants aged 25 years and under, and most were Caucasian (54 per cent, N = 7). The majority arose from incidents involving acquaintances (62 per cent, N = 8), though three complaints arose from alleged attacks by strangers.

Of reports of rape which the complainant later retracted, it is significant that in over half of the cases (N = 8; 62 per cent), it was not the complainant's decision to contact the police. Someone else decided to call the police or, in two cases, pressured the complainant to do so.

When one young woman, for instance (Case 78), came home late from a date with 'hickies' on her neck, her mother asked her repeatedly if she had been raped. The daughter kept saying no, but her mother said she did not believe her. Finally, the daughter decided to go along with the rape allegation, since her mother seemed so convinced, and the police were called. After questioning, she later admitted that sex had been consensual. Background details recorded on the file note that this teenager's sister was, at 15, already a solo mother, and that there was a real fear of being physically beaten by her father – factors which could help to explain both the mother's insistence on the incident being rape and the daughter's decision to accept this explanation of events.

Some of the cases involved situations where the person reporting the incident presumed a rape to have happened when it had not.

Case 65, for instance, was recorded on the police files as 'two false complaints of rape by above subjects' and involved two Pacific Island teenage sisters who returned home late from a church dance. Their mother found out that they had spent time with two young men, and decided to take them to the doctor for the morning after pill. When the doctor discovered that the younger sister was a few days short of 16, he phoned the police. Never at any stage did either of the young women say that the sex was anything other than consensual, and nor did their mother think this was the case – she was focussing on damage control given the lack of contraceptives used at the time. However, the police records categorised this incident as a false report of rape, which was cleared as 'no offence disclosed'.

In four of the cases reported by complainants themselves which were subsequently withdrawn, the police speculated on the file as to the possible motives that underlay these allegations.

In Case 86, the complainant, who was married and mentally ill, had sex with an older man, and arrived home late to her husband. Her account of events states that this man proceeded sexually after she had asked him to stop; the police believe she invented the rape excuse to cover her lateness, which was completely out of character, as was her having sex with anyone other than her husband. The complainant certainly agreed to withdraw the rape allegation, but it is hard to ascertain from the file whether sex had or had not been fully consensual.

Two cases involved the classic false rape scenario of an alleged rape in the street by a stranger. Both involved young women, aged 16 and 17 respectively, who were emotionally distraught at the time. In one case (Case 98), the complainant feared the end of her lesbian relationship and invented the rape allegation in the hopes of gaining sympathy from, and reconciliation with, her girlfriend. Although not charged herself with making a false report, the police said they had recorded her details on NIS[34] for future reference. In the other case (Case 99), the complainant admitted that she had falsified a rape account in a desperate attempt to get some attention from her father. He was dying of cancer, and had stopped speaking to her, and she was trying to find a way to get some sympathy from him and her mother for her distress. The file notes on this case are interesting and suggest a police response that was understanding and compassionate. This may possibly be related to the case being dealt with by members of a Child Abuse Team, who typically receive fuller training in trauma effects and victim interviewing than most detectives. The complainant in fact wrote expressing her gratitude:

> To all the members of the team,
>
> I wish to take this time to thank you all so very much for the way in which you dealt with me on the 28th.
>
>   I also wish to take this time to apologise for wasting your time with my childish way of getting attention so that I could hurt my parents and they would take notice of me.
>
>   I cannot tell you how sorry I am and now I have to face the truth that someone could of (sic) been attacked and seriously hurt while you were dealing with me and your time could have being spent on a case where you were truly needed.
>
> Many thanks for your understanding.
> Good luck for the future.
> Yours sincerely
> [Complainant's name].

Another case in this category also appeared to be handled relatively well by the police officers and detectives involved. This is worth examining, since it is easy to imagine this complainant being given very different treatment by some criminal investigators, because of the negative stereotypes she could evoke.

The complainant in Case 165 was a Caucasian woman, a solo mother in her thirties with a list of convictions from age 16, mostly for drug-related offences. Witnesses walking on a beach notified the police after this woman, bleeding from cuts to her legs, told them she had been raped by a group of Russian seamen and now her handbag was missing. She was taken to the hospital and kept overnight for observation, because she had fallen on the rocks and was in a highly intoxicated state, due to either drugs or alcohol. She told the police that she had been working as a prostitute on the street in the early hours of one morning when three Russian sailors picked her up, whereupon she went with them to a house where each of them had sex with her. The complainant says they refused to wear condoms, despite her telling them that she had Hepatitis B and C. She continues in her statement:

> So the sex was a business thing and they said they would have to go back to their boat at [port] to get some money. They took me in the car down past the British [a ship] and out on the wharf there. The ship they are on is rafted up third from the quayside.
>
> I didn't go on board the boat because I am not that sort of girl. I stayed in the car.

She wanted cash to buy her own drugs, but one said he could give her morphine and she went with a carload of them to a beach where, she said:

> There seemed to be Russians everywhere. There were 3 or 4 in the car with me and about another 10 turned up. Peter was doing all the talking and said that he had more clients for me. I told him No. I don't know how I ended up in the rocks and the salt water, I can't remember.

The detective questioned her about having told the people who came across her that she had been raped, then notes:

> She denies suggesting to the witnesses that she had been raped. I believe she told the people at [place] that she had been raped so that she would get some urgent attention.
>
> In her circumstances and the state she was in she would otherwise have been ignored.
>
> When being interviewed at the time by [detective] and again the following day, there was no mention to Police of rape.
>
> With the view of charging her with 'False Allegation' under the Summary Offences Act 1981, 3 months, $1000 penalty, I note that the offender must know that her statement will be passed on to Police.
>
> In the circumstances I believe there would be difficulty with that as she quickly dispelled the notion of rape when she spoke to us. I have cleared the Sexual Violation K3 and False Statement K4.

What the complainant herself said was:

> I didn't tell the people I had been raped, I said I had been thrown on the rocks. I had earlier told the Russians that this is New Zealand and if they didn't pay a prostitute and didn't treat her properly, it was rape ....
>
> I don't want to make a statement about it because I don't feel up to it. I want you to get my bag back and to give those Russians a fright.

In relation to the last point, the detective observed on the file:

> There was no point using Police and interpreters at $50 an hour to try and locate unknown Russians that may or may not know about [complainant] falling or being pushed into the tide.

It could be suggested that if the Russians haven't already had a fright, then bearing in mind her health, they may get one in the future.

Also noted was the fact that advice was given to the complainant regarding what to do in situations of non-payment, and her clothing returned. The detective concluded that

> ...she seemed vindicated with what sympathy and attention I have given her.

In the above case, it is clear that the complainant's credibility was greatly diminished by her status as a street prostitute and drug user. It is difficult to ascertain from the file whether she did or did not say to the passersby that she had been raped, and whether in fact she had been. However, some of the police who dealt with her seemed to be prepared to acknowledge that she had been the victim of an unfortunate incident, even if it was not a rape. The police officers involved were still able to view her as a possible crime victim despite the existence of factors which diminished her credibility. This demonstrates greater understanding of some of the issues surrounding the context and effects of victimisation than was evident in some of the previous cases examined.

Overall, analysis of this category indicates a complexity of reasons often underlying reports of rape which the complainant later states to be false. Over half of the cases studied here involved situations where the alleged victim had been pressured to tell the police about an incident, sometimes in circumstances where a third party presumed a sexual violation had occurred when in fact none had. Teenage girls, scared of the wrath and possible physical chastisement of their parents, may go along with such assumptions initially, only to find themselves trapped in a lie. Alternatively, the confusion and ambiguity surrounding sexual negotiation and forceful seduction may mean that, in some situations, the complainant feels as if she has been victimised and is genuinely unsure as to whether she was raped.

From the cases involved in this sample, there were no cases of malicious or vengeful accusation. A few tried to conceal their sexual conduct from others by making a rape allegation, or allowing one to be inferred, but the principal motive in these cases was clearly one of self protection. There was also minor evidence suggesting that emotionally distressed or disturbed women may, at rare times, create a fictionalised account of rape to try and attract sympathy or assistance. Most of the cases studied here, however, turned out not to be completely fictitious acts but were more likely to arise from wrongful interpretations by third parties, which were mostly speedily resolved by police investigative efforts.

Summary of case analysis

How an individual detective responds to a rape complainant, then, is complex. The variation between police officers is matched by the variation of complainants, their personal characteristics, and the nature and context of what they are reporting. It is difficult in practice to assess each situation on its own merits, and the police rely heavily on stereotypes to assist in the general exercise of discretion (Reiner, 1994; White and Perrone, 1997). In relation to sexual assault offences, this is evident in appraisals of victims' characteristics and culpability, and in the assessments made by officers regarding complainants' credibility (Allison and Wrightsman, 1993; Burgess, 1999; Estrich, 1987; Gregory and Lees, 1999; Kelly, 2002; Lees, 1997). As the police file analysis showed, this process itself involves subjective evaluations and interpretations, which may vary enormously depending on the particular officers involved and their relationship with a particular complainant.

The study of police files reported here shows a dominant mindset of suspicion underlying police responses to reports of sexual assault. This analysis revealed a wide range of factors that influence police perceptions of complainants' credibility, particularly when clusters of variables are apparent. Thus, whereas drunkenness on its own may not diminish victims' credibility, drunkenness in connection with other factors, such as previous consensual sex with the offender or the concealment of cannabis smoking, may tip the scales of credibility. The scales of justice apparently sit waiting, into which are placed factors which will either enhance or diminish a victim's credibility. The factors are weighted differently, and while a factor counting against the complainant may tip the balance seriously one way, factors in her favour may correct the balance again. Thus the negative attributions associated with being a sex worker or an alcoholic may be compensated for by factors such as prompt reporting, co-operation with the police and visible signs of injury or resistance (Gregory and Lees, 1999; LaFree, 1980).

The police do, in fact, have to tread a fine line between the victim and the accused as they attempt to preserve the balance of justice and guard against the possibilities of wrongful conviction. However, an overzealous commitment to the rights of the accused may unwittingly tip the balance the other way. The police may become in effect the adjudicators, applying their own judgments and interpretations to individual cases. Within this context, factors identified as determinants of complainants' credibility assume enhanced significance and can result in the premature closure of investigations. Whether or not an offence actually occurred is different from whether or not it *can be proven* to have occurred; for victims of rape, the first concern is understandably the more pressing, but because of their role in the prosecution process,[35] it is the latter which is of primary importance to the police.

Overall, the analysis presented here demonstrates that the historically pervasive attitude of mistrust in women's testimony continues to be evident in police processing of rape complaints. This study provides clear examples of situations where the complainant obviously knew her word would be suspect, and was aware that there were aspects of her background or behaviour which would lessen her credibility in the eyes of the police. Should she attempt to conceal such aspects from police knowledge, however, and have her efforts detected, then ironically her very attempts to bolster her credibility will result in it being irrevocably reduced. In this respect, victims of rape are caught in a double bind situation, whereby they know they will not be regarded as credible if they are perceived as 'immoral', yet will be viewed as even less credible if they are detected trying to conceal their 'immorality'. Either way, their allegations are viewed as beyond belief.

This chapter has considered the police position from comments made on rape investigation files. The next chapter presents material obtained directly from interviews with detectives themselves.

5
Having 'a nose for it': How Investigators Investigate

> I prefer five clean murders to one rape case. The more you investigate and get into it, the stickier it gets. ... Murder I can understand, but I can't really understand rape.
>
> (Detective, quoted in Burgess, 1999, p. 3)

Introduction

There are comparatively few studies that have involved interviewing detectives specifically about their involvement in sexual assault investigations. Those studies have yielded interesting results, although have typically involved small sample sizes (e.g., Gregory and Lees, 1999; Temkin, 1997, 1999).

As a result of my earlier involvement in research with rape complainants, I had been involved with the New Zealand Police in contributing to the development of a nationwide police policy on sexual assault investigations. The first version of this policy, known as the New Zealand Police Sexual Assault Investigation Policy, began a two-year lead-in period in February, 1998. The policy stipulated that a sexual assault coordinator should be appointed in each police district, and I decided to interview some of these persons. My intention with this research was to obtain the views of police detectives who had devoted considerable thought to the issues involved, and who had worked on a broad range of cases and with a variety of staff.

Method

The interviews with detectives were undertaken as a means of obtaining contextual information on the police to assist in interpretation of the file data. Initially four sexual assault coordinators in various parts of the country were approached, selected to provide some coverage of both urban and rural areas.[36] Most of these, however, nominated staff members whom they also felt it would be useful to interview, because of their experience and insights in this area. As time progressed, and I began the interviews with the women attacked by Rewa, it also became both possible, and useful, to undertake interviews with four of the detectives involved in this particular investigation. The final sample comprised 12 detectives in total.

Characteristics of the sample

It must be stated from the outset that the 12 detectives interviewed cannot necessarily be viewed as representative of detectives in the New Zealand Police overall. This sample was intentionally selected because of the expertise of its members in the area of rape and sexual assault investigations, and comprises staff with extensive experience within policing generally.

Of the 12 detectives interviewed, ten were male and two were female. In terms of age, one was in his fifties, eight were in their forties, two were in their thirties, and one was in his/her late twenties. One was Māori; the remainder all identified as New Zealand European. Most had served the majority of their time within the police within urban areas (N = 7); four had experience within both urban and rural areas; and one had worked only in rural and provincial areas.

In terms of length of service within the police, 5 detectives had between 10 and 20 years; and 7 had between 20 and 30 years. As regards their level of rank within the New Zealand Police, two were Detective Inspectors, 4 were Detective Senior Sergeants, three were Detective Sergeants and 3 were Detectives.

All those interviewed had been involved in numerous sexual assault investigations, with several listing these as in the hundreds. Four had also been involved in Operations Park and Harvey, the large-scale investigations established to apprehend serial attackers Joseph Thompson and Malcolm Rewa.

All of the above factors mean that the views presented here are not likely to be indicative of the views of detectives generally. Those interviewed were, in fact, asked to comment on the attitudes of staff with whom they worked, since differences often became apparent. The detectives in this sample, then, have generally had greater training and experience in sexual assault investigations than the majority of their colleagues, and most have a stated commitment to providing the victims of such offences with optimal police service, wherever possible. These factors undoubtedly affected their responses during the interview; thus the views represented here are likely to display greater awareness and sympathy towards rape victims than those of detectives generally.

Issues addressed

In the interviews with detectives, I used an interview schedule to guide the question line and to ensure some uniformity in the issues covered, while at the same time allowing the detectives considerable scope to influence content and determine the order of when topics were discussed.

My principal aim in conducting interviews with detectives was to deepen my understanding of police beliefs surrounding rape and sexual assault, and how those beliefs influence police procedures. The main issues canvassed included

- beliefs concerning the frequency of false complaints – both their personal beliefs as well as their perceptions of those held by staff with whom they worked;
- examples of cases they believed to have been false complaints and their understandings of the motivations underlying false complaints;
- police procedures and recording practices in their district; and
- their thoughts concerning the implications for police training and staff supervision.

The major themes emerging from their responses are presented here, illustrated by quotes from comments made during the interviews.

'Real' rape

Major definitional issues often emerge within the area of rape and sexual assault, and the police have been criticised at times for having a working definition of 'real' rape which they apply to cases brought before them (Chambers and Millar, 1983; Du Mont *et al.*, 2003; Estrich, 1987; Gregory and Lees, 1999; Kelly, 2002). Such a view was reflected in the comments of some of those interviewed in this study. D1,[37] for example, referred to sexual assaults always being treated seriously, then qualified this comment to specify stranger rapes in particular:

> I can say that it's always seen as a serious investigation without any doubt. As far as intruder rape goes, it's ... at the moment the position in [city] is that it's assessed almost on a par with a homicide as far as how it should be investigated .... I guess there are different types of rape. I mean, the rape of a child or the rape of someone who has been dragged into the bushes is probably going to get a more strenuous and a greater input, perhaps, than someone who, look she has been with a guy all night drinking, and I mean, they are still investigated with a view to prosecution. But at the end of the day I think intruder rape is seen at a higher level just because of the nature of the attack and the potential for the repeat of the crimes.

Stranger/intruder rapes clearly fit into the category of 'real' rapes, being viewed as reprehensible acts committed by the kinds of 'evil villains' whom many police have joined the force to catch. D5 expressed this distinction well when asked how he felt generally about being assigned a rape case to investigate.

> I guess it depended on what type of rape it was and if it was a stranger rape, of course it's right up there with the homicides, but when it's a domestic rape it doesn't become such an investigative challenge. It's usually, well, the offender is kind of there. It's a matter of getting the case together and working out whether you've got enough to go to court on. It's not rape. An investigator, I guess, has challenges identifying the offender, that's the big challenge.
>
> So the driving force in you is that – I mean what do you join the job for at the end of the day is what you've got to ask yourself? I was a young kid straight from school when I joined. So I was just under 18 when I joined and I was very moralistic and I'd change the world and what was and what wasn't going to happen and I guess it's always remained…. I mean, the job hasn't changed. I mean, we all talk about how the job has changed and how hard it is and we've lost our place really. But if you bring it back to the core job, our job is still the same and it's to keep the Queen's peace and keep people safe and look after the decent folk.

Another detective (D6) revealed, in his answers to my questions, the extent to which he assumed 'rape' meant stranger–intruder rapes.

> D: You know, people say that we only get, scratch the surface of the sexual complaints, sexual violation that goes on there. I don't think we do, I think that most genuine rapes are reported to the police.
>
> J : When you say that do you think, is that only in regard to stranger rapes or….
>
> D: Yeah, yeah, oh yeah. I'm not talking about family rapes or boyfriends.
>
> J : Oh no. I don't mean so much child abuse, but say, you know, rapes between partners, spouses?
>
> D: Oh no, no, I'm not talking about that at all.
>
> J : I mean, are they reported more often do you think now than they used to be, acquaintance rapes, marital rape?
>
> D: I've only ever had one woman, one married woman complain of marital rape…. It's the only one I can recall in my whole career, of a woman complaining of rape in the marriage. But I sat down and had a talk with her one morning at her place, you know, the husband was away. He got locked up for assault, I think or something, because it was a domestic situation. He'd been locked up for an assault and was at court and I got the job, you know, because he was in custody. So I

shot round the next morning to talk with her. So I had a talk with her in the morning and she was telling me about it, but then told me that she'd alleged that she'd been raped by him for years, you know. Just non consensual sex I would call it.

This detective went on to comment:

D: I suspect that there's probably a lot of that sort of non consensual sex happening in relationships.

J : It doesn't tend to get reported still?

D: Well, I don't know, Jan, I would imagine it probably doesn't. I'd imagine, oh, I don't know – I mean, it's going to sound awful but I call that a non consensual sexual encounter as opposed to rape. You know what I mean and I know it's probably semantics, isn't it, and it's only playing with words. I mean, rape to me is what the Rewa victims went through and what Thompson's victims go through. Whereas some woman who's living in a relationship, if she's living with a guy who's violent towards her, I mean, she has options. You know, she can get out. I know the, we have 'battered wife syndrome' and on and on it goes, but they still have options. But Malcolm Rewa's bloody victims didn't have an option and Joe Thompson's victims didn't have an option and that's, so that's why I, in my own mind, make this distinction.

Later in the interview, this same detective commented on the difficulties involved in investigating non-stranger rapes and began to speculate on why he had dealt with so few:

D: I think if it's not a stranger there's more, it's not as easy as – you're talking now like a date rape or something like that. It gets a bit more difficult you know. But to be honest, we don't really, we never seem to deal with many of those down here. Most of the ones – oh, I suppose we still get a few of those where, you know, they go to the pub and get pissed and go home and have sex with someone and then wake up next to them the next morning.

J : And that doesn't happen a lot?

D: No. No not really. Most of them are, like, ones where they, most of them round here are either intruder ones or they've been abducted by some guys driving past in the car who've grabbed them or they've been hitch-hiking....So the genuine ones just seem, they, they're not that difficult, you know. But probably because we, maybe because we don't deal with many of those acquaintance type rapes and relationship rapes. That could say something about the police, couldn't it? Because if we're not dealing with them it's perhaps, you know, obviously people aren't reporting them so there could be something wrong with the way, there could be something said about the way the police look at it and that's why the women aren't reporting those type of crimes, perhaps. It's just a thought. But getting back, so the ones – you know the genuine ones jump out and hit you and the others, the other ones, well, whether you prosecute or not is going to depend how or probably a lot on how keen the cop is. I mean, if you've got a lazy bloody cop he's going to make any excuse he can find to not bother doing any work on it. But the majority of the guys in the CIB aren't like that now. Well, they aren't, no one in the CIB's like that. You don't go to the CIB unless you're the sort of person that's motivated and, you know, pretty keen to lock up baddies. You know, that's why you go to the CIB, that's why you want to be a detective. So most, you know, all detectives are like that.

I have chosen to quote the above detective at length because he expressed so clearly what many others hinted at in the interview. The concept of 'real' rape continues to live on in the minds of many police, and hooks up with their perceptions of who the real 'bad guys' are. The kinds of men who may commit date or partner rapes do not usually conform to the image of the stereotypical rapist, and may even bear a close resemblance to the men they know, even to themselves. It is difficult in such circumstances to identify the perpetrators of these offences as the villains whom they joined the police to pursue and whose conviction and imprisonment they seek. 'Real' rapes are perpetrated by 'real rapists', not by their buddy or the guy next door. One detective chose to distance himself from stranger rapists by referring to them as 'animals', a distinction which some police obviously find comforting. However, such a view minimises the pain and trauma suffered by those women raped by men they know – in other words, the majority of rape victims.

It is also important to affirm that a small number of the detectives interviewed expressed views which indicated that they also questioned the distinctions often drawn between different kinds of rape. For example, two senior detectives noted with concern the ways in which some men are emerging as serial date rapists, specialising in selecting victims whose credibility they know will appear questionable. One placed Morgan Fahey[38] in this category, whom he saw as using his credentials and status as a doctor to protect himself for years against accusations from emotionally unstable or drug addicted patients.

This detective (D4) also stressed that there was a distinction between what could be termed 'moral rape' and 'legal rape'. In his experience, many victims reported having been raped in situations where it was clear that the alleged offender had in some way duped or misled them, or otherwise wronged them. Often, however, the way in which consent had been obtained or intercourse accomplished did not meet the legal definitions of sexual violation. In such cases, the complaint could not be proceeded with; nevertheless, this detective felt it was important to convey to the complainant that it was understandable that she *felt* like she had been raped, and that she could be viewed as the victim of a 'moral rape' even though legally no action could be taken against the offender. He said he communicated this perception to some victims.

> I don't say it unless I know it's true. I'll say, no, you've been raped. There's no doubt in my mind that this has happened but we haven't got any evidence that's going to convict this guy. He denies it. He's in fact got three mates that said no, he didn't do that, it wasn't him and two of them said that he did something else. So we haven't got a show. We believe you though, but we haven't got enough. If we thought we had enough we'd have a go, we really would. (D4)

Number of false complaints

All the detectives interviewed were asked to estimate the proportion of rape complaints which they believed to be false. Not all would commit themselves to a definite figure, and the responses of the six who did indicated an extremely broad range. These ranged between one detective who said 10 per cent and another who estimated that 80 per cent of all rapes reported were false 'in one way or another'. Others estimated 15–20 per cent; 20 per cent or more; between a quarter and a third; and over a half.

Comments from the detectives are provided below, where possible placing their estimates in the context within which they were made.

> Oh, I would have said less than 10 per cent in my opinion but it's really a guestimate. Some people say 30–40 per cent but I think that's way too high. When you say more in sexual assault compared to other offences, you do actually have to compare the offences – like, there have been more in sexual assaults than there would have been in robbery or aggravated robbery, of which there's very few. Would there be more in burglaries? I don't know. (D11)

> I mean, you'd probably deal with rape or sexual assault allegations, you'd probably deal with at least three a week. And I've always said I would, as an estimate, as a rough guess and without any research, I would say 80 per cent of them are false in one way or another. Some of them are absolutely a complete fabrication. Others are – the rest of them all fit into the category really where the victim has had sexual intercourse with someone and then has to explain themselves to Mum or Dad, or husband, or boyfriend. In the time that I've been in the CIB I've dealt with a number of those that are complete and utter fabrication, just a total lie. (D6)

Oh, I don't really know. Just if I was to say over the last ten rapes that have been reported to this office, probably three or four have been false. Three anyway, I suppose, yep. (D10)

One detective's initial response, when asked to provide such an estimate, was to say:

> D: Are you putting the acid on me, Jan! Um, at one stage for me it was three out of every four were not valid.
>
> J : OK, what do you mean by not valid?
>
> D: The offence was not as they described it, like there might have been more to do with consent issues or they might have held things back that might have evened up the story, that it might not have been rape or there might have been custody issues involved.

A senior detective, responsible for supervising large numbers of staff in an inner city station, spoke candidly about the extent to which he believed inflated perceptions still existed of the proportion of false rape complaints occurring.

> D: There still is – unfortunately – a prevailing belief that too large a number of complaints that come into the police are false and I disagree with that totally. I believe – there are false complaints, have been, will be in the future, totally false. There's no doubt about it, there are some – but not to the extent that it is commonly believed there are. I think, what I think happens is that a person works on a false complaint and because it's such an important investigation, it has such an impact on people, when they discover it actually is false or can prove it, because I believe you've got to prove they're false. You can't just have a gut feeling they are, but some people think you can, but once you've proved it is, that has – it guts people. It absolutely guts people and it works on them so much in their brain that they get tunnel vision for later on and all they have to have is a little inconsistency for them to think, oh, this is another bloody false complaint which is another thing I've briefed staff on. A 100 per cent of victims that come in here will always give an inconsistent or something wrong with their version of events the first time, without fail. But that's no different to an aggravated robbery, or other things. (D11)
>
> J : So you think any victim ... ?
>
> D: Always gets something wrong, always.
>
> J : Why?
>
> D: Well, they've just been put under the most incredible shock and stress, and trauma, you can imagine, how the hell can they be expected to get

everything right? They won't be able to be expected to remember everything. I mean, I was just reading something on memory the other day and it actually says that when you're put under that stress you can remember quite a lot of detail on actually what happened but the peripheral stuff you don't remember as well. Well, simple little things about what bus they caught. I mean, they might get that wrong and he says, oh, false complaint. They can't remember what bus they bloody caught, what a simple thing to remember.

J: So that would be enough for some detectives to write it off, do you think?

D: Perhaps not enough, but plant a doubt. Drunk as well, doing something silly and you add the three things together and they come up with 100 you know, when they should only add up – well, wait a second, this person's just gone through an incredibly traumatic experience, we'll reserve judgment until we've done an investigation. At the end of the day, any properly conducted investigation will discover whether a complaint is true or false in my opinion.

It is both significant and alarming that, at a New Zealand national police training course in 2003, when one detective claimed that 80 per cent of rapes reported were false, this comment was not disputed by others present and several nodded their assent to this figure (Pers. Comm., 2003).

Discussions about numbers inevitably led to speculation concerning reasons and motives.

Motives underlying false complaints

Gregory and Lees (1999) observed in the United Kingdom context the apparent paradox of police investigators seeming to be lacking in investigative curiosity about the factors underlying false complaints. One New Zealand detective exemplified this attitude when I asked him, in relation to women who had admitted making false complaints.

J: What sorts of reasons do they give?

D: Well, none. Well, we don't ask, we don't ask why. It's not the done thing is it? You can't just say to them, well, why, you know .... I mean, do you?

Another attributed the principal motivation to be the woman's need to be noticed, stating the main reason for false complaints as being.

D: Well, it's generally – it's attention seeking. Something's gone wrong with their life, their boyfriend's been ignoring them or they can't get a bloody boyfriend or there's a whole raft of reasons. I don't know what they all are but there seems to me to be – that attention seeking thing seems to be the key.

J : Right, yeah. But in terms of the attention that you get, I mean, you're liable to end up with quite a few pissed off police officers aren't you?

D: But they don't think about that when they make the complaint. All they think about is, I'm going to have them all over the place and they're all going to be interested in me and they don't think of the consequences. (D9)

Others tended to suggest the kinds of stereotypical motives often put forward elsewhere – for example, the young girl late home, or the wife covering up her infidelity. Thus one detective said:

I think, going back to why people would report a rape when they haven't been is the fact that they have compromised themselves with their behaviour and their partners have found out. To me, to me that's been my experience. That's probably one of the biggest reasons .... But yeah, there have been a few where, you know, they've either been late home and hubby's suspected something. (D10)

Similar comments were made by other detectives. D3, for example, said:

I know heaps of people who've, young girls who've become pregnant and they have to tell their parents, they'll say to their mother or something, 'I was picked up one night but I don't know who it was' and before she's finished, the next thing's the phone's gone, 111 [emergency number] is started. And you're on there interviewing for rape and it sounds nice, and then we sit down and someone will talk her through it. They'll say 'no it wasn't'. You know, that's how some of these generally start, just talking to someone.

Mention was made by some detectives of false complaints that they believed to be motivated by malice, the classic 'revenge' motive. One described it this way:

Sometimes they want to cause grief to somebody else, somebody who has pissed them off. I have had a couple like this, actually. In both situations the women had a psychiatric history and were on medication and they had stopped taking it and were getting out of control anyway and the boyfriends had pissed them off and they had laid these complaints and it was just to get at the guy. (D2)

Another said he had encountered two such cases in his entire police career. The example he gave involved a young woman who claimed to have been detained and raped by a man when she went to visit a girlfriend, found her not home at the time, and then asked the alleged offender if she could use the toilet. This detective described the case from his perspective:

> She lived not more than, literally not more than 140 or 150 yards away. She'd gone from her place on a warmish night to the friend's place, 'can I use the toilet?' So later I'm saying to her, 'well, how come you needed to use the toilet in such a short space of time?' It may be strange but I sort of think about those things before I go out, you know. I guess that was my training, perhaps I was over parented. But it occurred to me, you know, you just don't go out and then several aspects of the thing, of the investigation just came to life from talking to his girlfriend, which I had a bit of trouble doing. She wasn't going to let me in, I really just conned my way into her lounge and sat down and started taking a statement and before she knew it she'd made a statement to me. And I don't enjoy deceiving people like that but it turned out that her statement was quite crucial and me establishing that was a false complaint and that girl was a very promiscuous girl who was known to people in the neighbourhood to be one who would engage in any kind of sexual activity that you wanted her to and she had gone round to this guy who was a tattooist and had promised him sex for a tattoo. Both those events happened but for some reason she decided to say, I think, it was concern about her boyfriend finding out, that prompted her to say that she'd been raped. (D3)

The woman's father held a position of some influence in the local community, and was not impressed by police treatment of his daughter. The detective described this man's visit to the station.

> And he came in here, thumped the desk, 'My daughter was raped, what are the bloody police doing about it? I'm happy to support you in the public arena and fight for resources, I want something done about it!' I thought, jeez, am I going to break this man's heart and tell him that his daughter's a promiscuous young woman who nothing happened to and who deliberately engaged in intercourse with this guy willingly? But that was really a malicious complaint against a particular individual. She maintained, she was adamant that the rape had happened. I probably should have charged that cow because she accused this guy of rape and actually he's since hung himself. Now whether there's a connection there is something I'll never know. But I wasn't able to charge her. He hung himself. So that's the end of him. (D3)

Several detectives believed that women seldom made false claims involving someone whom they knew. In their experience, it was rare for a woman to name an alleged offender in a case which turned out to be false. This somewhat belies the myth of women being inclined to 'dob in' any and every male for rape. One detective, who had a reputation for being a hardnosed, old school investigator, seemed almost embarrassed when he made the following comment.

> In my experience – this is a terrible generalisation; I'm happy to say it in here because it's not going into the media – but if a woman comes in and complains that a guy has raped her, generally speaking he's raped her. I mean, if she knows the guy and they've had sex and she walks in and says I've been raped by him, it's very rare that she hasn't been raped. People just don't make that up about people. Well, they do sometimes but it's not common. (D9)

Some suggested that, if a woman did name a man whom she falsely accused of raping her, it was usually for a reason. In other words, it was because he had used her or wronged her in some way.

Other detectives cited possible psychiatric or psychological factors that may underlie false rape allegations; one detective, for instance, talked about those who made false complaints as often being:

> Mentally disturbed women. Fantasisers. Women that come in and have been raped and they haven't been near a man for years. (D11)

The comments of some detectives indicated an appreciation of the social and psychological factors usually involved in false accusations. As D2 commented:

> There are a whole lot of factors occurring in the complainant's life that are spinning them out of control and it can be financial, it can be their self esteem factors, it can be sometimes psychological factors, it can be a whole mixture of things, relationship factors or they are pissed off that things are not going their way, just lots of things like that. I don't think there would be any one thing happening to make a false complaint. Alcohol is sometimes a good reason, a good factor....So I wouldn't say there was any one factor, I'd say it was a combination and it is centred around the complainant.

Recognition of emotional and psychological factors led many of these detectives to advocate compassion in the police response to such women. One of the more senior and experienced detectives interviewed expressed it this way.

> In some false complaints of rape you have got to understand why it is people make false complaints you can actually deal with it properly. So

when a woman comes in and makes a complaint of rape, it doesn't make it false but it doesn't make it genuine either. But those that are false, you don't go in with your heavy boots on and tramp all over the victim, you have to have compassion and understanding. You might have a sick person, whether she is making a complaint out of a mental illness or an unresolved trauma that she hasn't resolved as she doesn't know how to and, not the training, but the assistance of the medical authorities, the counsellors that explained what it is she, what her problem is but it has manifested itself into a false complaint which we know is false or suspect is false. So you have to know how, you have to understand the false complaint before you can actually deal with it in a particular way. (D8)

Police responses to false complaints

The question of how to respond to perceived false complaints is a difficult one for the police. They must be mindful of the possibility that their perceptions may or may not be accurate, and are faced with having to determine the best way of establishing the 'truth' of the situation. For some of the detectives interviewed, this would mean simply challenging the complainant about any perceived inconsistencies or apparent flaws in her statement, hoping for an admission or retraction.

Most of those interviewed said they did not personally believe in 'grilling' complainants, with D6 expressing his belief that interrogation style interviews no longer occurred.

Well, people say, well, you understand then why detectives might grill or give a victim such a hard time at the first stage of the interview. But I think we've grown out of that in the police, you know. That happened 20 years ago but I don't think it happens now because I think we're a little more professional now and we, you know, we listen to the victim, we take that in, we do the preliminary interview, get the information and then investigate what she says.

Several detectives admitted, however, that they were aware of colleagues in the police who did still practise interrogation-style techniques.

But there is still some people out there, some police, that do give complainants a hard time because, for example, one might say to them, well you're going to get a hard time in court, no one's going to believe you because that's the way the system is. Now whether that's being negative because of the police environment they're working in and they've become negative or whether they're just trying to do something they're not trained at. That's probably more to the point. But yeah, there's some police there that say, well you know, you're going to get a hard time in court, and I know that happens. And it usually happens basically at the front counter when the woman first comes into complain to some joker on night shift who's probably a bit tired and has got to take a statement. But I don't think, it's not that often. (D10)

D9 maintained that the ability to read and interpret body language was important when testing the veracity of a complainant. He said:

You've either got a nose for it or you haven't and you know the old story of which side they're looking for the inspiration about what they're telling you? When someone's talking to me, I can tell. It's if they're looking to make something up they look up to the left – to their left, and if they're searching their memory banks, they tend to look up to their right. I think that's how it goes. Yeah, body language does really come into it quite a bit.

Some expressed strong concerns about the impact of showing complainants that they had doubts about the veracity of their statement and advocated extreme caution and sensitivity in such matters. D6, for instance, said he was often appalled with how rape victims were treated in court and believed the police needed to guard against doing the same.

You know, they deserve the best we can give them. Let's not shit on them straight away, even if you know they're lying, get their story and then do your job properly, do your investigation thoroughly and then you can go back to them and be straight up and down with them and say, look, you know, this doesn't tie up with that and this is not right and there's these inconsistencies here, we need to know the real truth. But if you don't do your investigation properly then you can't do that. And there's nothing to be gained just sitting down with the victim and saying you're bloody lying. You're not telling me the whole truth, I need to know the whole truth. Well, what do you gain? You know, you get the victim off side and then they go away and tell their story to their girlfriends and then you get this, the whole thing, where women are too frightened, or not too frightened, they just don't want to come to the police with their complaints.

One strategy suggested involved the need to preserve a positive relationship between the complainant and the detective whom she had made the initial statement to, in order to safeguard at least some feeling of trust and rapport with the police. If inconsistencies had to be confronted, the suggestion was made by one detective that the confronting should be conducted by a different detective, a little like the 'good cop, bad cop' scenario. This way, hopefully, the women's confidence in the entire police force would not be undermined should one detective put her through an 'inquisition'.

> You can't have the same detective that interviewed her suggest to her that the complaint is false and the investigator that took the complaint of rape 'cause the victim has the association of that detective and … she trusts the detective and we need to maintain that trust always. You have to have someone else who goes to her and puts the falseness of her complaint back to her. Now she might do two things, she might roll over and accept it and cry, but she might go the other way and that is aggressively and violently, not physically, but verbally, dispute our interpretation and vent her rage out on that police officer. Now, you don't want the rage being vented to the police officer that she has put her trust in, in telling this complaint … so you put a stranger in there, you put another detective in there so she has always got an ally in the police if she wants to come in five days later and say. 'Oh, I'm really sorry that I told you about that complaint. You treated me well, not like that bastard that came in the other day – he was really rude to me.' See what I'm getting at?
>
> So that's why you have two people, 'cause you still have to think, you can't cut off her knees and chop her head off, this is a victim we might need on our side in years to come so you don't bloody kill them. Horses for courses, that's why we need the understanding of the complaint so we know how to deal with it. (D8)

One detective maintained that the detectives he worked with were able to obtain a victim retraction in at least 50 per cent of cases involving false complaints.

> It depends on how you package it, how you approach it, you know. With empathy, its definitely the way to go, there is no use yelling and screaming at people, that's just … those days are gone and some days it just firmly entrenches their position that they have already lied to you. (D12)

Detectives differed quite markedly in their responses regarding whether or not women who made false allegations should be charged or not. A few said categorically that they should be charged.

> I charge them because I think they do a lot of harm long term. I mean, they cause so many problems and not just the work, but it puts all these people – it causes a lot of these other things that in the past, we've gone through the hoops because of these people and perhaps unnecessarily. (D5)

Often the detectives specified that the underlying motive or state of the woman would be the main factor determining their course of action. Thus D4 was clear that

> I think if it's malicious and done for criminal reasons they should be dealt with in the court. That's a small percentage. If they've done it out of confusion, dysfunctionality, drink, drugs, other problems, then they should be dealt with on the basis that it's a problem rather than a crime.

Some stated, however, that in their experience most false complaints did not name a suspect. D9, for instance, said:

> In my experience most of them – most of the false complaints that we get where we end up charging the woman, there has been no person there at all. They've scratched themselves and basically are attention seeking. Nothing has happened to them.

When I asked if such cases were rare, he replied:

> They're not rare but um, but they're not common. Yeah, they're relatively rare. Yeah, it takes a lot of courage for a woman to go into a police station and say to some big burly cop that she's been raped, knowing she's going to be put through the wringer and medically examined and the works.

Two detectives cited examples of cases where they had recommended that the woman involved should be given diversion.[39] In one of these situations, the detective stated clearly his reasons for advocating such a course of action.

> I said [to Prosecutions section], I don't want her going to the open court. I don't believe that's entirely appropriate, because of the conviction and just the boy that cried wolf, isn't it? Now what happens in two years from now, or ten bloody years from now, if she gets raped and the police look at her history? It doesn't say what the false complaint was about but a good investigator is either going to ask or get the file out. If he says to her, I'm going to get this file out, you'd better tell me about it, she will say oh yes I made up this false allegation that I was raped and that's going to blow her credibility right out of the window and I'm very concerned about the ramifications of prosecuting someone.... But certainly, if she had nominated somebody and that person had been caused public embarrassment, like their workmates knew they had been accused of a rape, I don't think that that comes into it then. That's a prosecution. (D3)

Several detectives queried the utility of the police taking women who made false complaints through the court system. D8, for instance, maintained:

> We very rarely take false complaints of rape to court. What does it achieve? It's time consuming for us to pursue a prosecution where there is no crime; this victim may be a victim for her own reasons. She might have put herself in a position, she regrets it very much, what's the point of kicking it out? She has had a hell of a telling off from us, she has probably had a grilling, she has been abused by us, politely, but still abused by us, had a telling off. So what's the point in going to court?
>
> We don't tend to take false victims to court simply because we want to get our own back. It doesn't achieve anything, it just ties us up. It means we have to, its another court case we have to prepare and takes time away from our normal duties ... the court would probably let her off, she has already got a warning from us, she is getting kicked out the door and a flea in her ear in no uncertain terms and that is probably for the satisfaction of us. A detective can vent his rage through his mouth, we don't need another court case.

Some detectives noted that often it appeared that those making false allegations suffered from some intellectual or mental disability, and queried the wisdom of putting such persons through the court system. One said that they often considered laying charges but usually refrained from actually doing so.

> The decision to charge is not often made and I'd say this is because of the victim being unstable. Like, we had an IHC victim who complained to her mother or teacher that she was raped. You wouldn't charge an IHC person. It's just a waste of time. Then you'll get the mentally unstable ones who have, for some reason they've been suffering from a lot of mental stress, or psychological stress, who will claim they've been raped and what's the point of putting them through it? You're probably going to push them over the edge. (D10)

Others spoke of the need to try and address the underlying problems.

> Well, I mean there are many ways you could respond to it. I respond to them by talking a bit to them about their problems and why are they like that, 'cause if it's financial – look, here is the number and let's ring these people and go and see them for budgetary advice; because if you are having problems with relationships, let's go and see these people here; and give them numbers and give them the opportunity to remedy it themselves so they don't get caught in that situation again .... It's important

that you follow it up – if they are making false statements you have got to look at why. (D9)

From comments made, it appears that more women might be charged if the police considered that sufficient evidence was available. A central factor underlying the few prosecutions each year for false complaints involved difficulties in corroborating such cases. One detective (D9) said his station seldom charged the women.

> ...because it's so hard to prove and it's so easy for a woman to come in and say – a big tattooed bum bloody leapt out of the bushes in the park and raped me and ran off into the darkness and I've never seen him since, and it's so hard to refute that. I mean especially if they go into the park and lie down on the ground and roll round a bit and put a scratch on their face and put a bit of mud in their hair and then come down to the police station. It's very hard to knock that over.

Another detective commented in a similar vein that a deterrent to prosecution would be the time required in preparing a case for court.

> It depends on how much work is going to be involved in blowing their story out of the water, to be honest, because I mean, if you are going to have to spend another 100 man hours proving them to be not telling the truth, a liar in this case and then charging them with the Summary Offences Act which is, I think, 3 months and a thousand or 6 months and two thousand, so very low on the scale cause there is no crime as such and um is it worth it? Or do you just clear it as a warning or just 'no offence disclosed', and just move on because we are just so busy? (D12)

One potentially problematic area for police relates to the transition in status from a woman being interviewed as a complainant to being treated as an alleged offender. At some point in the proceedings, her status changes in the eyes of the police. This tension was acknowledged by at least one of the detectives interviewed:

> That's another area which is a bit difficult to sort out because you do get some complainants come in, you know their complaint is a bit suspect for whatever reason. Whether they've got a husband and they've been caught out playing around or who knows what the reasons are really. And then you re-interview them as a suspect, I suppose, not a complainant, but you know you put the hard word on that their complaint is not true and get an admission and an apology. Then there's the decision well

you've mucked us around for a couple of weeks, do we charge her with making a false complaint or not. And then you've got to take into consideration what the effect of charging them would have on them. And they've already either been through some psychological trauma or problem which has brought them to the station to complain in the first place. So it's not going to benefit anybody. (D10)

Another senior detective also expressed strong views when questioned concerning his stance on this issue.

D: I'm not a fan of charging people with false complaints.... I mean, there are some that you should do, but my personal view is that you err on the side of caution charging them rather than not, because I would hate to ever deter a legitimate one coming on because especially when they're in a situation where they're thinking, 'Jesus, no one's going to believe me! Wow, that woman got charged last week for a false complaint, maybe I won't bother', sort of thing. I'd rather not run that risk.

J: Right, because you're worried about, that it will deter others from reporting?

D: Deter others. I can equally agree with a lot of people of my rank around the country who would say the opposite. No, we want to deter all those ones that are false and save ourselves hundreds of thousands of investigative hours. I mean, there's arguments both sides, it just depends where you sit with it. I certainly don't say they're wrong with their view and I don't think I'm wrong with my view.

J: It's a balancing act, isn't it?

D: Yes, absolutely, and there's some of them I'd have no hesitation in charging.

J: So have you been involved in cases where the complainant's been charged?

D: No.

J: Never?

D: No.

J: Right.

D: But that doesn't mean I wouldn't. It just depends on the circumstances.

J: So what would motivate you to?

D: First of all, you'd have to have a very strong case. You'd have to have a lot of good evidence. And I haven't seen one yet where we had enough evidence to prove it, so I probably stand back a bit more than

> we normally do because it's such a huge one to get wrong. Huge. And
> I think you're better to sort of, let it go, than to get it wrong. (D11)

The overall impression gained from the detectives interviewed was of significant variation in their views concerning what responses were appropriate. While some felt justified in 'throwing the book' at certain women who made false allegations, others questioned what gains would be made by such actions and expressed concern about possible consequences further down the track. These could involve, for example, someone labelled as a 'false complainer' later actually being raped but being disbelieved because of her previous false allegation, through to other victims being deterred generally from reporting sexual assaults.

The possibility also exists, and was acknowledged by some, of the police being wrong in their assessment that a woman was lying. In many cases of date and acquaintance rape, especially, there are two parties presenting different versions of events and little other evidence. Numerous examples of this kind of scenario were presented in Chapter 4, showing the difficulties faced by complainants in convincing the police of their victimisation. Men accused of rape rarely agree with the accusation; thus, in the face of her assertion and his denial, whose account prevails? In practice, the woman making the allegation is challenged the most rigorously concerning her account of the events.

Testing the veracity of a complaint is often a delicate and complex task and, as was evident in cases examined in the previous chapter, the possibility exists of cues being misinterpreted or having overly much significance attached to them. One detective (D11) commented that expectations held by the police regarding complainants' testimony were sometimes unrealistic.

> D: Just the fact that anyone who comes in here will not, cannot, possibly be expected to remember everything, get everything in some sort of logical sense, or chronological sense, because of what's happened to them. I was never told that, or didn't understand it. We go into policeman mode when dealing with the victim.
>
> J: What's that? How would you describe that?
>
> D: It's that we want the facts now, here, in logical order, we want to know what happened after that, this one first, and we want to get the whole thing now. And with a lot of victims we can get that, but of course, with rape victims you don't get it as easily because of the stress.

A senior detective with the Offender Profiling Squad provided a good example of the ways in which strange behaviour by the complainant can erroneously be interpreted as suspect by the police. The example is included in full because of the insights it provides into the police psyche and the way in which information can easily be misinterpreted, sometimes simply for the police to be able to close a case.

We tell the story of one of the Park[40] victims whose mother was 71 and she was IH and the girl as a result was also intellectually challenged and she lived in Otara, she was a Pakeha girl and she'd been attacked for the second time. Hadn't been raped, but there was assault with intent to rape. And of course, that immediately gives you the problem of forensic. Immediately you've got no forensic as far as he's concerned and you've got no proof that a rape was going to occur. Where you've got semen, at least you've got, you can say well, okay, intercourse has taken place and then you've got that. So attempt is always arguable, no matter what the charge is and this particular girl – the mother, it was a shocking house. Went in there and the detective sat down and the girl sat down there and he was sitting there and the first thing she did was, she got up and she went to the fridge and took out a handful of raw mince and started eating it in front of him. The detective, in fairness to him, took a statement from her and took the details and he treated it as attempted murder because she was pretty badly smacked around in the head, and he went back to her later on and thought well Mum's mad, she's half crazy, what did happen, and it was suggested perhaps that Mum had attacked her. And you've got to try, because you're trying to rationalise the irrational sometimes and when you're dealing with people like that you try and figure out: has there actually been someone in here or not?

Because it was an unsolved attempted murder, they sent a senior detective around there to speak to Mum, put it on Mum, because somehow they'd come to the conclusion that Mum – because there'd been domestic problems and we thought it might have been just – because she was so badly beaten and ended up in going to hospital that perhaps they'd just covered up and said there was an intruder in the house, to cover up the violence of an unsatisfactory relationship between this mother, and that's how it was written off, I think.

Now I actually stumbled on that file because I was pulling out all the intruder attacks in Otara when I was doing Park and that file was one of them. So I pulled the file out, and I pulled the open report and it just gives a quick summary that they believed the mother was responsible and there wasn't an intruder there and I of course took that as read and I threw it on, I think I had all the files at home in those days and I was kind of reading them in bed, you know, and I threw it on the ground and it fell open with a photograph of a table underneath this window, with the old window that pulled out, and Thompson pulled out and went in. Under the window which was his MO, always put something under the window. I picked it up again and had a look at it and there was actually a job sheet in there from a neighbour who had allegedly seen someone running away.

> I thought, well, I don't know, it seems a bit of an easy result here for the police just to get rid of this file and then further on into the file there was a job sheet by a dog handler who had tracked and the witness, the neighbour's view of this offender into a school at the back, which Thompson went to, all schools. I thought this is ridiculous. I had a look at it and I included it in as one of Joe Thompson's attacks and it was one which he admitted to. He did it both times; he attacked that girl twice. (D5)

The above scenario shows how the factors of intellectual disability and somewhat strange and off putting behaviour on the part of the complainant created sufficient doubt for the initial account to be rejected and for the family to come under suspicion instead. It was virtually a chance discovery by a detective on another investigation that led to this case being re-examined and to the complainant's version of events finally being upheld. As this detective said, it's important for the police not to read too much into how the complainant behaves when still in shock.

> The point of the whole thing was: it doesn't matter how the victim reacts to you, because, as you know, every woman acts differently to stress, and some of them are going to be a blubbery mess, some of them are going to over compensate with confidence, and some of them are going be antagonistic towards the first police, like whoever comes in – 'piss off'. One of them did that, in Park. Another one's going to throw their arms around you as their saviour. So I mean, it's going to be all that and everything in-between. (D5)

This same detective also cited a case in the Malcolm Rewa[41] investigation, where a woman reported and actually named Rewa for a rape in 1987. He produced an alibi, and the local police, despite knowing he had a previous conviction for attempted rape, wrote off her complaint. Michelle[42] said, in an interview for the *New Zealand Woman's Weekly*, that she was devastated when the police said they would not be pursuing their investigation of her case, and added.

> They [police] weren't treating me seriously. As far as they were concerned, I was just some bimbo. I wasn't important enough for them to go to any trouble. But I was a decent young girl who'd got in with the wrong crowd. And it wasn't as if I was out at a party with him when I was raped. I was home in bed. (Quoted in Fleming, 1998, p. 22)

Michelle's boyfriend was a member of the same gang as Rewa, and was in fact a 'mate' of Rewa's. The 'alibi' on which the police depended was nothing more than her boyfriend's testimony that 'If Hammer[43] says I was with him, then I was', combined with his refusal to sign a statement to this effect (Fleming, 1998, p. 23). Nine years and 24 women later, Malcolm Rewa was arrested. Michelle rang the police team working on Operation Harvey.

> I told the policeman my name and said, 'This man raped me in 1987 and got away with it.' The detective said, 'Yes, Michelle, we know.' They had my file there, and finally someone believed me. They really believed me. (Ibid.)

Michelle's case demonstrates well how police assessments of a victim's character and credibility can, at times, impede their ability to see her as a legitimate victim. Fortunately, at least amongst some of the more experienced detectives interviewed, this perception appears to be changing. Some acknowledged, for instance, that they had come to realise the ways in which certain women may be more vulnerable to rape or may engage in riskier behaviours than others, and how this should in no way detract from their entitlement to police service and protection. A female detective described a case that was nearly dismissed as a false complaint.

> I didn't attend the initial scene; it was dealt with by the night shift crime car, a detective and a constable, and it was a prostitute and she was really drunk when they saw her and her clothes had been tattered and that sort of thing and they couldn't get a straight story from her because she was really drunk and they had her in for an evidential medical examination and the doctor had done the Woods test which is shining a light on her. This guy hadn't actually had sex with her; he had ejaculated all over the back of her legs and pantyhose and the Woods test didn't show any semen. I came to work the next morning and got the file and the reports of other police officers, what they were saying, you know this absolutely reeks of no, you know, this just didn't happen and all that sort of thing, and so I spoke to this women later in the day when she had woken up and she was a bit more sober and I was still really iffy, going on what the cops had said who were first at the scene, that sort of thing.
>
> I actually spoke to her about this being a false rape complaint and that sort of thing and she was quite adamant that it wasn't and did get upset with me. I can honestly say it was the first time I have actually seen the Woods test where there was no semen so I was 'what are you doing?' and all that sort of thing, and she just stuck with it. So I re-interviewed her and got another statement from her that provided a bit more detail and I thought, I am going to send everything to the ESR because I just want to be truly sure and it came back from the ESR and there was lots of semen there and I just felt awful because I had just relied on this Woods test that the DSAC doctor had used so yeah, it was a learning curve for me, that I will still go with how I feel with the complainant and go from there.

I went back to her and sort of apologised to her and explained to her why I was concerned about it and the Woods test and the ESR examination and all of that and she was really good about it. And she could see where I was coming from and we still keep in touch. (D2)

This detective also said that ten days after this woman had been attacked, a man fitting the same description attacked another prostitute working in the same area. At the time of the interview, a suspect had been identified and the detective said she was fairly certain the case would proceed to court.

Complainants' credibility

The interviews with detectives reinforce that often the central issue at stake is the complainant's credibility. To what extent does she present as an authentic and credible victim? In practice, this often translates to mean: to what extent does this complainant present as an authentic and credible *person*? What is her social status? Has she been in trouble with the police before? Does she have drug and alcohol problems? Underlying these kinds of questions may be an assumption that only certain, socially 'approved' kinds of women can be genuine victims of rape. The rest are at best, dubious; at worst, sluts and liars.

Police officers inevitably engage in assessments of complainants and how they present, especially in comparison to the characteristics of the alleged offender. The use of stereotypes to inform the exercise of police discretion generally has been well documented and is in many ways understandable (Reiner, 1994; White and Perrone, 1997). Where it becomes problematic, however, is when adherence to judgmental stereotypes may blind some officers to the 'truth'. This is what men like Morgan Fahey will often rely on when they select victims whom they expect the police will appraise as somewhat dubious.

Some of those interviewed spoke about certain kinds of behaviours which were perceived as risky and 'inviting trouble'.

One situation like that would be those girls or women that let their hair down, so to speak, and put themselves in a situation like a gang environment. You know, like there's been a lot of cases I've been involved with where you've just got to ask yourself: why the hell did you go there? Because the writing's on the wall. (D10)

Alcohol related issues often prove to be particularly problematic. As was evident in Chapter 4, and substantiated by research conducted elsewhere (Amir, 1971; Crowell and Burgess, 1996; Russell, 1984; Warshaw, 1988), many sexual assaults occur in contexts where both the complainant and the alleged perpetrator have been drinking and, in situations of high alcohol consumption, it is initially hard to obtain good interview data from the parties involved. While some detectives acknowledged that it was not appropriate for men to have sex with women who were too drunk to consent, and that this amounted to rape, nevertheless a woman's drunkenness could count against perceptions of her as a credible victim.

In discussing the issue of consent for drunken victims, one detective (D3) compared this to the age of consent generally:

> The big grey area that comes in is this consent thing and whether intoxicated people can consent. They can't in law; like whether people under 16 can consent, they can't in law. But in practice they do, you know there's not many 16 year old virgins out there now, are there? Really, when you see young kids and their sexual behaviour. I know from what my daughter says about some of her friends and the activities they get up to with boys and that. It's actually pretty frightening.

The above comment suggests that, for this detective at least, although the law states one has to be 16, and sober, to consent, in practice, he feels this did not accord with his experience. Given the views expressed here, it is interesting to speculate how detectives with views such as his might respond to a drunken teenager complaining of rape.

Concern was expressed by some over the extent of risk taking behaviour engaged in by some young people, particularly after heavy alcohol consumption:

> Let's face it, when you're in your teens and your young twenties, whether you're men or women, you're taking risk taking behaviour, and when you're doing that you often put yourself in situations where you increase the odds of something happening to you. It's as simple as that really. So, alcohol is usually the reason why they take risks they normally wouldn't have. (D11)

Furthermore, the extent of alcohol involvement could also complicate police investigative procedures. As this detective went on to comment:

> It does add to the challenge to it, because memory comes into it. Most of – well, a large proportion of the victims come in somewhere between the hours of 11pm and about 3 or 4am. They've usually been up since about six or seven o'clock the previous day, so they're tired as, as well as that they're normally drunk and sometimes incoherent, obviously in shock, traumatised and so all in all that's a great recipe for not actually being able to get things that accurate. (D11)

Many of the detectives noted the frequency of alcohol involvement in rape complaints, particularly between persons known to each other where the difficulties often revolved around consent issues. One senior detective strongly believed alcohol to be a contributing factor in sexual assaults generally, arguing that those most at risk were

> Drunk women under the age of 25 basically, for both actually, for consensual – or for stranger and non stranger. Definitely. I mean, I tell my staff when I induct them, 95 per cent of women that come in here complaining of sexual attacks will be under the age of 25 and they'll be drunk. Ninety five per cent of the men that come in here and complain of getting beaten up will be under the age of 25 and they'll be drunk, too. It's just that men get their heads kicked in and the women get sexually violated. Because they're the people that are out there on the street and available as targets. (D11)

Another detective gave an example of the kind of case which he considered to have arisen completely from the victim's intoxication, and which would be impossible for the police to proceed with. In this particular situation, two sisters were drinking together at the pub, a guy gave them a lift home, one sister went inside and the other chose to stay in the car. As the detective described it:

> She just got so drunk at a pub and she went off, went home with this guy and woke up at four in the morning alongside some guy she'd never seen before in her life. Screamed rape, you know, ran out of the house naked to the next door neighbour's. But you know, we didn't deal with that as a rape. We investigated it: you've got to do the work, you know, and you've got to do it properly. You can't just, what I'm trying to say is, you've got to do your investigation properly and then when you've done it properly, if you've done your job properly, you will establish the truth, whether it's genuine, whether it's completely false, or what – what little fabrications there are in there on the way, you know. And that girl in [suburb], we didn't proceed with a prosecution in the end and she wasn't happy with that but we would have got nowhere with that.
>
> At the end of the day, you know what I mean, we didn't write that off as 'no offence disclosed', we just write that off as – how did we write that one off? Off the top of my head I can't remember how we wrote it off but simply that, I mean there's just no point in proceeding with the investigation. It was just that she woke up at four in the morning or five in the morning and saw this big black man next to her that she'd never seen before in her life, because she was so pissed the night before she couldn't remember, and she was terrified and jumped out of bed and took off.

I mean hell, you know, imagine trying to take that to trial. I know that you know if she's drunk she can't give informed consent, but it's fine in court but it's fine when they talk about it in the clear light of day. But hell, you stand up at trial and you get this victim up there who says, 'Well, I can't remember much and I was at the pub and I got pissed with my sister.' Then the sister gives evidence and says, 'Well, look, we were at our place at the front gate and I said come with me, and she says no, I'm going with this guy.' It doesn't look good and I think, you know, you'd find it very, very hard. (D 6)

For complainants, as we saw earlier in the discussion of police files, fears concerning how the police will respond to knowledge of their drunkenness can impact heavily on their disclosure. For example, a complainant who is worried that the police may judge her negatively may try to minimise her estimation of how much alcohol she had consumed. From a police perspective, however, her actions in this regard could further count against her. Now, as well as being a drunk, she is seen as a liar as well.

Some detectives spoke about the demeanour of the victim, but mostly in ways which suggested that they knew this was a complicated variable to assess in rape victims. One detective (D12) emphasised the ways in which his understanding had changed over the years, so that he was now less likely to be influenced by some of the traditional police indicators of credibility and authenticity. Instead, he prefers to look for evidence and corroboration of the victim's story, rather than attach too much significance to factors such as demeanour. As he expressed it:

So the key issue for me is corroboration, to a lesser, a much lesser extent, is credibility. Because professional women get attacked, prostitutes get attacked, people who have been abused previously get attacked, people with criminal convictions get sexually attacked, so it would be very unfair to say that you have to be white, you have to be between 20 and 40, you've gotta have no criminal convictions and that sort of stereotyping. You can't do it. And that's what you have to keep reminding our staff at times, they are junior staff they do get impressions placed upon them by staff who are more experienced and cynical and it's amazing how the sort of effect that can have on people and that is what you try to encourage at the end of the day, that they have their own mind and can make up their own opinion rather than just going with the flow, 'cause it's just wrong to go with the flow. So yes, corroboration is the key thing for me. (D12)

A senior detective provided an example of a case which the complainant had pursued through to the Police Complaints Authority in her efforts to have her account of rape believed.

The guy that was the offender is an icon down there. He played provincial rugby, he was a big rough character, everyone loved him but deep down he was an arse hole and there were job sheets there from other [guys'] wives who said when their husbands went away he always seemed to turn up at the doorstep seeing if they wanted anything and occasionally he would put the hard word on them and in fact one woman said he said, 'oh, if you let me in the sack things will go better at the College for your husband' and all this sort of shit so he was a. His attitudes were there to be seen but the cops down there didn't want to see them because they liked him.

Well, she was a bit older – she was – a lot of these people, they'll say, 'oh, she's a bloody psycho' and often they are. But because she's a psycho doesn't mean that she's a bloody viable target for some arse hole to go and rape. He probably sized her up – she was a bit of a police groupie, this lass, and this guy obviously thought 'oh she hangs around with the cops I'll give her one and she'll never complain'. And that wasn't the case at all. It turned out she was a virgin; although she was in her early 30s, she'd never had sex. And two [cops] went to bed and left him up with her. And it's clear to me from reading it that they were uncomfortable with his behaviour and they buggered off to bed to get away. And they both lied about what had happened.

When this complaint was made [the detective], who's an old rugby man, just said 'no way'. And then all the guys said, 'oh she's a bloody psycho, that tart, she hangs round all the football teams and hangs round the cops' and so they had this animosity if you like towards this woman from the outset and they let it colour their thinking and their judgment ....

They'll never get him convicted – never, because it's been so long ago and she did all the wrong things afterwards. Afterwards she never complained to the other two cops the next day.... She went to Australia on holiday and then told a friend in Australia, 'this policeman raped me and I didn't feel I could do anything because all the police like him and they wouldn't believe me', and it was a sort of self-fulfilling prophecy she had set up really. (D9)

Another detective spoke of the way in which inconsistencies could alert the police to a possible false complaint, although the possibility of misinterpretation also existed. What was more important was the existence of corroborative evidence.

You've got to be so careful because sometimes you'd get discrepancies from genuine complainants too. It's only going through all the evidence, really, and what supports it and what doesn't and there's usually some signal event in the course of the inquiry and you go aaaah this is a bloody false complaint. And it's like a big alarm clock going off. A classic example is someone who says she's been raped in a bloody park by somebody that walked up behind her and then you go and find she's been at a nightclub and then you find that at the nightclub she was dancing and kissing this guy and getting really bloody hot with him and then it suddenly starts to gel, well, hang on a minute – yeah. (D9)

Police procedures

From the descriptions provided of police procedures, it is clear that currently there is very little consistency between different areas of the country with regard to the processing of sexual assault complaints. The specific aspects focussed on here relate to police dealings with the complainant, since these are the central concern of this book. The general requirements remain the same; for example, obtaining a statement from the victim, probably arranging for her to have a forensic medical examination, explaining to her the reasons for proceeding or not proceeding with the case and so forth. However, considerable variation appears to exist in relation to how such requirements are managed.

One controversial area within the police relates to the optimal time at which to obtain the complainant's statement (Epstein and Langenbahn, 1994). Traditionally, police practice worked on the assumption that the statement should be obtained immediately upon reporting, and gradually this changed in New Zealand to a procedure whereby the medical examination was prioritised, for evidential reasons, and the statement was obtained directly following this examination. Feedback from complainants, however (Jordan, 1998a), indicated that taking their statement following the medical examination invariably meant that it was obtained at a time when they often felt exhausted, traumatised, possibly affected by alcohol or drugs and generally not particularly coherent. Since the statement forms such a critical part of any ensuing court trial, some police have begun to question the 'hand me down' wisdom of their predecessors. This was evident in the interviews when some detectives discussed the traditional approach while others spoke of the advantages of delayed statement-taking. Some admitted that determining the order of these procedures could be difficult.

> The biggest problem I have – and I think we have – investigating rape complainants is the period of taking the statement and the medical being done okay. It's a confusing area because a statement can take hours to take from a distraught victim and usually you've got a doctor called in and on standby and as time ticks on with that statement going on, they're getting impatient about where's this person I'm supposed to be examining. And

it usually happens with inexperienced staff that the doctor will get the victim to her surgery as quick as possible, and that leaves the police in a situation with not really knowing what's going on, because it hasn't been committed to paper and nothing to work on and that area is a little bit untidy, if you know what I mean. You've got the investigators screaming out for a statement so they can go and do a scene examination, pick up exhibits. Just a preliminary, a one pager would do. Yeah, one page.

But it's hard even to get one page off women who are really emotionally, you know. You've got to console them and then bring them around and then give them a cup of coffee which is all part of the process and they mightn't even talk for an hour. They might just sit there sobbing and you know they've been raped but they can't relate the experience right there and then because of post trauma stress and all that, I suppose. You've got a doctor screaming for them to come down to the surgery. Where is she, you know, I've been called out. And there's always the difficulty of what do you do first, do you take a statement off her first or do you get her to the medical first? And then you go to the medical and the doctor says: what happened? And then you say, well, we haven't got a statement or anything yet. But you've just got to work through each of those cases as you can. (D10)

Several stressed that the complainant was often not in the best state of mind to be interviewed at the time of the initial complaint. Thus one experienced detective maintained:

As far as the medical examination goes, obviously the earlier the better, it has to be done. But as for a statement being done immediately, if she's not up to it, what's the point? Because what you've got is a tired person who doesn't really want to be there. And I mean, that's the key to getting a statement from somebody. There's no point in getting a statement from someone who you haven't got a rapport with and you're not, she's not relaxed. Because apart from anything else all she wants to do is get out of there and she'll cut it short, she'll miss things out and she'll perhaps not be concentrating – I mean, getting things out of the old noggin at any time can be hard for some people, and if you're not focussed on it you're not going to get the stuff out. So I haven't got a problem with her being interviewed later on. (D5)

Another detective had even prepared a briefing paper for his station on the merits of delayed statement-taking, such was his conviction that this approach was preferable to requiring an exhausted complainant to spend hours trying to provide police with a clear, consistent account of every detail about what had happened to her. He maintained that police insistence on taking a statement when the woman was exhausted was abusive and counterproductive.

> At the end of the day, all those things are what the army do when they torture people, don't they? Sleep deprivation and blimmen all that sort of thing, and we do that to our rape victims! And so I think – there's been a number of reasons for that [immediate statement-taking]. I mean, there's been certainly a culture within the CIB where you wouldn't want to be seen as duck shoving so the nightshift crime car who deal with those people wouldn't want to leave it to the early shift because they don't want to be seen as doing a duck shove. Whereas now I'm trying to get through to them, well it's not a duck shove, what you should do is actually take the details of what happened, what they can remember at that time, but don't sit there for hours typing on a blimmen typewriter with detective's skills at typing at two words a minute because that just prolongs the agony for the victim. Get the details down in a note book, pass it on to the early shift. Bring the victim back in 18 hours later when they've sobered up and have got a bit clearer memory of what actually happened. (D11)

Discussion of the possible merits associated with delayed statement-taking prompted one detective to provide a clear, recent example of where he believed the police seriously erred in not providing a complainant with that option. In this particular case, a young woman alleged having been raped late one night by two men, and the police insisted on obtaining a statement from her as soon as possible.

> The statement taken by the police officer was appalling, absolutely appalling. He was a detective constable and a very, very good one but he tried to interview her after she had been up 16 hours or something like that. And after she'd been drinking. And he got the medical off her and then he tried to interview her, so it was always going to be a bad interview as she was at the end of her tether .... That was a classic where we should have sent her home and she would have come back much clearer. She didn't even read the statement, she told us, she didn't even read it, he walked out of the room while she was there, she just signed it, was too tired, couldn't be bothered and there was some particularly concerning points in that statement that made us wonder if it was valid or not. Words like penetration and things like, victims don't use those words for a start and I mean to such a point where you look at the statement and you say: this isn't true. But the whole point is: it isn't her statement, it's his statement, his words. We sent it to Auckland to the criminal profiling unit and they came back and said we have put the scan process over it and it's not correct, the statement is not valid, it's not true. They are absolutely

right, but it's not her statement, it's the police officer's statement. So sometimes we have to get around it and she went through a pretty hard time
over the first couple or three days, to be quite honest in respect to that, and
it was all because of the initial officer's statement off her, which wasn't
fair on her.

Investigation of the case cited above could easily have been terminated
because of the way in which the complainant's statement was obtained by
the police. Fortunately, in this particular example, good supervisory practice
meant that the circumstances surrounding the taking of the complainant's
statement were queried and she was re-questioned. Two offenders were eventually convicted and imprisoned for this offence.

Overall, then, comments from the detectives suggested that currently
this is a time of change within the police. While some felt it was important
to obtain a statement quickly, many were questioning this practice. This is
consistent with the guidelines included in the New Zealand Police Sexual
Assault Investigation Policy 1998; however, interestingly enough, although
all these interviews were conducted in late 1999 and 2000, not all of the
detectives interviewed knew even of this policy's existence.

The policy also included guidelines pertaining to the conducting of the
medical examination; again, this was an area where some disagreement
existed over the preferred procedures.

Medical examination

Being medically examined for forensic evidence after being raped is one of the
most arduous processes any crime victim has to face (Green, 1988). In England,
there has been extensive criticism of the way in which such examinations are
conducted (Gregory and Lees, 1999; Kelly, 2002; Temkin, 2002) and police
have endeavoured to manage these better, in part through making rape examination suites available. The standard of these suites, and their utilisation,
appears to have been haphazard (Gregory and Lees, 1999). In New Zealand,
considerable effort by concerned medical practitioners led to the formation of
Doctors for Sexual Abuse Care (DSAC). This organisation provides specialist
training for doctors willing to be called out to conduct examinations of rape
victims, and DSAC doctors are part of an inter-disciplinary team with police
and support agency representatives. The efforts made to improve complainants' experiences of the forensic medical examination have been reflected
in markedly higher satisfaction levels of New Zealand rape complainants with
this process than has been evident for their English counterparts (Jordan, 1996,
1998a; Gregory and Lees, 1999). Hence in Liz Kelly's recent overview for Her
Majesty's Crown Prosecution Service Inspectorate, she identified 'the availability, skills and attitude of forensic examiners' (Kelly, 2002, p. 24) as ongoing
areas of concern within the United Kingdom.

From the interviews conducted with the detectives, it appeared that one issue which still causes some dissension in New Zealand relates to whether or not all women reporting a rape should be immediately and routinely referred for examination, or after some initial sifting out of complaints that were perceived to be false. Some detectives insisted that arranging the medical examination had to be the first imperative, saying it needed to be organised:

Straightaway. Medical examination is the first thing and the most important thing. You can't really delay that. (D4)

Another said:

Because you take every victim, every complaint, at face value, you would go to a medical, you'd go to a medical examination fairly early or as early as you can. Normally, anyway, you would so I guess, yeah, I mean, I think medical examinations are always on course.... As far as the medical examination obviously the earlier the better, it has to be done. (D5)

One detective, for example, maintained that it was too early in the proceedings for the police to have adequate information on which to refute the complainant's account, and suggested that the medical examination itself could assist police in their decision-making.

D: Yeah, the thing is no, you've got to go ahead. You've got to. We tend to go ahead because the decision that it's false isn't actually made until a lot further down the track. I mean, you wouldn't just, you wouldn't want to make that decision that quickly.
J: Even if it looks dicey.
D: The medical examination will help you. That comes first, the medical examination and a medical examination can indicate that it is false. It doesn't always. But conversely, it can indicate that there's definitely trauma here, there's physical evidence there that suggest that. (D4)

Another was equally adamant that the medical examinations were too expensive to be conducted unnecessarily, and believed it was his duty to insist that there be some initial screening of complainants before these were arranged. He made this point in the context of discussing a recent complaint which he had quickly determined to be false.

The woman was intoxicated, she was actually quite objectionable as well, particularly to me, and I knew that, we were short staffed, we were going to have to do a scene examination and a whole lot of enquiries and tie everybody up for many hours and up I decided at that stage that I would confront her early on and when I think about it that is how I have always done it. It's the way you do it. And you have to do it in a way where they don't feel, you know, in case you are wrong, they are not going to feel put off by the police in your approach and as I say, I sort of have a sort of a sense in a way that I do it so I am not accusing or making anything up. You don't need to do any of that, you don't end up turning them into an offender, but you are interviewing them as an offender for a false complaint. You do have to draw a line: look police resources are really scarce at the moment and I think the thing of going right through the medical if there are clear signs that the thing is dodgey, I don't think its a good idea. Calling a doctor out, it's five to seven hundred dollars for a medical examination and the actual resource cost is really high. I think as long as it's said in the right way, if you can ease them into it and just explain, say, sometimes people react strangely or unusually, or maybe it happens in another way, and sometimes say, well there are a couple of things here that just aren't or seem a bit anomalous or whatever you are going to do .... (D1)

Not all detectives, therefore, agreed that the medical examination should be undertaken in every case. Moreover, some detectives still expressed a preference for the statement to take priority over the medical examination, advocating:

Take the statement before the medical generally. It depends on your victim and how traumatised she is and that sort of thing, but I would generally take the statement first .... Generally I prefer to do the statement first, that is my preference. I like to think that it gets it all out of the way initially and you can do it all in 24 to 48 hours. Sometimes I'll leave taking a statement until the next day, just so she can get a chance to get herself together and do the medical but you just have to weigh up if the physical examination is going to be worse for her than actually sitting down talking about what happened sometimes and generally I will assess it for the female. I would talk to her about it and see how she feels. (D2)

In many cases, however, it should be pointed out that this question becomes irrelevant because of delayed reporting. A forensic medical examination is of most utility if conducted within 72 hours of the incident, although is generally advised for up to seven days afterwards (Fancourt *et al.*, 1994). Many rape victims, however, report incidents outside this timeframe, with historic complaints being not uncommon occurrences. In the 1998 study, for instance, 40 per cent of the complainants had reported the incident after more than seven days had passed (Jordan, 1998a).

No offence disclosed

Given my interest in the reasons underlying the police decision to proceed or not with a rape investigation, I was particularly interested to hear what these detectives had to say regarding when they would file a case as 'no offence disclosed' (K3[44]). Their responses indicated considerable confusion surrounding what should be filed in this category, and what it meant.

Several were emphatic that this category should apply only to fabricated incidents. D3 exemplified this perspective.

> I'd have to be really certain that it was a proper K3 situation and a 'no offence disclosed' situation, that the complainant was lying, before I'd put a K3 on it. Because that's what it means. No offence disclosed yeah. And so if someone has come to you and says that an offence has happened and you're in a position at the end of the investigation to K3 it, then he/she must be lying because the two things are mutually exclusive of each other.
>
> If you've got an offence that you can't clear because you can't identify the offender, that is not a K3. That offence still happened and it's an uncleared crime because you've got no offender stats because you don't know who he was. If you've got a situation where you decide that your victim is lying, that's when you've got a K3, a genuine K3, and it's the only situation that one should apply it to. It's not for files which you can't, which you decide for whatever reason that you can't take to trial. That's not a K3.

D12 basically agreed but suggested that the 'no offence disclosed' category may also include cases where the complainant subsequently withdrew the complaint. He also implied that the major purpose of this category was to provide a way for the police to increase their clearance figures.

> Somebody comes in and reports being sexually violated, we investigate it, and they either withdraw their statement for various reasons, or they get charged in relation to making a false statement or there is overwhelming evidence to support that it is not a valid complaint. Even though they don't get charged, we would K3 it, 'no offence disclosed'. It's a stats thing; if a district had 50 unsolved sexual violations that wouldn't be very good, would it, so to get around it you K3 it – it clears the stats.

This view was confirmed by another detective, who observed in relation to the K3 category.

> There's no clear guidance as to what you're actually supposed to put in it. I mean, statistics is not something that people get tied up in knots about as to what to put on there. 'Say, what's this one go under?' Unless you've got a very finicky boss and I would suspect that there isn't a great deal of thought goes into what one goes in there as long as there's a clearance of some sort. I wouldn't put any emphasis on it. I would have suspected that 'no offence disclosed' grouped together a whole lot of things – false

complaints, no offence, 'it happened – no evidence' and 'I don't know what happened'. That would have gone in there as well. (D11)

One detective also stressed that he felt this category was overused within the police, with potentially dangerous consequences further down the track.

> Because what happens – I'm thinking defence now. What happens if I clear that 'no offence disclosed' – where's a file – the file cover sheet says so and so victim. Alias offender so and so. Text: sexual violation. All right. And you come across to the statistics and it's cleared, 'sexual violation – no offence'. Now if I was a switched on lawyer and five years down the track the offender gets locked up, I'd be asking for a copy of every page of that file and I'd be producing that statistic page to the court, to say the police have cleared this as no offence and now they're going to have a second bite of the cherry and put him out. (D10)

A related concern, raised in Chapter 4, is how the police may be influenced if complainants whose cases were cleared 'no offence disclosed' subsequently make a rape allegation against anyone else. From comments identified in the analysis of police files, any hint of a complainant having been involved with a previous suspected false complaint puts a question mark over any complaints she later makes. Given that many detectives clearly equate the 'no offence disclosed' category with false complaints, despite clear indicators that it is used in many other situations, this could clearly have detrimental consequences.

What is apparent is that the police often clear complaints as 'no offence disclosed' which were withdrawn by the complainant. As some detectives themselves noted, a victim's withdrawal or retraction of a complaint does not necessarily mean she was not the victim of a sexual offence. As one noted about rape complaints made to the police:

> Certainly there's lots that come our way that just go nowhere, you know, where the victims withdraw. But then again, they may not be false, you know, don't get me wrong there. A lot of women – not a lot, but there a few that after making the initial complaint, you know, they will get hold of you a couple of days later and they don't want to go through with it and you can understand that. The trauma, the trauma of the rape, they've probably talked to other people that they know who have heard stories about women getting grillings in the trial, and it still bloody happens despite all this bullshit about protection from the law, about the grilling of the victims. Their sexuality still gets put on trial there and it pisses me off but that's the way it is. (D6)

This detective spoke also of the need to be cautious in trying to ascertain how legitimate some of these cases were, then noted:

> Mind you, the danger in that is that genuine rape complainants often would be happy to walk away. Having had a taste of what's involved, I'm sure a lot of them would be quite happy to just pack their bag, walk off into the bloody sunset and never mention it again. (D6)

One point made by several of those interviewed was that the lack of consistency and the complexities involved in dealing with sexual assault victims raised training and supervision issues for the police.

Training and supervision issues

A supervisory issue identified by some detectives involved the need to assist staff in managing the impact of false complaints. While some said there was no problem in doing this, others expressed concern that experience with false allegations could leave some officers feeling 'burned' and cynical. One detective said he felt it was important to encourage staff to go and see someone, such as a counsellor, and debrief.

> I think it's a staff issue. You should be looking after your staff and we are not always going to be able to see, especially those early signs when guys are under it. I mean, I have done it, and I have encouraged my staff, you know its no big deal, you don't have to be a big brave detective any longer, it's good to go and talk about these things.... But that's what I think. I think they should all be getting debriefed once a year minimum and if they need it more they should be able to come to me and we just sign it off. (D12)

The issue was raised by some that not all detectives were suitable to interview rape complainants. This could be hard to identify, one said, given that no detective is likely to admit to having difficulties in this area. The possibility of specialist units was dismissed by all those interviewed, however. Even though some felt such units would be desirable, the practicalities and resourcing issues involved meant these were not considered viable.

Instead, some argued for better training of those involved in interviewing victims. One senior detective, who has been involved in CIB training, lamented the paucity of good training given to detectives concerning the effects of rape trauma on victims and the various ways this may affect how they present. He felt it was particularly important for supervisors, at a minimum, to have this information so that they could monitor the processing of rape files by more junior detectives.

If we don't have understanding of the victims of crime or of human behaviour as crimes occur, then you don't have the ability to test whether the investigative practices are right or wrong. A cop comes along, does the investigation, queries it and says it's likely this woman has laid a false complaint. Now, you might get a supervisor that is none the wiser and says ok this is a false complaint, or you might get a supervisor who says, hang on a minute, listen to this victim, how was she treated? Her behaviour is brought about by the trauma and stress she was under at the time, not because she has laid a false complaint. She is behaving that way because she has no ability to do anything else but try to survive the crime; this is how she deals with it. So if you have an enlightened supervisor who thinks that way, when he gets this report that says it's a false crime for the wrong reasons, he can say na na na na this is not a false crime, it's a true crime, carry on, and the reason why we carry on is because this victim is genuine. We have got too many supervisors, too many, that don't have the knowledge they should have, therefore they make the wrong decision. (D8)

Other issues were raised pertaining more generally to detectives' involvement in rape investigations which also indicated a need for greater training and staff supervision. One potential danger highlighted drew attention to the emotionally intense relationship that can sometimes develop between detectives and rape complainants. In discussing this, one detective remarked:

It can be a terrible strain on us because sometimes they [rape complainants] get very attached to us, some get fixated....So you put little plans in process, plans that can hopefully deal with it if it gets too out of control. Like, you make sure you are never alone with the victim or you are always in a very public area once they reach a certain stage in the investigation. You have to become a little bit more distant because otherwise they can get the wrong vibes and, I mean, there are occasions where policemen have got involved in relationships [example given]. You do get very close, well some of us on some occasions do get very close to our victims and it's very hard not to but that's why we do so well. 'Cause we have such an interest in it and you are dealing with people and I would suggest that very few officers who just turn off can get the same sort of result....

It can be a real danger especially if the woman, or man, but generally woman, has come from an environment where for years and years they have been in a position where they have tried to please. So it can muddy the waters a little and is something I don't think we receive enough training on. And personally I think that that is why you have to have close supervision of your staff....Remember, you are dealing with detectives who are human. As well, some of them may be going through relationship trouble or they may be single or they may get such an empathy with the victim that they feel they are the only person who can resolve this person's trauma, so it's a two way street. And there's a real concern in there that we have to address. (D12)

It is easy to see the potential complexities in such scenarios, where typically young, vulnerable, female rape victims can become emotionally dependent on the contact and support provided by strong-looking, caring, male detectives. Training specifically aimed at fostering awareness of the dynamics involved would be advantageous, combined with wise staff deployment and careful supervision.

Conclusion

The interviews with the detectives provide information from the perspective of those involved in every day decision-making concerning rape and sexual assault allegations. Their comments indicated that a diversity of views exist, even within this small group of detectives who were specially selected because of their expertise in this area. It was clear, for example, that some of those interviewed adhered to strong notions of what constituted 'real' rape, while others emphasised growing concerns about the rapes perpetrated by some men against dates and acquaintances. Estimates regarding the proportion of false complaints also varied immensely, and some detectives expressed anxiety regarding how quickly some of their colleagues might conclude a rape complaint to be false. Further evidence of continuing adherence to negative stereotypes of women was apparent in comments made by some regarding possible motives for false complaints. Little serious thought appeared to have been given to this issue, lending support to the view that beliefs in the frequency of false complaints have been overstated for so long now that few detectives seem prepared to question the basis for this particular tenet of police folklore.

It seems reasonable to extrapolate from the fact that some of the detectives interviewed held stereotypical attitudes about rape victims to suggest that such views are likely to be evident in other officers also. Moreover, this view was confirmed both in observations made by the detectives about staff they worked with, as well as in comments made on the police files examined in Chapter 4. Strong suggestions were made by some that extensive, specialist training was currently lacking in New Zealand, and that there was an urgent need to equip detectives with greater understanding of the effects of trauma on rape victims.[45]

It was clear from what the detectives said that, despite the existence of the New Zealand Police Sexual Assault Investigation Policy, little agreement exists nationwide concerning police practice and procedures. Much of what occurs at a local level appears to be shaped by individual officers and supervisors, suggesting that such persons may be key figures in achieving future consistent policy implementation.

Comments made by the detectives who had been involved with the Malcolm Rewa investigation indicated that they felt the police had learned a lot from their interactions with the women he attacked. In particular, they felt they gained much greater understanding of how to manage and support rape complainants through investigation and trial processes. In turn, they felt that these women benefited from the police's increased awareness and their provision of dedicated personnel. The victims of a serial rapist are, in fact, likely to receive optimal police treatment because they conform so well to the 'real' rape scenario, and are essential tools for the police to apprehend the offender, in cases which attract high public and media attention. The next chapter presents the views of the women themselves as they reflect on their experiences with the police.

6

Perfect Victims/Perfect Policing? In the Words of the Women

To a man, rape may possibly be considered a myth, or else an insidious lie, dreamt up to entrap him, or both of these; to a woman it is neither myth nor lie, it is a frightening reality.

(Muriel Schulz, quoted in Mills, 1991, p. 207)

Introduction

In 1998, serial rapist Malcolm Rewa stood trial for a total of 45 counts involving 27 women whom he had attacked between 1987 and 1996, with all but two of these attacks occurring within suburbs of Auckland city. His trial lasted three months, at the end of which Rewa was convicted on a majority of counts, mostly for Sexual Violation by Rape, against 25 of the women.

In the months after the trial, I was privileged indeed to be given the opportunity to meet with some of the women whom Rewa attacked.[46] They were keen to tell their stories, and to see some positive outcomes emerge from the ordeals to which they had been subjected. The result was that I interviewed 14 of these women, obtaining in-depth qualitative material relating to their experiences with the police and trial, the effects of the attack and their recovery processes.

Methodology

At a rape conference in 1996, a senior detective told me that he thought the women whom Rewa had attacked would be excellent to interview for my research on rape. Unfortunately the trial was still a long way off so the women would not be free to speak until after that, even if they wanted to.

Two years later this same detective phoned me. His message was brief and to the point – the trial is over, the women are moving on with their lives, and some are keen to see something positive come out of this experience. Would I like to meet with them? He gave me one woman's phone number to contact, having already obtained her permission to do so, and with her cooperation an initial meeting was held at her place between myself and five of the women. Together we decided to extend my research to include their input, with several of the women offering to review my existing interview schedule and adapt it to their own experiences.

Also discussed at the meeting were practical issues concerning, for example, whether and how to contact women not at the meeting, and where and when to hold the interviews. The woman who was hosting the meeting that afternoon, Patricia, offered her place as an interview venue and sent a brief report of the meeting to others who had attended a post-trial lunch at her place. These women were asked if they were interested in hearing more about the research and, if so, their permission was sought for me to be given their contact details. A policewoman who had been extensively involved in supporting the women through the trial attempted to contact the remaining women to see if they were interested in hearing about the research. This was to ensure that, if possible, every woman was given the opportunity to participate if she wished.

From these contacts I had 18 names to follow-up. The remainder had, in most cases, left the country, apart from one woman who wanted no further contact about the case and another whom the policewoman decided not to contact because of her disturbed mental state. Most of the women spoken to initially agreed to participate, apart from three women who changed their decision between the time of the initial contact and the time of the proposed interview.

One woman, for instance, decided once the Burdett[47] murder retrial was over that she wanted to leave it all behind and changed her mind about being interviewed the following month. Another woman made a time to be interviewed, did not show up, and when I rang raged down the phone at me. All I could do was validate that this had to be her choice, that there was no compulsion and that it was important that she decide what was best for her. While I felt that I managed to respond clearly and positively to her, I found her verbal abuse of me profoundly distressing and disturbing, as a journal entry from that day reflects:

> I feel so sad tonight, like the whole size of this project and all the pain Rewa has inflicted has just bowled me over. How can one man cause so much suffering, so much anguish? It's been really hard today and I've wondered if I should be doing this at all. When one woman screamed down the phone at me and said Rewa had taken over enough of her life and she didn't want to talk to me or have any more to do with it, I just felt shattered. I cried and felt guilty and felt like she was so angry with me, but then she can yell at me and make me disappear but she could never yell at Rewa and make him vanish, or yell at the police and get them to leave her alone. But that is how I make sense of it tonight.

Fifteen women were interviewed in total; this number included fourteen of the twenty-seven women whose cases were heard in the 1998 trial, plus a woman whom Rewa had been convicted of raping in 1975 who was called to appear as a witness in the later trial.

The interviews tended to be emotionally intense and, despite the subject matter, were also quite uplifting, for both interviewee and interviewer. In order to minimise potential stress for the women, I was careful not to ask questions about the sexual assaults themselves; however, in some cases the woman herself chose to disclose aspects of this in the course of the interview. I was also keenly aware of the importance of maintaining a clear definition of my role as a researcher/interviewer so as not to be perceived by the women as a counsellor, nor to take on that role myself. At the close of each interview, I checked out with the woman how she was feeling, whether she had someone she could ring if it later became apparent that the interview had stirred up issues for her, and ensured I had contact numbers available to pass on if required. As it turned out, all of the women had their own supports – partners, friends or counsellors – in place. One woman, for instance, had felt shaky before the interview and rescheduled it to allow time for her to meet with her counsellor first. Another arrived in a slightly distressed state, insisted that she wanted to go ahead, then sobbed on and off throughout the interview. After the interview we spent some time discussing the possible need for her to return to counselling and I ensured that she was able to check that her partner had arrived home before she left. Many of the women commented afterwards that they experienced the interview positively and it helped them both in terms of gaining a sense of closure as well as appreciating the extent of the progress and recovery they had made.

With the women's permission, the interviews were all subsequently transcribed to facilitate analysis. A separate file was created for each of the women containing my interview notes, the transcript and notes from her police file. This material I then analysed by identifying themes and issues in the women's accounts and experiences.

The remainder of this chapter presents a profile of the women and an overview of their feelings concerning the ways in which the police responded to their victimisation.

Profile of the women

The women whom Malcolm Rewa attacked ranged in age from 15 to 43 years of age. Table 6.1 shows the ages of the total number of women whose cases went to trial, compared with the ages of the women who were interviewed for this research. Although women in each age group were interviewed, proportionately more of Rewa's older victims were included in the interview sample than those aged under 20. This is probably a result of the fact that

Table 6.1   Ages of the women at time of attack

Ages of the women	Number in each age group	Ages of the women interviewed
15 and under 20 years	5	1
20–29 years	7	4
30–39 years	10	5
40–45 years	5	4
Total	27	14*

Note: * Excludes the woman attacked in 1975 for whom Rewa had already been convicted.

Table 6.2   Counts of indictment against Rewa

Offence	Number of counts in total	Counts involving the women interviewed
Sexual Violation by Rape	32	15
Attempted Sexual Violation by Rape	2	2
Assault with Intent to Commit Sexual Violation	5	2
Aggravated Wounding	3	0
Abduction	2	1
Murder	1	0
Total	45	20

the younger women had fewer attachments or dependants and were more transient, and therefore harder to locate following the trial. Police said some women had in fact moved overseas, and one young woman returned to her homeland. Twelve of those interviewed identified themselves as New Zealand European, and two as Māori or part-Māori. Two of the women were full-time mothers; three were full- or part-time students, and the remainder were employed, many in professional or managerial positions.

In terms of when the incident occurred, seven of the women interviewed were attacked between 1989 and 1992 and seven were attacked between 1993 and 1996. Rewa stood trial on 20 different counts relating to these 14 women – 10 of Sexual Violation by Rape (in addition to which, he was charged with raping three of the women twice and one three times); two of Attempted Sexual Violation by Rape; two of Assault with Intent to Commit Sexual Violation; and one of Abduction. Table 6.2 lists these in comparison with the total counts for which Rewa was indicted.

Police responses to women victims of a serial attacker

When I first discussed with police personnel the prospect of interviewing some of the Rewa victims, I was impressed by the detectives' descriptions of the ways in which they sought to support these women, especially through the trial process. Rewa was not the talkative, cooperative offender that Joseph Thompson had been[48] and it was clear that a difficult court case lay ahead. The police assigned several dedicated complainant officers whose prime responsibility was to liaise with and support the women in the lead-up to the trial and during its process. Considerable effort was spent in preparing the women for their appearance in court. This included such measures as arranging an individual meeting for each woman with the prosecution team and taking care to 'match' the women with whichever one of the three crown prosecutors it was felt she would have the greater rapport. A room was set aside for the women at court to provide them with private space, and steps taken to try to familiarise them with court layout and procedures.

The additional care being taken began earlier in the process for some of the women. Once it was established that a serial rapist appeared to be involved, measures were adopted to maximise the opportunity for the collection of evidence and to provide good support for the victims from the point of their initial contact with the police. Part of this process involved the police being open to hearing what the women needed and being responsive to their concerns. One detective commented afterwards that he and his colleagues were on a 'learning curve' throughout this process as they struggled to provide the women with optimal levels of support. He commented also that

> The kind of treatment these women got was the kind every woman who's been raped should get.

This remark prompted me to consider whether or not it might be useful to ask these women to describe police processes from their perspective. If these were the women whom the police had tried their hardest to 'get it right' with, what was the outcome? What worked, from the women's point of view, and were there any gaps or omissions which still needed attention? These women largely fitted the stereotype of the 'perfect' victim in that the majority were attacked in their homes, whilst sleeping, by an unknown assailant who forced entry to their house.[49] Added to this was their status as victims of a serial attacker, which provided the police with an additional impetus to achieve excellent service delivery. What, then, could be learned from the study of these modified police processes? In other words, did the 'perfect' victims feel they had received 'perfect' policing? If so, how could this inform future police planning and service delivery to victims of rape and sexual assault. If not, what would, from a victim's perspective, have made it 'perfect'?

The women's perspectives of the police response

Overall, the women rated the police highly: their views were divided equally between those who stated they were 'very satisfied' and those who said they were 'satisfied' with the police response.[50] Their overall assessment, however, was in nine cases somewhat better than how they rated the police in relation to their initial experiences of reporting and statement-taking. While only one woman declared herself 'dissatisfied', eight others said they felt that the treatment they received from the police improved over time. As the police themselves indicated, the measures they implemented leading up to and during the trial were favourably received and appear generally to have increased the satisfaction ratings they received. Analysis of the women's experiences of the specific measures and procedures adopted is, therefore, instructive in providing feedback for police personnel in the planning and implementation of victims' policies, particularly with regard to sexual assault victims. What is also significant, however, is that the experiences of the women were not uniform. The obvious dimension on which this is apparent relates to women who were attacked earlier in Rewa's 'career': they tended to be treated more routinely than his later victims. In addition, the same policy or procedural guideline is not necessarily implemented in a uniform manner, nor does it impact identically on different victims, or on victims at different stages of the recovery process. These dimensions add a complexity and richness to the analysis of the interview material which follows.

The transcripts of the interviews were read and appraised, using grounded theory analysis (Glaser and Strauss, 1967) to elicit the women's responses and identify key themes arising from their experiences of police procedures. These themes are presented below, illustrated with quotes and examples provided by the women.

Positive aspects of the women's treatment

I. General police attitude

Belief

The majority of the women confirmed that, as one might expect from the features associated with these attacks, the police never appeared to doubt or disbelieve the woman's account of what happened. Jennifer's[51] response was typical.

> I was reasonably happy with the way I was treated, with respect, there was never any doubt that what I was reporting wasn't true or anything. I never felt threatened or anything.

As noted in previous chapters, police belief in a victim's credibility has frequently been related to such variables as the perpetrator being a stranger; lack of victim provocation (e.g. the victim being asleep at the time of the attack); victim resistance and the extent of visible physical injuries sustained; and victim credibility as assessed by factors such as occupation and socio-economic status (Du Mont *et al.*, 2003; Harris and Grace, 1999; Kelly, 2002; Lees and Gregory, 1993; Stace, 1983). From a police perspective, most of Rewa's victims scored positively on all these traits. Even one woman, Karen, who had known Rewa previously, through a mutual friend, felt that this did not intrude on the police's response to her:

> There was never any doubt, to me it appeared there was never any doubt in anyone's mind that I'd been raped by someone who'd broken into the house, it was cut and dry which was good from my point of view....
>
> I don't know whether it is the circumstances of mine that made it obvious that there was nothing to disbelieve, the fact that I went to a policeman's house afterwards probably helped. I never at any stage felt that there was any doubt about what had happened, I never at any stage felt that the fact that I knew Malcolm Rewa influenced the way that the police dealt with me, as far as integrity goes, I only have the highest praise for them really. I don't think that's necessarily true for everybody. I think I'm aware of those feminist issues, I was aware of those things.

There were, however, some exceptions to this overall trend, which are examined later in this chapter when outlining negative aspects of the women's treatment.

Support

Many of the women commented on the importance for them of feeling supported by the police, and of feeling that the police were on their side. Such support could be evidenced in practical ways at times: for example, by the police providing the women with lifts to and from the police station or court; and in one case by their lending Isabel, who was a student, a mobile phone so that she could continue her studies and be called when she was required at court, rather than spend time waiting down at the courtroom. Isabel commented that, given the high emotional costs involved in testifying, such a facility was 'one of the perks'.

> The side effect of this was that I used the mobile phone quite a lot to have lengthy conversations with my cousin and I might have rung up my husband and my mother as well. So, I was a bit naughty really, I was talking on the phone so much they might not have been able to get through! Some of the other students have mobile phones, why shouldn't I? Walking around on campus talking to a hidden friend, it's really good! (laughs)

Practical gestures such as this were appreciated by the women and helped them to feel as if they mattered and their evidence was important. Feeling *emotionally* supported by the police was also mentioned by some of the women. One way in which the women said this was evident lay simply in police reliability – that the police returned phone calls promptly, and did what they said they would do. Ann related how she felt about this.

> I think the police did really well. They were always on call if you wanted to find out what's happening and you'd ring up and you'd either get Chook[52] or one of the other guys, and they'd say oh, Ann, no, she's off doing something but I'll get her to call you as soon as she gets back and they'd always do that, you know, when they're wrapped up in such a big case like that .... I think they treated us well.

Ann felt that it may have been easy for individual complainants to become lost in a court case as large as this one; on the other hand, the very fact that this was such a big, high profile case may have prompted the police to be especially attentive to the needs of their principal witnesses.

Being validated by the police was specifically mentioned as important by several of the women. Shelley, for example, recounted how when she phoned the police she was afraid that Rewa was still hiding somewhere in the house. She feared that he was waiting for her in the wardrobe and wondered how the young, male attending officer would respond when she asked him to go and check for her. Shelley said she was very appreciative of the fact that he appeared sensitive to her feelings and went to check without looking at her as if she was crazy.

> I believe that he thought I was being totally appropriate in asking him to do that and he did it without any raising of eyebrows or anything.

Other women mentioned the importance of gestures from the police, such as having their presence acknowledged whenever they walked into the court. Patricia observed of the lead investigator:

> Every single time you walked in, whoever walked in, he stood up in there and he greeted them. Yeah, that was part of it, it was all good stuff, the treatment that we got, it was all really good.

Patricia went on to speculate regarding the police:

> What were they trying to achieve by treating all of the victims so well? Positiveness (sic) and confidence, wasn't it, so they could get up on the stand and be confident and trust in who they are, and that's what happened.

And that is what needs to happen from the minute of the attack....It happens from day one, it doesn't happen from when they realise that they are trying to hang this dork at the other end....Afterwards it needs to happen to get that trust, that positiveness in every little thing, and you do that by getting it right with the little things and all of a sudden you've got it in the big things as well.

For Karen, it was important to have the police acknowledge the feelings she had towards Rewa and help her put these in perspective. She spoke appreciatively of the way in which she felt supported when she went to court to see Rewa take the stand.

I got there, it must have been just before a break. The courtroom had sort of a barrier, so I'd walked in the door and down the side I could just kind of see him[Rewa] from the side and I felt really aggravated, really nervous about it. It was like I'm going to see him, I can't believe it, I didn't know what it was going to be like. There were a lot of police there, hanging off his every word. Since it was very early in the piece he was probably telling the sad story about how his mother had died when he was a child and getting quite upset and all the rest. It must have been just before the morning tea break I think, anyway, then the judge said it's morning tea time. I'd sat down and I went to get up and I can remember standing quite close to him but I wasn't in his line of vision and I just wanted to kill him, I felt so overcome with emotion and being so close to him, I just wanted to kill him, I just wanted to scream, I really wanted to just abuse the hell out of him.

As I was standing there, feeling all this anger come up and threatening to overtake me, Steve Rutherford[53] appeared, grabbed me, walked me out and said to me 'It's not worth it', he said, 'if you yell out, it would be you that gets removed from the courtroom, not him. The bastard's not worth it.' It was like, it kind of dissipated, it was like, thank you Steve. So, then I went out and had a cuppa tea.

They're all so matey, the police. It's a real boys' thing. They're all joking and carrying on – we had Steve Rutherford making us cups of tea, he's probably never made a cup of tea for a woman in his life, I'd say! They looked after us, I didn't feel like I was up there by myself or that I shouldn't have been there or that I was in the way or anything like that. I felt that if I wanted to be there, they were happy for me to be there sort of thing.

Other women also echoed Karen's sentiments, expressing their amazement at times that they received such supportive treatment from some of the big, burly, 'bear-like' (as one woman said) male officers involved in the investigation.

Place of interview

Several women also referred to their appreciation of the police being sensitive regarding the most appropriate place to conduct interviews with them. Not all the women had identical feelings regarding this, placing the responsibility on the police to determine the most appropriate venue, in consultation with the individual woman concerned. For some, it was important that the police travel to them and interview them in their home, while others preferred the option of discussing details of the incident in, what was for them, the more anonymous setting of a police station. Gabriel, for instance, noted that:

> I especially appreciated the personal visits in my own home. I felt good about the detective coming to see me and me not having to go to the police station, you know, that it was done in my own home. That the time was arranged before hand, when she would come over. I felt really comfortable about that.

Jennifer felt that, from an evidential point of view, it was useful to make her statement to the police at the crime scene, although acknowledged that this could be hard.

> J: I think it's a lot more vivid for you when you're standing in the house, you remember more things than sitting in a police room or an office or something and just trying to remember it all the way through.
>
> JJ:[54] So how was it for you to go back and do that?
>
> J: People have a real expectation of how some people ....I suppose to a certain degree, you're probably still a bit shocked, still in a bit of shell shock, it was okay, it didn't worry me. To me it didn't feel any worse than sitting in her office and telling her, but I could certainly see that for some people that might be quite different.

Sensitivity to children's vulnerabilities emerged as a potential source of concern, with some of the women who were mothers expressing their appreciation when the police were careful in the comments made and questions asked while children were present.

Being seen as a person by the police

The earlier rape research I conducted had identified the vital importance attached by complainants to feeling that they were viewed by the police as persons, not case numbers (Jordan, 1998a). This sentiment was reiterated by the women interviewed in relation to Rewa's attacks, and may have been heightened in significance for some because they shared a common offender and feared they could be reduced to a number. Helen acknowledged this when she praised the police team involved with the investigation and the efforts they went to:

> H: I felt sorry for the police in terms of they were so understaffed, they were bloody tired, they were. They were good, they were really good, I couldn't fault them for the amount of staffing they had and the amount of time they put in. You weren't just a witness, you were actually a person to them, which was nice, so they were good, I can't fault them.
>
> JJ: That's really good.
>
> H: Yeah, it is good, I was pleasantly surprised really!
>
> JJ: Had you thought that you might be just a witness?
>
> H: Yeah. Number 202, or whatever I am (laughter).

Helen noted also how, in the lead-up to the trial, it was important for the prosecutors also to see the women as individuals. Following meetings arranged by the police for the women to meet the prosecution team, she related:

> ... even the crown prosecutor said, 'From seeing you people', which the police initiated, 'from seeing you, we've realised that we're actually dealing with real people here', rather than 'we've got a mass of 27 bloody women we've got to try to get through court', y'know, sort of thing.

Continuity

An aspect often mentioned by victims concerning their interactions with police relates to officer continuity being viewed as desirable (Gilmore and Pittman, 1993; Gregory and Lees, 1999; Jordan, 1998a). Complainants whose case is passed on to other investigators without explanation report feeling aggrieved – unless, of course, they feel better served by the officer to whom they were reassigned! Generally, however, victims express a desire for continuity and the opportunity to establish an ongoing relationship of trust with individual police. This issue was recognised and specifically addressed by detectives involved with the Rewa investigation. While some of Rewa's earlier victims did experience a lack of continuity in their dealings with police, efforts were made to correct this with the later victims. Some were assigned one primary officer to deal with from the time of reporting, and in the long (almost two year) lead-up to the trial, all the women were dealt with by dedicated complainant officers, as outlined below.

Specific measures introduced as part of the Rewa investigation and trial

At least one of the women victims involved in the Rewa case challenged the police regarding what she perceived as their tardy communication at times.

Trial dates were being set and deferred and changes were occurring which were not always being communicated to the women, and she pointed this out to the investigation team. She said she felt gratified by their response, which indicated a willingness to try to see the situation from the victim's perspectives.

Specific measures were introduced by the investigation team aimed at ensuring high levels of victim support and preparation for court. These included the police providing the women with the following.

- Dedicated complainant officers;
- Bulletin letters and updates;
- Pre-trial meetings with the prosecution team.

Each of these measures is addressed below.

Dedicated complainant officers

Dedicated complainant officers comprised, at any one time,[55] two women detectives whose prime responsibility was to liaise with and support the women. These detectives were assigned full time to the investigation team, and given primary responsibility for maintaining regular contact with the complainants, supporting them practically and emotionally, and being an information channel between the victims and the rest of the police and prosecution team.

In Jennifer's case, which was one of Rewa's last attacks before his arrest, she was introduced to one of the dedicated officers, Sandy, the day following the incident.

> And at that stage, she made it very clear that the plan was that she would be the only person, as such, that I dealt with in any going back and forward, that it would all come through her generally.

She commented that, whereas:

> … at the time you just go along with the flow …. Looking back now, I'm pleased that it was only ever one person, except that Sandy left.

All of the women, however, said that although initially they may have been dealt with by numerous officers, often manifesting a range of abilities and temperaments, it was useful to have greater continuity as the trial date approached. For many, these women detectives played a vital role, and in some cases were chosen by the women to be their support person when they gave evidence in court.

Letters and updates

In response to concerns expressed earlier in the trial lead-up period by some of the women, the police began to issue occasional, bulletin-type letters.

These were posted to all the women in an attempt to keep them informed of developments, explain delays in trial dates, and provide revised time frames and other information. Many of the women commented favourably concerning this practice, and felt that these letters were useful for the information they contained as well as in signifying recognition of the importance of the women to the case overall.

> S: The letters were very good at staying in contact with you. There was one not long after... once you've been through all that stage of identifying things, there was a letter that came and said this is what we think is going to happen blah, blah, blah.... Leading up to the trial, before they actually got in contact with you, there were another two letters. I think, it was good, it told you what was happening and when they expected it to happen etc, etc, and always a 'please feel free to contact us', with their numbers, if you need anything.
>
> JJ: So would you say from that, that you feel like you were kept informed of the progress of events by the police?
>
> S: Yeah, yeah, I would, it was pretty good.
>
> JJ: That sounds...
>
> S: Quite professional really, isn't it! (laughter) That's not like a government department at all really!

Pre-trial meetings

Concern has been expressed in many jurisdictions regarding the possible dangers arising from prosecutors not meeting complainants before the day of the trial (Bargen and Fishwick, 1995; Gregory and Lees, 1999; Kelly, 2002). Criticism has also been expressed by victims involved in court cases of how, in their capacity as witnesses, when they do eventually meet the prosecutor, this is usually in a very rushed manner (McDonald, 1997; Young, 1983).

The size and complexity of the Rewa investigation, coupled with the expectations and demands often voiced by the women themselves, prompted the police to invest greater energy in pre-trial preparation. Several months before the eventual court case, arrangements were made for each woman to meet, on her own, the major police and prosecution team. This meeting enabled her to meet the three different prosecutors involved and establish who she would be most comfortable with in court, as well as providing an opportunity to have any questions she might have about the forthcoming trial answered by some of the key players. One of the dedicated police women detectives accompanied the women for this meeting, and the visit was combined with, where possible, a tour of the courtroom; alternatively, the courtroom visit occurred nearer to the trial date for some women, depending on courtroom availability.

Many of the women welcomed this commitment of time and energy by the police and prosecution team. As well as enabling practical issues to be

resolved, the gesture was interpreted by some as signifying recognition of
the victims' centrality in the forthcoming trial. Gabriel, for example, said she
appreciated the opportunity for pre-trial dialogue with the prosecutor.

> It was more Simon Moore who introduced himself as prosecutor for my
> case and he was just very, very helpful and 'stay for as long as you want,
> come back, call and ask any questions, it is not a problem'. Very helpful,
> and I was there for an hour and he explained quite a lot to me in that time.

Jennifer's comments were typical when she recounted how useful she found
the trial preparation.

> When we went along to the second meeting, we actually went along to
> the courtroom, he [prosecutor] gave you a diagram which you took away
> which said: here will sit dah, dah, dah. Here will sit the jurors, this person
> will be here…. They were very good at that.

Likewise, Frances noted how particularly helpful she found the pre-trial
briefing:

> I suppose the whole thing of going through the courtroom, you know,
> the jury sits here and he'll be here and you'll be here and there's people
> behind you who will be police or reporters…. It gave me a feeling, before
> I even got there, of who would be in the courtroom, where they would
> be and that sort of thing, so that was actually useful, rather than walking
> into a room I'd never been in before and that sort of thing.

Whilst valued as a procedure overall, some aspects associated with these
meetings were criticised in terms of process, a point elaborated on further in
the next section.

After trial function

The constraints of law made it impossible for the women to have much contact with each other, at least until after they had testified in court. Some of
those who attended other court sessions, such as Rewa's evidence on the
stand or the judge's summing-up, began to chat with each other, and on the
night of the jury verdict several of the women sat with and supported each
other. What many felt, however, was that the other women were their present but unseen companions. Once the trial was over, and Rewa had been
sentenced, a luncheon was organised at Patricia's apartment for all those
who had been closely involved in the trial. As well as any of the women who
wanted to attend, invitations were extended to the police and prosecution
team, along with their spouses and partners. The luncheon provided the
opportunity for a collective debrief, as well as being an occasion to celebrate

and congratulate each other for surviving the court ordeal. Not all of the women were able to, or necessarily wanted to, attend this function, with about 15 of the total being present. Those who did go spoke favourably of the occasion and the contribution it made to their own sense of closure to all that preceded it. Shelley, for example, in acknowledging the role played by the police in her post-rape recovery process, spoke of the importance of this occasion.

No, the police certainly had a role to play in that and they were very ... like certainly, when I was in court, they were very positive and said I did a really good job, all that jazz. It was really good to see at the end, at this after match function, that they were all here. That was really important to me, to see them, you know, with their wives and they were all there. It was a kind of nice round off really.

Negative aspects of the women's treatment

While the women I interviewed all rated the police positively overall, nevertheless most rated at least one or more aspects of their treatment negatively. Identification of the negative features experienced provides the opportunity to develop a more textured picture of police–complainant interactions and the factors important in shaping these dynamics.

Not being believed

Whilst most of the women were relieved that the police appeared to have no difficulty believing that they were legitimate victims, not all of Rewa's victims were responded to in this way. Kathleen, for instance, related how she felt judged and disbelieved by the police detectives who interviewed her shortly after she was raped.

K: Well, about three days after it happened I was up at the station and they [detectives] turned around and said, 'Come on, Kathleen, we know you were making all this up, we know you were having an affair and you were having sex that morning and it got a bit rough and you just made all this up, just so your husband doesn't find out ... '. My God! What I said to them I probably can't repeat, but I told them what to do with themselves. So I walked home with them literally following me in the police car saying 'We're sorry, we're sorry, blah blah blah', and when I got home they would be hanging off the phone saying, 'We know that's not what happened' and 'We just had to see what your reaction was and if you hadn't reacted like that then we would have been a bit suspicious ... '.

JJ: So how did you feel?

K: Oh, I felt like punching them! I really felt like: My God! You know....

JJ: So that just came completely out of the blue for you, so until then you felt like…

K: Yep I've giving them all the information, they are getting on with it, they are keen, they are on to it and then this sort of drops out of the sky! In my wildest imagination I couldn't have come up with anything stupider…. I felt so insecure, they don't believe me, my God. I said to them, 'Look', I said, 'that's it. I've had enough of you guys. If you won't help me, I'll catch him and then you'll be arresting me' sort of thing. I was so annoyed, I was so absolutely frustrated, but that was only like for that day….

Kathleen was the victim of one of the earlier rapes for which Rewa stood trial in 1998, and it was evident from talking with her that she and her partner (later her husband) were initially viewed as having questionable credibility by the police. She believes this arose principally from negative police perceptions of her partner's involvement in drugs and the music scene. The police thought that, at minimum, her partner knew the identity of the man who raped her and suggested that he had been directly implicated in her attack. Not surprisingly, such insinuations impacted harshly on the pair's relationship, with Kathleen admitting that it took a long time before she was convinced that her partner had, in fact, had nothing to do with the attack. In her case, DNA evidence was obtained and linked to Rewa when he was finally arrested in 1996.

Similar issues associated with belief and credibility were evident in the case of another of Rewa's victims. Several of the police detectives involved in the investigation themselves told me about the police response to a woman raped by Rewa in 1987.[56] She was a young Māori woman, with gang affiliations to Highway 61 (the gang to which Rewa was affiliated), and with some previous criminal convictions herself. She actually named Rewa as the rapist but he had arranged an alibi to try to cover himself. Police at the time viewed his version of events as having greater credibility than hers and the case was not proceeded with.[57] Despite having a named offender in 1987, a further known 26 women were raped or sexually assaulted by Rewa before this woman's case was eventually heard in the 1998 trial, at which Malcolm Rewa was finally convicted of the crimes committed against her (Fleming, 1998).

Attitude of police

How the women felt the police perceived them and behaved towards them was of vital significance. Some of the women commented that they did not always feel that the police they dealt with were comfortable interviewing rape victims. At times they felt that police discomfort and embarrassment prevented officers from being able to ask the right questions, particularly in the case of a few, but not all, male officers. As Karen commented:

> He knew that there were ways to treat rape victims and things to ask and things not to ask and he was aware of that, but perhaps he didn't have it quite integrated into his interviewing skills.

Others spoke also of feeling like they were being treated a certain way:

> ...because on the police investigator's manual, on page 16, it said...

Several women also expressed concern that at times they felt the police viewed them judgmentally. For example, Kathleen was asked what she had worn to bed the night Rewa raped her. She told the police she had worn a camisole top and underwear to bed and recalled:

> I remember one of them saying to me, oh, is that all you wore to bed? That sort of male attitude – maybe if you had worn a winceyette nightie it might not have happened.

Interview environment

The environment in which police interviews are conducted can often be extremely important for victims. Several of the women interviewed said they were, in fact, appalled at how terrible the conditions were – as Shelley commented:

> It was absolutely disgusting. The chairs were falling apart.... We had to use our mobile phones. The window was broken, the air conditioning was half hanging off the wall, I mean it was third world, something you imagine you'd see in Istanbul or South Africa. And that actually had a huge impact on my mental alertness I think.

Some complained that, when they were taken to the police station to give their statement, they were interviewed in the same dingy, cell-type rooms that police use for interviewing criminal offenders. Such rooms were often originally designed to be intimidatory and produce feelings of sensory deprivation and isolation (Kassin and Fong, 1999), clearly rendering them of debatable merit as a comfortable environment in which to conduct the sensitive interviewing of victims of trauma.

Gabriel pointed out how she felt affected by the implicit messages of power and control conveyed in the interview setting, observing:

> I don't think they [interviews] should be done behind a desk. Do you know what I mean? It's like going into an office and someone going. 'Okay, well tell us about your rape thing'. It's like the power is in that

person's hands. You know, because they've got their desk and their pen and their box of tissues and you're sitting there, in this chair that you've never sat in before, in a room that you don't know, and I just, I don't know, I tend to feel that there should be some kind of space that is comfortable for complainants. And there isn't.

Karen also noted the inadequacies of the interview environment:

I think in an ideal world, it would be really good to have the interview take place, to have the medical and interview take place at some place that is a bit more comfortable. That would be the ideal scenario, rather than being taken to Central, which isn't a very attractive, user friendly place – and it's full of policemen!

Other women spoke of the lack of privacy and safety they felt whilst at the police station. Interview rooms often seemed to be semi-public areas, with interruptions being frequent. Suzanne felt particularly aggrieved by the lack of respect and understanding she experienced in this regard from the women detective who interviewed her.

S: She took me up into this room that had about a dozen desks that the police work in, and sat me in one of these and started doing my statement. She took three personal phone calls and continued to talk, I couldn't believe it. I told Chook because I just couldn't believe that she did this, took *three personal phone calls* while I was doing the statement with her. She continued to chat on, one of them she talked to for about 15 minutes while I was sitting waiting, about what she'd been doing the previous day and some friends that they'd met, and she just continued and I was just sitting there thinking, I just don't believe this! If I had been in my normal state of mind, and not been through what I'd just been through, I would have said. 'Excuse me, what the hell do you think you're doing?' I just couldn't believe that she was doing it, especially for a female to do it. [Emphasis in original]
JJ: Did it feel somehow worse in a way that it was another woman who was being so insensitive to what you'd just gone through?
S: Yeah it did, she should have known how I felt and she obviously didn't care.

Helen recalled her discomfort at interruptions that occurred when she was being interviewed by one of the dedicated complainant officers.

There was one point, these police guys kept bursting in to the room. She [detective] didn't have her own room to do the interviews in, and she was sharing with some policemen. I just felt really stared at by them, so that wasn't nice. I could tell that Sandy was pretty angry about them, she'd say, 'Excuse me boys, but I'm conducting an interview here, do you think you could leave?', and they were like. 'Got this work to do'. They knew what I was there for, so that was not good. I felt very degraded by that, I guess. So that wasn't good....

Helen also mentioned the vulnerability she felt when going to get herself a drink at the police station.

I went to make myself a cuppa tea or something because ... and the only place to make a cuppa tea was in the officers' mess, so there's a lot of people again around there. It would have been nice to have a little room that had a sofa in it, and a coffee cup, something so that you've got a bit of privacy. Because again, you've got this room full of men, big bulky men, and you're feeling pretty vulnerable at the time, and I think in terms of ... they weren't offensive or anything, it was just you're feeling vulnerable, you think everyone's looking at you, you've just been attacked, raped, you know, you feel yuck, and that just makes it worse really. You want to hide, so why not let someone, just at that time, just give them the comfort they need.

Other women also expressed discomfort at the way in which they were scrutinised by other officers, feeling surveyed as 'Rewa's latest victim', and spoke of how degraded they often felt simply walking through the station or in the police canteen. In Marie's case, she felt acutely embarrassed walking through a busy police station:

I had to go into Auckland Central for photographs.... They didn't have photographers who came to me, I had to go there. I had to go up several floors to the police photographer. That was terrible, it was awful. Walking in through the door, everybody looked. I did look pretty awful. That was really humiliating having to do that. Because I had marks around my neck where he (Rewa) tried to strangle me.

Similarly, Connie recalled how vulnerable she felt being taken into the police station dressed in her night attire:

C: They took me down to the police station in my nightie, that's exactly how I was dressed, in my nightie. I was dying to go to the toilet. I was dying to have a wash, but I wasn't allowed. They [police] said, 'No, you can't. Look, please, if there's semen evidence that we can get ...'. They took me down to the police station. I can't remember how long I was there, it seemed to be ages. I was not in any particular private area, because it must have been the start to the change of a shift, because people seemed to be coming and going and sort of staring at me.

JJ: How did that feel?

C: Lonely, just lonely.

Victim seen as number/case

As has been noted, the Rewa investigation and subsequent trial was one of the biggest rape inquiries ever held in New Zealand. Mostly the women said they felt the police managed it well in terms of treating each woman as an individual, but there were occasional slip-ups. Whilst possibly inevitable in a case of this magnitude, nevertheless such errors impacted harshly on the women involved.

A good example of this occurred when Karen rang and gave her name to the detective who answered the phone. He replied,

'Oh, you're number 61, aren't you?'. That was my house number. I said, 'yeah, lovely'. It was a small thing but it was like, 'Oh yes, thank you very much!'

Other women commented how remarks made, at times, by professionals involved in the case conveyed a sense of there being a stereotypical 'rape victim' whom they were being assessed and compared against. Thus Helen said.

H: It was even brought home to me, the perceptions are, even amongst these people, that women who get raped are not very intelligent, come from lower class backgrounds, are asking for it, are either prostitutes or dah, dah, dah ... and that's what they're saying, which is not good in a way, but that's the perception, I guess, out there. So they were saying, actually there's a lot of intelligent women coming through here.

JJ: So they sounded a bit surprised in a way when they said that?

H: Absolutely. But that's a social perception, you know that it's there. It's not just a belief, it's a truth, as far as I can see.

Police minimised attack and effects

Once the attacker was suspected or confirmed to be Malcolm Rewa, the women usually felt that they were well looked after and responded to by the police. However, some said such concern was not so evident while the attacker's identity was still being established. In Frances' case, she was attacked while she was out running early one morning. She managed to avoid being raped, and felt that the police initially trivialised the incident. Frances felt they dismissed the attack as being no big deal, when it clearly was for her and left her feeling shocked and highly vulnerable. She was, however, determined not to be put off running and began instead to run with others. Less than a fortnight later she was running in the same area with her companions when they came across a woman who had just been attacked. Frances told the police that it sounded like the same offender, and, after further police investigation, Rewa was charged with both these attacks.[58]

One of the most potentially fraught issues to arise in the context of rape reporting derives from the victim's confusion, or at times denial, as to whether or not she has been raped. The likelihood of such confusion occurring is understandable, given that while legal definitions assert black and white boundaries, the realities of sexual assault range along a complex continuum of behaviours. Research evidence suggests it is therefore not uncommon for women to be hazy as to whether or not they were raped, and to tend towards minimisation of their attack (Kelly, 1988; Kelly and Radford, 1996). In such circumstances, effective law enforcement will be dependent on the skills and sensitivities of investigators cognisant of these processes.

Suzanne hoped for such a response from the detective who interviewed her, but felt she received the opposite:

> I remember telling her about how he was pushing himself in, he couldn't get into me and it wasn't until later in the court that I realised that that wasn't recorded.... She focussed more on the attack side rather than on the sexual side, when both of it was important. She just focussed on that one side of things, and I think she wasn't really interested in it, to be quite honest...it was trivialised. I really just don't think she was interested. To her, it was just a minor assault because that's the way the statement ended up being. I just don't think she was interested.

Suzanne felt particularly aggrieved that, had the detective been more sensitive to what she was saying, she would have immediately been sent for a medical examination.

> I'm very, very disappointed and angry with the way it was handled, and also anybody in their right mind should have been sent for a medical after that, and she didn't! I told her what he'd done. I remember saying to her, in front of ___ [flatmate], I said to her, 'Look, I don't know exactly what he's done but it's really revolting, I feel damp'. I said, 'I really need to go the toilet' and she said 'Go', and so I went and she never sent me or anything and I said to her in front of ___ before I left, 'Am I okay to go home and have a shower?', and she said 'Yep, off you go, we'll be in touch tomorrow'. So I went home and I lay in the bath for an hour after I'd rung ___ (fiancee), and [he] was arranging to catch a flight up at this stage, and I lay in the bath for an hour because I felt so disgustingly dirty, and it wasn't until that afternoon [he] came up and he said, 'Have you had a check done?' I said 'No, they told me not to worry about it'. He said he couldn't

believe it, so he then spoke to the detective and I dealt with [different detective] and he was a brilliant detective, and he couldn't believe it either. They came and got me the next day, but it was a bit after the event.

What Suzanne's experience highlights also is the immense importance of the police role in assessing complainant testimony. For all sorts of reasons, a rape/sexual assault victim may minimise what has happened to her. This could be for reasons of psychological self-protection, cultural shame, fear, sexual reticence – in many ways, the reason is irrelevant. For the detective interviewing her, it is important to find ways of establishing rapport so as to obtain the fullest account possible. The detail may not emerge immediately, in which case erring on the side of caution is advisable when it comes to decisions about, for example, arranging a forensic medical examination. This decision needs to be taken by the police, not left to the victim to specify. As Suzanne said,

> If I was in my normal frame of mind, I should have questioned it further, but I thought, here's the professionals dealing with this situation.

Pre-trial preparation

One of the positive features identified in the previous major section related to the efforts made by the police and prosecution to prepare these women for the rigours of the court trial. Considerable energy was expended in trying to familiarise the women with courtroom procedures and supporting them through this time.

The pre-trial meetings that were held with the police and crown prosecutors were viewed as a positive initiative by the women. However, while the good aspect for them was that these meetings occurred, several expressed reservations regarding the way in which these were arranged. Criticism was specifically voiced about the lack of advance information given to each woman concerning the size and scale of these meetings.

Karen described the process leading up to this meeting:

> I got this letter from Steve Rutherford saying you're coming to meet the crown prosecutors and all the rest. Veronica came and picked me up from work, and we tootle off to the High Court, where I'd never been before. She said to me before we went in, she said, 'I'll just tell you now, there's quite a few people in the room. There's so and so and so…' and rattled off all these names which meant nothing to me.
>
> I walked into this room and there's like eight people, plus Veronica and me, so there was like 10 people in this room. Everyone was sitting not quite in a circle, they had the police here, the lawyers here and it's like…. I'm used to being in meetings and I was really pleased about that, and I'm used to talking at meetings so it doesn't worry me, but I think that for someone

that's not used to talking to a lot of people, it would have been a nightmare, there was way too many people there....

I had no idea who these bloody police were, sort of thing. I later found out they were all the top police from the inquiry and all probably had every right to be there, and certainly the 3 prosecution lawyers did too, but there was too many people. Apparently, I was only about the third one that they saw, and apparently the first person or the second person had really freaked out. She'd walked into this room full of men – *we're not good at walking into rooms full of men*. I think that's probably something that hadn't been thought of. It wasn't great.... I bet they don't do that again. [Emphasis added]

A feeling of daunt when the door to that meeting room opened was mentioned by many of the women. Gabriel referred to it as 'hellishly intimidating',while Frances said:

Well, all I would have needed to be told was 'there's this many police there and these other people' and then I would have known, rather than the door opened and it was, 'oh, look at all these people'.

As well as the measures already mentioned, a room was set aside for the exclusive use of victims and their support persons, in an effort to provide them with a safe space where they could try to relax, give vent to their feelings if need be, and gain some respite from possible intimidation by those supporting Rewa. In practice, this room (which was some distance from the courtroom) was not used as frequently, by some of the women at least, as the police's room. In part this was because of the close team-like environment which was created by the police and sought after by those women who spent longer times at court, often through choice rather than requirement.[59]

The feeling was also expressed by some that the process of preparing the women for court tended to happen when the police felt it needed to, rather than when the women might want this to occur. This prompted Helen to challenge the police to communicate more fully with the women during the lead-up to the trial, noting:

They probably felt that they were doing enough, but you live with something day by day, it's not enough, you need to know this guy is going to be put away or whatever you're feeling and he's not going to be out there, just those little silly things: 'Are you making sure he can't get out?', 'He can't get bail, can he?', because you don't know, I don't know the court system .... Do people like that get out on bail? You know, you don't know that. It would have been nice if there was someone to answer those questions and not feel silly about it.

Later in the interview she referred to her thought sequences once the letter arrived outlining the forthcoming trial:

> Because as soon as I knew I was going, you got the letter, then you start dreaming. It's like, oh my God, he's going to be able to come across there and kill me. You know, again, they're not logical but you want to know that there's ten people between you and him. Because if he can do it once, he can do it again. How do you know he hasn't got a knife, how do you know? Yeah, all really stupid things and maybe that might have helped me a bit to know, there's two bodyguards on either side, there's all these people before he can get to you... which I was told two days before and that's great, but if I had been told when I was actually starting to think about it.... But people can't anticipate if they're not inside your head, I suppose. They must have known from enough women, though, that you're going to have those sort of fears.

Concerns such as these raise questions about whose time frame is being adhered to, whose needs dominate the process and how can these issues best be resolved.

Lack of follow-up after court attendance

In contrast to the women's general appreciation of pre-trial input, strong dissatisfaction was expressed by some that as soon as they had given evidence, it felt as though all support was withdrawn. Whilst some rationalised this as understandable, in that the police and prosecution focus had now shifted to the next witness to take the stand, nevertheless it provoked feelings of betrayal in some women. Shelley expressed this sentiment well when she noted:

> There was no debrief after the court appearance which would have been really important to me. I mean, there you were, the most special person to the prosecutor and for the court and you were like queen for the day. It was very much that, you know, and there was media coverage and you stood in the box and there was all this and then it's like, 'Bye, next one'. A sort of disposable witness really. Just disposable, you know we've – you've done your dash and thanks very much, that's great, goodbye, without a thought to actually, this person's leaving with you know all sorts of things happening to her.

For Shelley and some of the other women, the need to have some kind of debrief arose following their court appearance. This was true for Marie also, who had to manage the added difficulty of taking the stand as the first police witness in the 1998 case, 23 years after Rewa's conviction for attacking her.

She recalls:

> I was quite happy with the way things went, the only thing I would say, I wasn't prepared for afterwards. After I had given evidence, I actually had a dreadful time the next 2 or 3 days, just the let down. I don't know, whether it was all the build up to get me there, I felt there was nothing, I was just left high and dry. Because I was the first witness, I got the impression, it might have been totally incorrect, but I got the impression that they breathed a sigh of relief, 'Oh, we've started, we've had our first witness on the stand, and the trial is under way'. I think they all went off to the pub to celebrate! I got the impression that it was you've been there, done your bit, now that's it, goodbye now, thank you very much. I just felt there was no follow-up. Now whether that should come from them, I don't know. I still needed the contact, I needed to know what was happening. I knew in my mind that they're really busy, they're preparing the next person to go on the stand, I've done my bit now, so they can put me to the side. I just felt that.... I just spent all the Thursday crying, which is probably just reaction. I had to have people with me, I was just a mess and yet I had coped with going in there, I had coped with the week, I had done everything, but nobody really was there for me afterwards.

In Frances' case, however, the time she most acutely felt the need for police/prosecution contact was following the delivery of the verdict. This was because, for her and one other woman, the jury returned Not Guilty verdicts against Rewa. Frances describes how she contacted one of the dedicated women officers that evening:

> F: I rang her because it was late at night when the jury came back in but I was up so I rang her at the courtroom and she told me then.... It was so late at night, she just said, 'Look, I'm really sorry to have to say to you that your verdict was not guilty'. It was a funny feeling, a really strange feeling. My sister in law said to me, it's almost now that you actually need to be speaking to someone about it. In those few days afterwards, it was a real feeling of ... that I did put it all behind me then it all got opened up again, and now it's left really open. It's not so bad now as it was when it first happened.
>
> JJ: In terms of that, did you get to talk to anyone, the police or the prosecutors afterwards, did they sit you down at all and give you some explanation about what they think the jury's reasoning may have been or anything like that?
>
> F: No.
>
> JJ: So in an ideal world, what would you have liked to have happened?
>
> F: Perhaps just sit down with Paul Davidson [prosecutor], I guess, and maybe for him to say why he thought I got that verdict. I think I was

quite surprised too, leading up to the trial there was so much ... there did seem to be, they seemed to be going out of their way so much to make sure everything was going to be okay for all the witnesses, and then afterwards there wasn't any contact, that was it, it's finished, it's over.

JJ: So how did that feel, what message did you feel like that gave you in a way?

F: I guess I was quite an unimportant part of it, it was that sort of message. When we had a thing a few months later here at Patricia's, I spoke to Gina [prosecutor] about it there, she came up and she made me feel better about it, she said we have no doubt in our mind that he was the one who attacked you. I actually really needed to hear that, but I needed to hear it sooner .... It would have just given me that affirmation that I needed at the time.

Other sources of dissatisfaction

Statement-taking process

One concern raised by many of the women, and which echoed that identified by women interviewed as part of my earlier rape research (Jordan, 1998a), involved their feeling that the police often persisted in taking their statement when they were exhausted. This practice was criticised by some of the women because it appeared to represent an adherence to police procedure at the expense of sensitivity to victims' needs. Persisting in continuing to interview in such circumstances could also result in the police resorting to putting things in their own words, instead of ensuring they obtained as realistic a picture as possible from victims. Such a practice not only undermined the women's sense of the validity of their experience, but could also have potentially serious implications later in the process – for example, when the women were questioned or cross-examined regarding their statement in court.

Jennifer felt the police tried to interview her initially 'when it was the wrong time and it was too late'. Shelley also described how exhausted she felt by the time the police began to obtain her full statement.

I think that – see, by the time I was giving my full statement, I'd spoken to the police on the scene, I'd spoken to the doctor and given the same statement to the doctor at the hospital and then I was doing it for the third time in a more extended way to the police and I think what really I would have liked to have seen happen was that statement could have waited. I think I really needed the time, I mean it had to be done. I probably would have performed better had I had some sleep and then come back and perhaps had it done in my own home or done it in a more comfortable situation.

Shelley also noted that the detective who was interviewing her knew she was tired and tried to speed things up for her, but this could have resulted in incorrect details or sequences of events being recorded:

> I did feel as we were going through that he was trying to kind of put the words for me, but I think he was just trying to be helpful rather than being objective about writing the statement. And there were some things that he read back to me that I said, 'No, that's not actually what happened', or 'No, that's not what I mean'.

One or two women expressed dissatisfaction regarding what they perceived as limited or inappropriate techniques that the police expected them to be able to utilise. Patricia, for example, had fought with Rewa and chased him down the road, in the process obtaining a good look at him. The police were keen for her to assist them by drawing a compusketch,[60] which she agreed to do. This proved to be a singularly frustrating experience, she said, which lasted more than three hours:

> They had an American profile programme in there, it had not one Polynesian, not anything, the closest thing to an Asian was an Eskimo. They didn't have anything that was slightly conducive with a Māori or Polynesian that you see on the street.

Other women observed how difficult they found the process of police interviewing and statement-taking because of the explicit nature of the information required. In response to a question concerning whether she felt she could provide the police with as full an account as she wanted to, Kathleen responded:

> No, because I couldn't divulge a lot of that information 'cause I didn't feel comfortable. If I had maybe a female there, or they had gone through a list of questions, like: Did this happen or did that happen, did he do that, it probably would have been a bit easier.... 'Cause there are some things like when he, the oral sex bit, I didn't know how to say what had happened. It was just sort of uncomfortable, horrible....
>
> I couldn't say a lot of the stuff I wanted to say or that I felt I needed to say but, yeah, I don't know, I couldn't, I just couldn't. You know, I felt embarrassed, I did feel embarrassed, yeah, that's the word for it, I felt embarrassed.

Retention and return of personal property

All of the women had items of property retained by the police for forensic examination. These included mostly items of clothing and bedding, including items used by Rewa to bind and gag them. The women understood the importance of these items being examined, but several expressed concern regarding the police retention, use and return of their property. Some of the women said that they were not always informed of the procedures to be followed, and at times heard nothing after their property passed into police hands.

One major source of discontent arose from the lack of consultation by police as to what the women wished to have happen to these items following their examination. While many said they did not necessarily want these items back, most felt they would have liked to be offered the choice. Shelley described the property items of hers which the police retained:

> They had all my bedding including pillows and duvet. My dressing gown, the clothing I was wearing at the time .... I just assumed that, I mean, they may have said to me, 'We're taking it for evidence', but that was all and there was certainly no clear explanation that I wasn't going to get it back and that actually surprised me because my duvet cost me, it was a set and they actually destroyed all the evidence afterwards and then I made a claim to my insurance company and they said no. It wasn't, I wasn't going to get a claim on it and so then I contacted the police who wrote them a letter and they came up with the money after the police wrote the letter. It was incredible, I felt it was incredibly insensitive. It was those sorts of things that really, really threw me. It was those extra little things, a few layers out....

Shelley also felt aggrieved that the next time she saw her pantyhose, which Rewa had used to tie her up with, was when they were displayed on national television following the release of the trial verdict.

Women whose property was returned often complained about the way in which the police managed this process, with some feeling that greater sensitivity could have been displayed by the officers concerned. For example, the police would suddenly arrive on the doorstep with the items in question, without the woman being given a choice regarding whether or not she did in fact want to see these items again. The likelihood of it being upsetting to see the clothes one was wearing when raped did not always seem to be appreciated by the police – it was simply time to return the property so it was returned. One woman, for example, found it distressing when her property was returned with crosses marking the spots where semen stains had been found. The condition of some items meant that, ideally, complainants would have been warned about the state of the goods in question. As Isabel said:

> They took away all the clothes that I'd been wearing when I was attacked and they gave them back sometime later, but I don't know why they bothered giving them back because they all had little holes cut out of them. They came back in those sort of evidence bags.

Raquel also had the pair of jeans she had been wearing handed back to her, without any advance warning, and with a big hole cut out of the crutch area. The material had been removed for forensic analysis. Raquel had been attacked and raped in her car; when the police had finished their examination of the vehicle, she was told to come and collect it. Her boyfriend went and was upset to find the passenger seat still down in the position Rewa had placed it for the rape. Furthermore, Rewa had cut this woman badly during the attack and the inside of the car was still covered with her blood, a fact which prompted a family dispute amongst all those close to her as to who could best manage to clean it, until in desperation Raquel herself arranged for it to be valet cleaned.

> That's another thing, another complaint, and I don't know whether we really have right to complain about this, but when I got it back it [her car] back, it was still … it had blood everywhere in it. I remember the seat still, the seat was still back, my seat that he put me back onto, the passenger seat was still down, they hadn't put it back upright and then when ___ [boyfriend] went to pick my car up he was really, really upset seeing the seat down because it made him think about everything, and the first thing he did was put the seat back up. He was really upset, it made me uncomfortable, I remember being uncomfortable because I saw how upset he was, that probably made me …. I was dealing with it really well, it hadn't really occurred to me how upset everyone else was at the time because I was still in my own little world, in survival mode, I wasn't really … it's hard because they can't always do the best thing for you because they're really messed up themselves. When you're a victim, you forget that there's a lot of other victims too, but you're the victim of the actual crime, but there's a lot of other victims emotionally and it's kind of hard when you're the victim survivor to relate to that, you don't actually completely understand what they're going through, they're busy trying to cope with it and understand what you're going through which is hard enough and you're not really capable of understanding what they're going through. But there's blood everywhere in my car and I had to take it back like that and get it cleaned, that was interesting.

As Raquel said, though, why could the police not have either cleaned it themselves or offered to get it done at the family's expense before they took receipt of the vehicle?

From the examples and statements described above, it is clear that while most of the women felt very positively towards the police, some police procedures and behaviours produced dissatisfaction. Even when they apparently conformed to stereotypes of the 'perfect victim', these women did not receive 'perfect policing'. For some, this sense of dissatisfaction could have been further enhanced by police personnel making serious mistakes in relation to the management of their cases and evidence. The next section documents some of these errors and the women's responses.[61]

Mistakes and errors made by police

The fact that mistakes were made is probably not surprising in a case of this magnitude. In the course of the lengthy investigation and trial procedures, there were at times lapses in communication, errors of judgement and insensitive behaviours. Examples of these, as described to me by the women, follow.

Shelley, who was raped twice by Rewa in the course of the attack, expressed concern that one rape charge was apparently lost between the time of statement-taking and the trial. It seemed to her that one page of her statement must have gone missing, since Rewa was only charged with the one count of rape against her. If he had been acquitted by the jury on this charge, she said she would have been much angrier about this aspect of the police management of her case. If the police had deliberately reduced it to one charge, then the reasons for this were clearly not communicated.

Shelley also said she had originally identified an item of clothing found in Rewa's possession as belonging to her, then some months later found hers still in her house. She told the police and asked them to delete the reference to this identification of clothing in her statement. No such deletion occurred. When the case went to court, the defence lawyer, Barry Hart, pounced on this occurrence, delighting in being able to show how 'mistaken' in her identification of the item Shelley had been and goading her as to how many other details she might be mistaken about. She commented:

> I felt a little bit let down by the police that there had been a communication problem and unfortunately the defence had that information and he really hassled me on that and he'd say, 'you were wrong with the camisole, are you wrong with anything else?', you know, so and I felt that I had been allowed, that they'd exposed me unnecessarily to that sort of questioning and I found that really, really hard to kind – I felt like I had to claw my way out of it really.

In other cases there was confusion sometimes as to whether Rewa's attack on an individual woman legally constituted rape or not. Such ambiguity is not unusual in practice, given that sexual behaviours occur along a continuum in reality (Kelly, 1988), rather than neatly falling into the polarised dichotomy advanced in law and examined in earlier chapters. In Rewa's case, this confusion was exacerbated at times by the fact of his erectile dysfunction, which obviously affected the extent to which he was able to achieve penetration. How the police responded to the women's accounts of his actions had significant ramifications later, and often determined how he should be charged: Patricia's case, for instance, was filed as an aggravated robbery initially, a factor which meant that her case nearly missed being linked to Rewa as the offender, although she expressed amazement at this oversight.

> P: One of those police told me that aggravated robbery leads to rape. You know, there are all these steps: there might be an aggravated robbery this year but next year they are likely to be a rapist, that they keep on the adrenaline as such, that they keep on. So they [police] should already know that, so if this sort of arrogant policeman would tell me that, why doesn't everybody know that? Why isn't it already in the system? So it got filed under aggravated robbery and that is when I said to Chook, how come it took you so long? You would think they would have found it when he had gone through all the files in [her suburb].
>
> JJ: Yeah, what did he say?
>
> P: Because it was filed under aggravated robbery and not attempted rape. Big gap, big gap. It's tunnel vision.

A scarf belonging to Rewa had been left at Patricia's address. The police took the scarf away, and she was sure that, since it looked like it had been round Rewa's neck for a long time, some forensic evidence would be obtained from it. Unfortunately, she told me, it seems that the police may not have noted that this scarf belonged to the offender, rather than the victim. For whatever reason, the scarf appeared not to have been forensically examined at the time.

> I don't know what went wrong but there was a big mess up with that scarf and that was all they had to go on and they blew it. At the time of the court it was mentioned that it wasn't there, it had been mislaid somewhere.

Suzanne feels she encountered a similar problem with the police concerning identification of a fingerprint outside her flatmate's bedroom.

> The chap doing the fingerprints said, 'I've got a really good thumbprint of this one, through the point of entry'. I said, 'Oh, great'. When Rewa was arrested, the police said to me … because I said, 'What about the thumbprint, as some kind of evidence?' They said no, it was my fingerprint, and I said no it's not, and they insisted it was, and I said I have never, ever been into [flatmate's] bedroom ever and I still haven't to this day, and I certainly never had my finger on that …. I actually got really angry in the end, I said, 'It's not my fingerprint!' In the end they said it was [flatmate's] thumbprint and [she] said I have never had my finger on that outside of the window, it was right there, we knew he got in that

window because the stool was there where he got in, it was right where he would have put it...because he put the screwdriver under it, we couldn't believe that they were doing this.... That actually did concern me, it was like they first initially said it was mine and then they said it was hers, and I know I've never been anywhere near her bedroom inside and out, so that was a little bit of a concern.

Connie recounted to me how absolutely exhausted she felt by the end of her statement. Her husband drove her to her parents' place, and as she walked in the door news of her attack was being headlined on the television news and the phone was ringing; it was the police requesting that she return immediately to the station. She felt scared that perhaps they did not believe her:

Well, that was my thought, that they didn't believe me. Despite the fact that it was on TV, that it had made the news, it's still not enough in your head to tell you, well it's on the news, they believe you, because I know what news is like, a story's a story, doesn't matter whether it's true or not. And I thought, Oh no, they don't believe me, what now?

Connie returned to the police station, feeling agitated. On her arrival, what she discovered was that the typist had spelt a word wrongly on the statement and the police simply wanted the change authorised and signed by the complainant. This seemed a small detail to the police but by then this experience was impacting hugely on her, adding to her already heightened senses of fear and vulnerability.

Several of the women expressed concerns in particular over the arrangement, or in some cases lack of arrangement, of medical examinations. Mention has been made previously in this chapter of Suzanne's anger when the detective failed to send her for a forensic examination when this might have yielded critical evidence. In Raquel's case, she feels the police made a potentially serious error of judgement in not sending her for an immediate medical examination to have her head injury assessed. Instead they drove her to the police station, saying they would have to arrange for a clinic to be opened for her to have the forensic examination:

That is what they told me afterwards, but in actual fact that had nothing to do with my head injuries. In actual fact the fact that I had head injuries, they damn well should have taken me to A and E now that I think about it....

I guess they probably felt that I was quite lucid and quite okay to...you know. But there was nobody there to check my pupils. You know when you have, you've got a difference in concussion and brain compression I mean who knows, who knows what had happened to me? It's probably a little bit slack on their part. I mean if I had been really badly injured they would have taken me to hospital, you know, but because I was walking and talking fine they didn't concede that there was anything wrong with me. God, I could have collapsed an hour later, you know.

Gabriel also had concerns regarding police liaison with medical personnel. In her case she was taken to the hospital to have her injuries examined, but feels that the police left her there without medical personnel being told how shocked and vulnerable she was likely to be feeling. Gabriel commented:

> I was quite disgusted about the fact that, when I was at the hospital, I was left in rooms by myself and wheeled out of rooms because there was no more rooms and left in a hall way on a stretcher for a long time. I found that very disturbing, because I couldn't get up without help. I just think that's terrible being left by yourself. At that stage there was no one available to be with me. And the fact that the X-ray person didn't know the nature of my, no one knew the nature of why I was there. Now I don't know whether that is because of the privacy of it all, like I don't know if the Police can go up to the nurses and say, 'Look, we've had this young person who … '. No-one seemed to know why I was in there. I had to tell them and that was not something that I really felt capable of doing.

What is apparent, in the above examples, is that many of the women were aware of potentially serious mistakes and significant oversights that were made by the police. Fortunately, these mistakes did not appear to seriously impede case outcomes (in this case, Rewa's conviction), although some women believed that potentially the police's errors may have had more deleterious effects. What emerges from the women's accounts overall, however, is that if the police have a fundamentally positive relationship with the woman from the outset, then such errors will be tolerated within the context of that relationship. Just as in any marriage or partnership, errors of judgment or communication may occur, but if the underlying bonds of trust are there then these are unlikely to jeopardise the fundamentally secure basis of the relationship. In other words, if the foundation of the police– victim relationship is strong, complainants will be understanding of the pressures on police and relatively forgiving when mistakes occur.

Some of the women noted that their experience of the police was more positive than they initially expected, although attributed some of the reason for this to it being such a significant inquiry. As Gabriel reflected:

> I don't know, just because I had a good experience, I mean, I'd never know what it would be like to make an individual complaint. Bearing in mind that when I was attacked, the Police already knew that there was a serial rapist out there and had a very good idea that this was part of it. And perhaps I did get a lot of special treatment, and then definitely

throughout the trial, in fact all of us did because it was so unusual and it had to look good because shit everyone was looking at them. It had to look good. Imagine if it wasn't handled very well? I mean, God. How would the country feel to find that there was a serial rapist and the police force were all over the place and didn't give a shit! It had to be handled very well because it was in the limelight.

What emerged for the women overall was general satisfaction with the police approach, coupled with an ability to give clear, specific examples of which aspects, from their point of view, were not handled well. As Shelley expressed it:

I'm very positive, I had a very positive relationship with the police and accepted a lot of their downfalls as well. In fact I know that their processes weren't often wonderful and you know having to deal with 30 of them at different times, I kind of accepted that because each one of them as individuals were really nice to me. And that's why I could accept it .... There were quite clear cock ups along the way ..., but the fact that there was that real sense of support and belief ... I didn't really feel too bad – I was angry about it but I kind of rationalised it.

Patricia noted also that while the mishaps may appear insignificant on one level, they all detract from the ideal of perfect policing:

So, it is all minor little things that are human failings really, but in a case like that, or yeah, in cases as big as that one, if you can close the gaps on human failings then I guess you would get a more perfect system and then everything is going to flow a lot easier, isn't it?

Implications of the research

The responses of the women attacked by Malcolm Rewa to their experiences with the police provide us with valuable insights into the concept of what, from the rape victim's perspective, constitutes 'perfect policing'. A clear understanding of victims' needs emerges from the interview data. This includes validation of many of the measures employed by police during Rewa's investigation and trial, as well as criticisms of some of the ways in which these procedures were managed.

Important aspects of police practice which were applauded by the women included

- the provision of dedicated women complainant officers;
- the ability to liaise with a police team of aware, sensitive detectives during the trial;

- the opportunity to meet the Crown Prosecution team in advance of the trial; and
- familiarisation with courtroom layout, defendant's position in the court.

Many of the women reiterated the paramount importance of issues of safety and privacy for victims of rape/sexual assault. Being believed, validated and reassured was also stressed, because of the need to counter the negativity and degradation of sexual violation. Several of the women spoke of the ways in which they felt so acutely dependent on the police, as professionals, to determine the proceedings. In suggesting how police might approach this issue, Helen said:

> It's almost like you have to try and think what the woman needs, because she doesn't know, she's not been through it before, she's not going to be able to make decisions for herself.

Can the police learn, as Helen suggested, to put themselves inside the head of a rape victim and anticipate what she needs? Or, to express this differently, can the police show empathy? For as Kohut (1977) defined it, empathy is 'vicarious introspection',

> the capacity to place oneself, both cognitively and emotionally, in another's shoes, to see or hear from another's perspective. (Orange, 1995, pp. 17–18)

Psychotherapists have long stressed the importance of an empathic response for creating a climate within which their clients can feel safe and connected enough to disclose personal information (Kohut, 1977; Orange, 1995). In similar vein, the police officer must demonstrate empathy if intimate details of a sexual assault are to be obtained, and trust and cooperation maintained. The overall positive response of these women to the police suggests that at least some officers were able to establish such rapport, at least some of the time.

This raises the question of what factors determine this ability to show empathy and sensitivity towards victims of rape – gender, training, personality or experience? The results of this research, combined with the data obtained in my earlier study, suggest the importance in particular of training and experience. In both studies, women often suggested the desirability of a specialist police unit to respond to sexual assault victims. Access to interview rooms and facilities designed with victims' needs in mind was also strongly advocated, rather than expecting traumatised individuals to adapt to the deliberately harsh cell-type environments designed for interviewing the perpetrators of crime. What must it be like for a victim of rape to imagine that the previous person sitting in her chair was possibly a rapist or child abuser?

The most significant aspect to emerge from the interviews with these women concerns the paramount importance of the police establishing a positive relationship with the complainant. Unlike many victims of rape, the majority of these women were regarded as credible victims and had their accounts believed by the police from the outset. An environment of trust was created which formed a strong foundation for a relationship that had to be sustained over a long period of time. The police recognised the centrality of Rewa's victims to the police goal of successfully prosecuting this repeat offender. The efforts the police went to in establishing a respectful and supportive relationship with the women proved to be invaluable. The sheer magnitude of this investigation meant that, on occasion, mistakes were made and insensitivities did occur. In a single complainant case, mistakes such as those cited earlier involving a lost scarf or wrongly identified fingerprint could cause the entire case to collapse. Fortunately, in a multiple complainant case such as this, isolated instances of bungled evidence were unlikely to prejudice the eventual outcome. While such mistakes might strain the relationship between the police and the woman concerned, if a good, solid relationship already existed then the women were usually willing to forgive such indiscrepancies. In other words, if the complainant already felt believed and supported by the police, then a mistake or inconsiderate remark would be assessed within the context of a fundamentally positive relationship. The capacity to forgive and to understand would be apparent. For example, if the return of a complainant's property was not handled well, the complainant may be aggrieved by that act but, hopefully, not to the extent that she would decide to end her relationship with the police. If, however, the relationship was already strained, and there was little trust or rapport between the police and the complainant, then one more sign of police disrespect or insensitivity might tip the scales. The result might then be that the complainant would decide 'That's it!' and withdraw the case or refuse to cooperate as a witness. It is the strength and quality of the police–complainant relationship that carries a case through to completion and, hopefully, to successful prosecution of the offender.

A major factor underlying the fact that the women attacked and raped by Malcolm Rewa were dealt with positively derives from Rewa's status as an offender. He was a repeat, serial offender, the kind of 'monster' rapist whom the police are highly motivated to apprehend, and there was extensive public and media pressure on the police to 'catch their man'. However, from my talking with police involved in this case, it appears that they began increasingly to see, from spending so much time with these women, how lacking in victim orientation they, as investigators, actually were. Hence, from interviews I conducted with senior police personnel involved in the Rewa investigation, as well as from the women's remarks, it is clear that the police learned to become much more consistently victim-centred in their approach and management of the women as the investigation proceeded.

In part this was because Rewa's latter victims were often able to be linked to him immediately (largely because of his modus operandi), and thus the offender's status and notoriety influenced police treatment of the victim and crime scene. What some detectives observed, however, was that the women whom Rewa attacked were mostly highly educated and articulate women who were able to verbalise their needs and reactions clearly. Thus when, for example, one woman complained about a poor lack of communication concerning trial dates, the police responded favourably and began to issue occasional written bulletins to update the women concerning case developments.

It is debatable how much this receptivity to complainant suggestions could be attributable to the size of the case and status of the offender, or the status of the victims, or to the police recognition that the only way Rewa would be convicted would be as a result of victim cooperation. Whatever the motive(s), the effect was that the police learned the necessity of listening to and validating the victim, and developed a much fuller appreciation of victim needs and vulnerabilities. Since the end of the trial, detectives involved in this investigation have become regular contributors to detective training courses held at the national Royal New Zealand Police College, emphasising in particular the importance of an empathic police response to rape victims.

At heart, those they lecture to may always primarily define themselves as hard-nosed detectives who are motivated to try whatever is necessary to catch serious offenders. Whatever the reason, part of what at least some police learned from the Rewa and Park investigations is the centrality of the victim to police success in their mission. Part of what needs to change is the expansion of the concept of serious offender so that this category includes not just the easily defined 'animals', as one detective called Rewa, but the much more typical non-stranger rapists, whose victims may often be viewed as imperfect victims and characteristically receive less than perfect policing, as the study of police files demonstrated.

In talking about perfect policing, it must of course be acknowledged that perfection as a concept is not an absolute; ideas as to what constitute perfection are diverse and situationally determined. What is perfect policing from the police point of view may be defined as that which nets the offender; whereas from the victim's perspective, perfect policing may be a broader, more complex concept. It may incorporate that which validates victims and their experience, provides them with support, and secures their safety, *as well as* involving the police doing whatever is necessary to help secure the arrest and conviction of the offender. This emphasis will vary for different women; there is no one, uniformly shared goal. For the police to reach their goal, they need to be able to ascertain, for every individual victim of rape, what she in particular needs from them, in order to secure her trust and cooperation, and their success in law enforcement. As Isabel observed in relation to the symbiotic relationship between her, as a rape victim, and the police:

> Okay, so they run the system, the police and the lawyers run the justice system, but they needed my help to do what they needed to do and they let me do it my way – a little bit.

7
'Getting it right': Reviewing Police Responses to Rape

> To get abuse listened to is the first thing: to get it understood is the next.
>
> (Elizabeth Robbins, 1907, quoted in Mills, 1991, p. 232)

Introduction

The results of the research presented in this book give cause for concern. They demonstrate the continuing impact of negative patriarchal beliefs and attitudes about women in the New Zealand police organisation and on the responses of some police to rape and sexual assault complainants.

The study of police files presented in Chapter 4 showed a dominant mindset of suspicion underlying the police response to reports of sexual assault. This analysis revealed a wide range of factors that influence police perceptions of complainants' credibility, particularly when clusters of variables are apparent. Thus, whereas drunkenness on its own may not diminish victims' credibility, drunkenness in connection with other factors, such as previous consensual sex with the offender or the concealment of cannabis smoking, may tip the scales of credibility. The factors seen to enhance or diminish a victim's credibility are weighted differently, so while a factor counting against the complainant may tip the balance seriously one way, factors in her favour may correct the balance again. Thus being a sex worker or an alcoholic may be compensated for by factors such as prompt reporting, cooperation with the police and visible signs of injury or resistance (Du Mont *et al.*, 2003; Gregory and Lees, 1999; LaFree, 1980).

Interviews with detectives, detailed in Chapter 5, largely confirmed these findings, although those spoken with had been selected for their particular expertise in the area of sexual assault investigations and, with some exceptions, tended overall to be less stereotypical in their attitudes. Nevertheless, their comments concerning detectives' interviewing practices with rape complainants suggested that many continue to subscribe to judgmental beliefs concerning the victim. Also highlighted was an overall lack of awareness concerning the psychological factors which may be associated with false rape complaints and poor understanding of the effects of rape trauma on victims' demeanour and behaviour. These issues prompted some detectives in particular to consider current training measures to be inadequate in preparing those involved in sexual assault investigations for the task.

Research presented in Chapter 6 on those involved in the Malcolm Rewa investigation, both complainants and detectives, showed some of the ways in which the police response to victims could be improved. The detectives said they learned much of benefit from the women attacked by Rewa, as well as from having access to books which detailed the effects of rape trauma on victims. The interviews with the women provided valuable material on their responses to police treatment and initiatives, and showed how, for these women also, it was important that the police believed them. The experiences of a few of the women signalled the difficulties some police have in believing women's accounts, as well as highlighting issues requiring greater overall police sensitivity and attention. One significant finding to emerge from this study related to the importance of having the police believe and support complainants not only to ensure case progression and victims' cooperation (Epstein and Langenbahn, 1994; Wells, 1991), but also to establish a baseline of trust which would predispose complainants to 'forgive' any mistakes or insensitive acts later made by the police in relation to the handling of their case.

The different studies presented complement well the existing literature on rape reporting and the police response, and confirm the results of previous research which sought to identify the principal factors affecting police judgments and reactions. Since most of the major studies in this area had previously been conducted in England (Gregory and Lees, 1999; Kelly, 2002; Lees and Gregory, 1993; Temkin, 1997, 1999), this research demonstrates that the trends observable there are also evident within the New Zealand context. The research aimed to elucidate the dynamics of the relationship which occurs, focussing in particular on the factors that affect police officers' perceptions of victims' credibility. A central concern, then, was the ways in which the police tend to construct rape narratives and interpret factors and cues associated with the victim. What do police routinely 'see' when different kinds of complainants approach them? What factors are seen as 'cues' and how are these interpreted? What is taken to determine 'truth' or 'falsehood'?

The results presented strongly suggest the influence, conscious or otherwise, of particular scripts. The relative infrequency with which most individual officers deal with rape complaints means these scripts are constructed only partly from actual policing experience, and are more commonly informed by the attitudes and beliefs dominant within the police occupational culture, and within society generally (Jackson, 1978). Moreover, it is likely that the personal experiences of individual officers can also be influential – for example, their own sexual assault experiences, as either offenders or victims, or those of persons close to them. The influence of such factors will not be uniform, since the same experiences impact differently on different persons, and can be mediated by other factors and interventions such as, for example, counselling or psychotherapy. An additional factor that needs greater recognition is the impact on detectives of continued exposure to serious crime. As one commentator has observed,

> Rape investigators can and often do become vicarious victims – stressed, altered, and in some cases destroyed by the crimes they investigate. (Reese, 1999, p. 241)

While the physical and potentially life-threatening risks of policing are frequently acknowledged, these may be overstated in relation to the emotional risks associated with this occupation (Doran and Chan, 2003; Reese, 1999). The traditionally 'macho' culture of policing, however, inhibits the recognition of such non-physical dangers and deters most individual officers from seeking professional advice and assistance in this regard. The wall of cynicism which many police officers build as a protective defence mechanism from the emotional rigours of the job may also produce cold, hardened responses towards others (Reese, 1999).

Previous experiences with complaints believed to be false may also be influential, and predispose some detectives towards greater scepticism and suspiciousness of rape complainants in general (Burgess, 1999). As some of those interviewed remarked, better practices of case supervision and debriefing may help to some extent in remedying the development of excessive hardening and cynicism following the frustration of being involved with an actual false complaint. Moreover, the observation was also made by some that not all detectives are necessarily equally suited to dealing with rape complainants, and those who are adept at interrogating offenders may not be best suited to the sensitive interviewing of complainants. The gender of the interviewing officer seemed less important than their attitude and level of awareness (Jordan, 2002).

Police perceptions of victims' credibility influence the stage that individual cases reach in the criminal justice system. The first contact that the police usually have with a rape complainant begins when she, or someone acting on her behalf, reports an alleged offence. The length of time that has passed since the offence occurred is taken into account, and, in cases of delayed reporting, consideration is also given to whether or not the victim told others about the incident (who may be called in court as recent complaint witnesses). Not telling anyone about the incident is often interpreted as dubious, despite extensive evidence demonstrating how difficult many women find the process of telling others about sexual assaults (Du Mont *et al.*, 2003; Feldman Summers and Norris, 1984; Gartner and McMillan, 1995; Gilmore and Pittman, 1993; Gregory and Lees, 1999; Jordan, 2004; Kelly, 1988; Koss *et al.*, 1987; Spohn and Horney, 1992).

There are also generally accepted beliefs concerning how a rape victim 'should' look and behave; women whose demeanour is outside that expected are often regarded with scepticism (Aiken *et al.*, 1999; Burgess, 1999; Burt, 1991; Du Mont *et al.*, 2003; Gregory and Lees, 1999; Kelly, 2002; Temkin, 1997). The expectation is that a 'genuine' victim will appear upset, vulnerable, submissive and powerless; she will look, in effect, like a 'victim' (Burgess and Hazelwood, 1999; Holmstrom and Burgess , 1974). Withdrawal and dissociation may be misinterpreted as signifying that she does not care, and using humour as a defence may be perceived as inappropriate. Most police expect a woman to share their predominant concern of wanting to identify and arrest the offender. Yet a woman who has just been raped may not feel excessively offender-focussed, at least in the initial stages. Instead, she may be more focussed on sur-viving, struggling to come to terms with what has just happened to her and how she can best cope and manage it. It is likely that the woman will be in a state of shock and may be numbed into passivity at the same time as the police feel catapulted into action. She is in re-action, while they are in action mode, and the potential for miscommunication and misunderstanding is colossal.

The police generally want her to have a medical examination immediately, considering this vital in their quest to 'nail' the offender (Adler, 1991; Gilmore and Pittman, 1993; Gregory and Lees, 1999; Kelly, 2002). They find it hard to appreciate that her concerns may differ from theirs. For example, that when she hears the words 'medical examination', she does not neces-sarily hear them as a chance to gain evidence against the offender for some future court case; instead, she is likely to hear something signifying intru-sion, re-violation and humiliation. Moreover, she may also consider, in her exhausted state, how this procedure will prolong the length of time before she is able to rest and try to sleep.

Many victims of rape feel apprehensive about whether or not the police will judge and blame them for provoking the incident (Du Mont *et al.*, 2003; Epstein and Langenbahn, 1994; Estrich, 1987; Feldman-Summers and Norris, 1984; Gregory and Lees, 1999; Kelly, 2002). As cases examined in Chapter 5 showed, if a woman presents as having been drunk or drugged at the time of the alleged rape, police may see that as contributing to her sexual violation, rather than condemning the way in which the perpetrator exploited her vul-nerability and diminished competency (Abbey *et al.*, 2001; Amir, 1971; Crowell and Burgess, 1996; Harrington and Leitenberg, 1994; Ullman *et al.*, 1999; Warshaw, 1988). Similar interpretations are placed on factors such as intellectual disability and psychiatric instability, suggesting that these tend to be viewed as diminishing the victim's credibility rather than as enhancing her vulnerability. What the cases examined in Chapter 4 portrayed, however, was a tendency to view intellectual or psychiatric impairment as factors which reduced the 'truth' value of the complainant's testimony.

How an individual detective responds to a rape complainant, then, is complex. The variation between police officers is matched by the variation in complainants, their personal characteristics, and the nature and context of what they are reporting. It is difficult in practice to assess each situation on its own merits, and the police rely heavily on stereotypes to assist in the general exercise of discretion (Reiner, 1992, 1994; White and Perrone, 1997). In relation to sexual assault offences, this is evident in appraisals of victims' demeanour and culpability, and in the assessments made by officers regarding complainants' credibility (Allison and Wrightsman, 1993; Burgess, 1999; Du Mont *et al.*, 2003; Estrich, 1987; Gregory and Lees, 1999; Kelly, 2002; Lees, 1997). As the police file analysis showed, this process itself involves subjective evaluations and interpretations, which may vary enormously depending on the particular officers involved and their relationship with a particular complainant.

The dynamics of the relationship between the police and a complainant are, therefore, pivotal, but need themselves to be considered contextually. Interactions between police officers and rape complainants take place against a series of backdrops, each of which can also potentially impact on the style and content of such exchanges. When police encounter non-police persons, they typically perceive them initially as 'other', as outside what is euphemistically called 'the police family', and more typically described as the police occupational or organisational culture (Brown and Heidensohn, 2000; Chan, 1996, 2003; Fielding, 1995; Holdaway, 1983; Reiner, 1994; van der Heyden, 1997). The 'them and us' mentality which can affect police–citizen encounters is present also when rape victims contact the police. If the victim describes or names an offender who is well known in police circles as a 'villain', then the victim may be treated in ways akin to a cousin or distant relative. She is not police, but she is not completely not-police because she and the police are now presumed to share a related sense of hostility towards the same person. Thus, if the offender is someone whom the police have no ambivalencies about catching (because he is already known to them, was vicious, or preyed on the excessively vulnerable whom the police feel protective towards), then the complainant is more likely to be perceived as credible. If, however, the police are able to empathise with the position of the alleged rapist, and find it difficult to feel antagonistic towards him, then they may turn their antagonism on the complainant. Either way, the police are the hunters, and their prey is not always the rapist; it may sometimes be the complainant. If the alleged offender wins the sympathies of the police, and the complainant loses them, then these subjective affinities are likely to influence overall perceptions of the case and of the complainant's credibility. Given such complexities, 'getting it right' becomes a major challenge indeed.

Reviewing the police response

A central factor to consider when reviewing police responses to crime victims is that the police organisation itself is not a uniform, static entity.

Rather, it is shaped by a range of factors and variables which change and evolve over time. These include, for example:

- issues of resourcing and the assessment of priorities within the police organisation itself;
- innovations in policing philosophy and practice;
- changing community expectations; and
- shifts in political opinion.

In international terms, the police response to rape victims in particular has been the subject of considerable pressure to improve police performance overall (Brown and Heidensohn, 2000; Epstein and Langenbahn, 1994; Gilmore and Pittman, 1993; Gregory and Lees, 1999; Her Majesty's Inspectorate of Constabulary and Her Majesty's Crown Prosecution Service Inspectorate, 2002; Kelly, 2002; Temkin, 1997). As noted in Chapter 3, various developments and initiatives have been introduced with the aim of making police reporting and investigative procedures more sensitive and responsive to victims' needs and emotional states. Some of these are examined in greater detail below, and assessed in relation to the potential they present for improved police performance and victims' enhanced satisfaction. This section begins with a brief overview of similarities in the structural positions of policewomen and women victims.

Role of women within the police occupational culture

A parallel process operates between the significance accorded to crimes against women and the position of women within the police organisation. Women were excluded from policing until comparatively recently, and have long been recognised as a minority group with minority status (Brown, 1998; Brown and Heidensohn, 2000; Doran and Chan, 2003; Gregory and Lees, 1999; Hale and Bennett, 1995; Heidensohn, 1992). Within New Zealand, for example, women constitute 15 per cent of sworn police officers overall, with 94 per cent positioned no higher than the status of constable in the rank structure, compared with 75 per cent of male officers (New Zealand Police, 2000). Criticisms have been made internationally of the way in which policewomen are deployed differently from male officers (Boni, 1998, cited in Brown and Heidensohn, 2000; Gregory and Lees, 1999; Hyman, 2000; Jones, 1986); promoted less often (Heidensohn, 1992; Waugh, 1994); and resisted by many of their male colleagues (Brown and Heidensohn, 2000; Gregory and Lees, 1999; Hale and Bennett, 1995; Waugh, 1994). Issues surrounding the sexual harassment of women within the police are being increasingly noted (Brown, 1997; Halford, 1993), and related to the masculine ethos and biases of the organisation overall (Brown and Heidensohn, 2000; Doran and Chan, 2003; Gregory and Lees, 1999; Heidensohn, 1992; Waugh, 1994). The difficulties associated with promoting other equal

employment concerns, such as access to childcare and challenging homo-
phobia, have also been identified as problematic and discriminatory in practice (Gregory and Lees, 1999; Hyman, 2000). Whilst such issues remain
apparent within the police organisation, women as victims of men's violence
will also share inferior status. Thus Gregory and Lees have observed

> There is a clear link between the requirement that sexual attacks are
> treated as serious crimes and the requirement that policewomen
> are treated as equal within the force. (Gregory and Lees, 1999, p. 201)

Where the issue of gender has been recognised at times, however, has been
in relation to the deployment of women officers.

Gender of police officers

Given that most rape victims are female, and that most of the police officers
criticised in earlier rape studies were male, the possibility of the gender of
the officer making a significant difference has been canvassed (Brown and
Heidensohn, 2000; Brown *et al.*, 1993b; Goodstein and Lutze, 1992; Gregory
and Lees, 1999; Jordan, 2002; Lees and Gregory, 1997; Pike, 1992; Pino and
Meier, 1999; Radford, 1987; Toner, 1982). The assumption has been made
that, as more women enter the police, their deployment on sexual assault
cases will automatically result in improved service delivery to victims.
Women victims, it was assumed, will find it easier to disclose intimate details
to another woman, and policewomen will have a 'natural' empathy with the
victims (Adler, 1991; Brown *et al.*, 1993b).

This assumption has resulted in some jurisdictions assigning greater
numbers of women to specialist rape squads. In parts of Britain, for instance,
dedicated units have been established staffed by specially trained officers,
most of whom are women but usually managed by a male detective (Brown
and Heidensohn, 2000). Where problems may arise, however, is when supervisors assume that female detectives will require less training and less experience than their male counterparts in order to manage sexual assault cases
competently (Easteal, 1993; Pollock, 1995). In such an environment, both
victims and female police officers lose out. The victims may receive less
informed, professional policing as a result, with sympathy and understanding by no means guaranteed or seen as a substitute for competency. For
women officers, such deployment can result in their being regarded as inferior and less competent than their male colleagues – an unfair comparison
when one set of colleagues is being appraised on the basis of training and
experience and the other on so-called 'natural' aptitude.

Some women do have strong feelings concerning the gender of the officer
they speak with; others do not. Contrary to popular assumptions, rape complainants do not automatically prefer to speak with female officers and,
when they do, do not always find them more understanding than their male

counterparts (Goodstein and Lutze, 1992; Radford, 1987; Toner, 1982). Most of those interviewed in my previous research (Jordan, 1998a, 2002, 2004) felt that gender did not compensate for experience, and were concerned above all with receiving a professional and caring response from the police. The negative experiences some women had with hostile and disbelieving policewomen raised doubts about assumptions of 'natural' sympathy and aptitude. Conversely, other women rated highly the sensitivity with which some male officers treated them. Gender-based assumptions, it seems, can be highly misleading, and 'common sense' assumptions can, in effect, make no sense at all. Where the gender of the officer is critical, however, is when the victim requests an officer of a particular gender. Given the difficulty many victims face in articulating their needs, the responsibility lies with the police to offer complainants a choice, wherever possible, between equally qualified officers of either gender. Where such a choice is not currently available, the police then have the responsibility of selecting and training sufficient numbers of officers to make this possible. This will only happen if the police make rape a priority area in relation to training, resourcing, management and performance appraisal.

Specialist squads

The issue of specialist or dedicated squads appears particularly pertinent to the policing of sexual assault, and has been explored within the United States of America context (Epstein and Langenbahn, 1994; Goodstein and Lutze, 1992; LaFree, 1989), and more recently in Britain (Brown and Heidensohn, 2000; Kelly, 2002). Research conducted with complainants concerning their experiences of being interviewed by the police makes a compelling case for specialisation. Clearly, when it comes to interviewing rape victims, not all officers can be considered equal in this regard. Issues of gender and training are not the only factors to consider. Attitudes, personal beliefs and experiences cannot be ignored completely. Whilst the argument can be made that a true professional will set these aside, the horrifying experiences of some complainants indicates that this does not always happen in practice.

The New Zealand Police currently advocate that all officers should be generalist specialists and there is very strong resistance to suggestions of having dedicated squads for rape investigations.[62] The hostility with which this option has been greeted suggests the possibility that more underlies this reaction than the stated reason of resources. Thus while resistance to the concept of specialist rape squads is typically articulated as a resourcing issue, in reality it appears to be more closely connected to assessments of police priorities and philosophy. Specialist units are often established in crime categories rated highly by the police, such as organised crime and drugs, and the area of child sexual abuse has long been recognised as requiring specialist selection and training. By comparison, adult women's experiences of sexual violation are accorded little priority, unless a serial sex offender is involved, or an offender whom the police are interested in for other reasons (such as gang involvement), or the specific victim's characteristics provoke public sympathy. While a dedicated rape squad may be impossible to sustain, or even to justify, outside of major cities, ensuring the availability of specially selected and trained police personnel to conduct rape investigations would be highly beneficial for police and complainants alike. However, cognisance should be taken of experiences in some jurisdictions where combined units were established to respond to reported instances of both child and adult sexual assault. Within such contexts the police prioritised cases involving children, resulting in few advantages being experienced by adult rape victims (Kelly, 2002).

Recent developments in policing

Police organisations around the world have been challenged in recent years to be more responsive to the public whom they ostensibly serve. Considerable criticism has been voiced concerning the extent to which the police obsession with crime-fighting has led to an excessive preoccupation with catching offenders, at the expense of such areas as crime prevention and awareness of issues concerning victims (Cameron, 1986; Trojanowicz *et al.*, 1998; van der Heyden, 1997; Walklate, 2001). Moreover, research addressing the effectiveness of traditional police practices, such as random patrolling, has produced generally damning results (Hough, 1987; Young and Cameron, 1989). Against this backdrop, 'community policing' (Bayley, 1994; Buerger, 1993; Greene and Mastrofski, 1988; Palmiotto and Donahue, 1995; Trojanowicz *et al.*, 1998) has emerged as a challenge to police perceptions of themselves as an alienated thin blue line, pitted against increasing tides of violence, lawlessness and social decay. Models of community policing vary greatly, but at the heart of most is a common goal of building greater partnerships between police and community, with a view to improving law enforcement success and promoting enhanced levels of citizens' satisfaction with police service delivery (Bayley, 1994; Buerger, 1993; Trojanowicz *et al.*, 1998).

Consistent with a community policing model is a redefinition of the public generally, and crime victims and witnesses in particular, as valuable aids in law enforcement (Trojanowicz *et al.*, 1998). Increasing emphasis is being placed on the need for high-quality interviewing of victims to elicit detailed information which will assist the police in the early apprehension of offenders (Hazelwood and Burgess, 1999). Such an emphasis, however, may appear unnecessary in the vast majority of sexual assault investigations, given the statistically high chances of the alleged offender being someone known to the complainant and usually able to be named and identified without the aid of sophisticated police sleuthing techniques or offender profiling. This by no means implies that community policing is irrelevant, however. The increased emphasis placed by this approach on enhanced police communication skills, problem-solving and accountability to the public should, ideally, be translated into improved treatment of crime victims. The New Zealand Police have embraced community policing in their official rhetoric; it remains to be seen in practice how, and to what extent, this will impact on police officers' treatment of sexual assault victims.

Police policy on rape

In 1998, the New Zealand Police introduced, for the first time, a written policy to inform the handling of sexual assault investigations (New Zealand Police, 1998). That no such policy had existed prior to 1998 reflects to some extent both the low priority attached to such investigations and police reluctance to acknowledge the limitations of generalist training for dealing adequately with a specialist area.

Moves to develop this policy began as a response both to increasing criticism from rape support services and to the results of research documenting rape complainants' experiences of reporting rape to the police (Jordan, 1996). These results had initially been presented at an interdisciplinary conference in March 1996, which a number of police had attended along with doctors, lawyers, academics, counsellors, support agency workers and interested members of the public. Some officers seemed genuinely shocked at accounts of highly inconsistent and sometimes hostile treatment of rape complainants, and shortly afterwards one was assigned to oversee the development of a policy. This process involved a lengthy period of consultation and negotiation both within the police organisation as well as with outside agencies.

The policy that was finally introduced stipulates police adherence to procedures that include assuming all sexual assault complaints initially to be genuine and referring the complainant without delay for a medical examination. The policy also suggests that the police obtain skeletal details initially from rape complainants and defer statement-taking until the victim has been able to rest and recover slightly.

If fully implemented, the policy would assist greatly in improving the quality and consistency of service delivery in this area. However, currently it appears that the fervour for introducing a policy has not been matched by equal enthusiasm for seeing it adopted and adhered to nationwide. The stipulated appointment of a police sexual assault coordinator in each district did eventually occur, but sometimes appeared to be a kneejerk response to a requirement that all districts send such a person to a seminar at the Police College. The views expressed by those present revealed there was considerable resistance to aspects of the policy and a desire to see it diluted in tone and application.

A two year lead-in time for policy implementation was planned, which ended in February 2000; over four years later, it remains difficult to see any tangible impacts arising from its introduction, apart from the establishment in 2003 of a training course on adult sexual assault investigations. Dispute over the policy's contents, in fact, has resulted in it being 'under review' for some years now. To date, no national coordinator has been appointed at the Office of the Commissioner to oversee the nationwide implementation of the policy. Whether or not such a person is appointed will provide some indication of the extent to which this is viewed as a priority area.[63] Meanwhile, opposition to the policy has not abated in some quarters, and, as I discovered when interviewing detectives, it seems likely that many are not even aware yet that a policy exists, let alone knowledgeable about its contents. From the victim's perspective, any changes brought by the policy's introduction seem largely imperceptible. For the New Zealand Police Sexual Assault Investigation Policy to be more than a token gesture of political correctness, substantive changes are needed to demonstrate to police officers that this is a priority area for service delivery and performance appraisal.

The dynamics of the police–victim relationship occur within the context of the police organisation overall. Police responses to rape complainants are therefore influenced by such factors as policy and strategy planning, deployment issues and police resource decisions. In turn, the police organisation itself is located within the broader context of the criminal justice system, and impacted upon by developments within its sphere.

Criminal justice system

The police occupy a pivotal role within the criminal justice system. They effectively control the turnstiles which filter members of the public into the system, and the exercise of police discretion is pivotal in its scope and influence (Gilmore and Pittman, 1993; Kerstetter and van Winkle, 1990; Lees and Gregory, 1993; Reiner, 1994). Within this arena, institutional processes operate amidst an environment of changing trends and ideologies, resulting in both legal and attitudinal shifts. Several of these themes are addressed briefly here, in relation to their potential impacts on police practice.

Victims' movement

Over the last 30 years, increasing criticism has been directed at the criminal justice system generally for its failure to meet the needs of crime victims (Doerner and Lab, 1995; Lee *et al.*, 1993; Walklate, 1998; White and Perrone, 1997). Our system has traditionally been oriented around identifying, locating, apprehending, prosecuting, convicting and sentencing offenders, with the victim being treated as an accessory to this aim.

Some significant developments have occurred in recent years. Increasing pressure has been placed on the criminal justice system to make victims more central within its processes. In New Zealand, this was partly evident in the passing of legislation in 1987 aimed specifically at crime victims.

The Victims of Offences Act 1987 stipulated, amongst other considerations, that victims of crime had certain rights, including the right to be treated 'with courtesy, compassion and respect for their personal dignity and privacy'; to have details of the harm caused by the crime conveyed to the judge in the form of a Victim Impact Statement prior to the offender's sentencing; to be kept informed concerning developments with their case; and to have the right to request notification of the offender's impending release, or escape, from custody (Lee and Searle, 1993).

Not all legislation is equally enforced, nor easily enforceable. The findings of the research conducted with rape victims (Jordan, 1998a,b, 2001) clearly demonstrates that the basic tenets of *The Victims of Offences Act 1987* are not being adhered to by the police. If they were, then such a proliferation of examples of the negative treatment of victims would not exist. Whilst some of the concerns raised by participants in this research related to the personal qualities and attitudes of individual officers, many arose from situations where information was withheld, property retention and return was bungled, safe environments were not provided, and, above all, respect for the needs and wishes of the victim was absent.

The brutal impacts of the traditional, adversarial justice system on rape victims were increasingly acknowledged throughout the 1990s (Koss, 2000; Lees, 1996; Scutt, 1998; Thomas, 1994). In a recent article, US rape researcher Mary Koss noted:

> Inherent features of adversarial justice within the courtroom also shape survivors' experiences, such as the environment of formality, the sequestering of witnesses who may also be the family and supporters of the victim, attorney questioning that exacerbates self-blame, and the perpetrator's unmovable stance that he is not guilty of a crime. (Koss, 2000, p. 1335)

Research data obtained from nearly one thousand criminal trials showed that the majority of rape victims believed that rapists had more rights than they did, that the criminal justice system was unfair, and that they were not given adequate information about their case, nor input and control regarding its handling (Frazier and Haney, 1996). Concerns such as these have promoted greater debate over the issue of whether or not legal reform measures can dramatically improve the current system, or whether an alternative approach needs to be developed (Bronitt, 1998; Goldberg-Ambrose, 1992; Henning and Bronitt, 1998; Koss, 2000; Lees, 1996; Smart, 1995; Taslitz, 1999; Thomas, 1994; van de Zandt, 1998).

Sentencing issues

Public concern in the 1980s that rape offenders were receiving nominal sentences resulted in changes being made in New Zealand in 1993 to extend the maximum penalty for rape to 20 years. This was a political move, designed in part to demonstrate an awareness of the serious impacts of rape in a climate where feminist criticism was strong. This move now, however, appears to be in danger of backfiring. It has contributed towards complacency in some quarters that enough has been done about rape, and even that the pendulum has swung too far in favour of the victim (Goodyear Smith, 1995; McLoughlin, 1997). The fact that average sentences for rape are actually in the vicinity of eight years, not twenty, is ignored. Nor are the difficulties inherent in achieving convictions in rape cases acknowledged, despite being of international concern (Harris and Grace, 1999; Her Majesty's Inspectorate of Constabulary and Her Majesty's Crown Prosecution Service Inspectorate, 2002; Kelly, 2002; New South Wales Department for Women, 1996).

Little likelihood exists, however, that victims would be served well by longer sentences. Harsh sentences on statute books, even if they were enforced, do little to address the problem of rape if most victims either refrain from reporting rape, or do so only to feel revictimised by the trial system and to see their attacker acquitted. Despite so-called improvements, rape continues to be characterised by low reporting, high attrition and low conviction rates (Gregory and Lees, 1999; Harris and Grace, 1999). Moreover, even if an offender is convicted, doubts are sometimes raised over his guilt by those who consider he was 'framed' or the victim of a woman's vengefulness. Although seldom urged to doubt a not guilty verdict, nor to spare a thought that a raped woman has possibly been re-raped by our 'justice' system, the public seem increasingly to be urged to regard rape convictions with scepticism (McLoughlin, 1997). A handful of cases of supposedly proven wrongful convictions have been manipulated for political mileage by those determined to champion the rights of men accused of rape and abuse, who use such cases to 'prove' that the criminal justice system is weighted in favour of the victim. Such cases attract widespread public interest and media coverage, precisely because they reinforce traditional views of women as malicious liars and men as bumbling Romeos.

If a man accused of rape is in fact innocent, then his being arrested and charged is clearly a terrible travesty of justice. If, however, he was not convicted when he was actually guilty, then that would also have been a travesty of justice – yet the latter occurrence, although far more common, is seldom acknowledged. This is, of course, related in large part to the justice system being overtly weighted in such a way as to minimise the chances of wrongful conviction – hence the adage that it is ten times better to let a guilty man go free than an innocent man be convicted. Wrongful conviction of the innocent always appears more injurious to the public good, but the question still needs to be asked: *for whom* is it better if a guilty man goes free? Certainly not for the victim of his offences, who has lost confidence in the justice system, been retraumatised by a court appearance, and fears retribution from her attacker as well as public shame and humiliation for now being perceived as a liar and false complainer. The victim's life may be destroyed, but our system has traditionally not held victims in high regard so that outcome appears of little consequence. This old adage that we hold so dearly, when applied to rape cases, emerges as yet another way in which laws have been written and interpreted to benefit male offenders at the expense of female victims.

The findings of the research presented in this book are not only theoretically interesting, but also have clear practical implications which need to be considered. These relate primarily to implications arising for the police, although inferences can also be drawn which may be worth considering by victims, victim advocates and researchers. Some of these are explored in the following section.

Implications of this research

Implications for the police

Training

There are extensive and urgent implications for police training arising from the findings of this research. These relate particularly to the widespread divergence in officers' understanding regarding the range and variability of the effects of rape. Misinterpretation of victim behaviour and demeanour appears commonplace, and signifies adherence to stereotypes regarding how victims 'should' present (Burgess, 1999; Freckelton, 1998; Gregory and Lees, 1999; Lees, 1997; van de Zandt, 1998). These attitudes appear currently to receive scant attention in training (Beckett, 2000; Her Majesty's Inspectorate of Constabulary and Her Majesty's Crown Prosecution Service Inspectorate, 2002; Kelly, 2002), where awareness and understanding of victims' needs remains a secondary consideration to offender-based concerns.

Based on the findings of this research, the following suggestions in relation to training are made:

- increase the amount of time spent on victim-oriented issues and concerns;
- utilise more frequently the expertise of other professionals working with victims, such as doctors, counsellors and support agency workers;
- sensitise all police officers to the effects of rape and how trauma might impact on complainants and affect their demeanour and interactions with others;
- train detectives in particular about widespread variability in the effects of rape and post-traumatic stress disorder;
- equip all investigators with specific skills for sensitive victim-interviewing;
- use a wide variety of means to examine, and challenge, the prevalence of rape myths and negative attitudes towards sexual assault victims generally, as well as stereotypes of 'legitimate' victims;

- expand officers' understanding of repeat victimisation, to foster greater awareness of the reasons behind some women making multiple complaints of sexual assault;
- enlist specialist trainers to improve officers' understanding of intellectual and psychiatric disability, and of the increased vulnerability of these women to abuse and violence;
- address the issue of alleged false rape complaints by acknowledging the inflated nature of beliefs concerning their frequency and exploring the reasons for these; and
- enhance understanding of the possible reasons underlying actual false complaints and suggest appropriate courses of actions to follow (for example, referrals for assistance to appropriate agencies).

In addition to the above, specialised training and education to promote a fuller appreciation of the dynamics involved in sexual assault cases is advocated, and commented on specifically in the next section.

Education concerning the nature of rape

In law, rape is clearly distinguished from non-rape; in life, it is not. It is therefore not surprising that many police adhere to stereotypical definitions and understandings regarding the nature of rape (Burgess, 1999; Gregory and Lees, 1999; Lees, 1997; Young, 1998). It is, however, reprehensible that such views are not challenged and replaced with greater appreciation of the complexities associated with this offence. Included in this should be information designed to challenge prevalent myths and misconceptions regarding who is raped and in what contexts, as well as material illuminating the difficulties often faced by complainants in defining what happened to them as sexual assault and reporting those responsible. Current appreciation of such issues appears slight and impacts negatively and destructively on complainants, eroding their trust in the police in the process.

Public perceptions of the police have taken somewhat of a hammering in recent times. In New Zealand, as in Britain and the United States of America, allegations of police racism have been rife, with strong dissent being voiced over police involvement in the killing of a young Māori man, Steven Wallace, on 30 April 2000 (*The New Zealand Herald*, 2 May 2000). In 2001, several shocking cases involving police officers as perpetrators of rape have been exposed for public and judicial scrutiny. These have included the conviction of one officer for a rape he perpetrated while off-duty, as well as the trial of a detective for pressuring a woman to commit indecencies on him in exchange for leniency (*The Sunday Star Times*, 20 May 2001). Shining the media spotlight on these police officer rapists is important in terms of public accountability, but such knowledge may deter some women from feeling safe about approaching the police with a rape complaint. Some of the detectives who were interviewed also referred to colleagues whom they knew to have raped, and who had been apprehended on sexual violation charges. (See also Note 68, p. 254)

Such examples suggest the need for greater education of officers concerning sexual negotiation practices generally. Indeed, how can we expect police officers raised in a social climate characterised by the legacy of patriarchal thinking examined in Chapter 2 *not* to need some form of re-education? The police's role as enforcers of the law demands that they should be urged to reflect on the basis for these laws and have some awareness of the ways in which gender inequalities are related to criminal offending and victimisation. Professional and accountable policing, in my view, means that this should not be regarded as an option but as an essential prerequisite to the informed investigation of sexual violation offences.

Supervision of staff

Staff management and supervision is a central aspect of most occupations, and this is particularly significant in occupations, such as policing, which are characterised by high levels of interaction with often distressed members of the public. From examples included in this book, it is clear that individual officers appear to have considerable autonomy and discretion, and that levels of supervision vary in intensity. As some detectives indicated, as evidenced in comments made in Chapter 5, this often comes down to the priorities and management styles of individual supervisors. In practice, this means that there is widespread variance in degrees of consultation, monitoring, and post-incident debriefing. While debriefing may be regarded by some as an optional extra, and is addressed here in a separate section, good management is a necessity, not an option. Greater attention needs to be given to equipping those in management positions for the task and to specifying good practices to be followed to ensure greater staff consistency in investigation procedures. Whilst the New Zealand Police are making positive efforts regarding the updating of a Manual of Best Practice, and are increasing the training given to sexual assault investigators, the danger is that such material will simply appear and disappear, unless supervisors consistently reinforce and reward such practices.

Staff debriefing

Comments made by some detectives indicated that currently few procedures exist for assisting individual officers in managing the frustration and cynicism which may result from dealing with a deliberate false complaint. Whilst stories emerged of individual officers feeling 'burned' and possibly embittered by such cases, often understandably given the resources and emotional energy devoted to them, there was little acknowledgement of the ways in which this might impact on later complainants. In one or two cases, supervisors had temporarily removed detectives from interviewing victims while they 'got over it', but there appeared to be little recognition that they may need assistance in dealing with such negatively charged experiences. One possibility would be to foster greater consistency amongst supervisors in debriefing detectives during and after *all* sexual assault investigations. This practice would acknowledge the additional complexities and demands involved in managing such investigations and, in the case of deliberate false complaints, provide the opportunity to assess with individual detectives possible options for limiting any negative consequences which might arise. Such options could include time-out, liaison with support agencies, or team or individual debriefing with qualified professionals.

Implementation of rape policy

Around the world, police departments are endeavouring to appease the concerns of victims rights advocates by introducing policies designed to ensure the respectful, informed and sensitive treatment of crime victims (Epstein and Langenbahn, 1994; Gregory and Lees, 1999). While such efforts on the part of the police are to be applauded, the danger is that the improvements made will be deemed sufficient to correct previously identified faults and inadequacies. An English rape crisis centre worker, Marian Foley, has cautioned

> The police view that they've now 'got it right' around rape and can move on to other issues is disputed by many of us involved in rape crisis work. (Foley, 1996, p. 173)

Similar views have been expressed by academics involved in rape research, who note with considerable concern the fact that changes made by the police appear to have achieved little in improving complainants' experiences (Gregory and Lees, 1999; Temkin, 1997, 1999).

As noted above, the New Zealand Police introduced a policy in 1998 specifically designed to achieve greater police consistency in this area. Policies, however, are simply sheets of paper with words written on them, and their mere existence does nothing to change attitudes or behaviours. Their utility lies in establishing a basis against which to evaluate the consistency of performance and promote greater professional accountability. Six years on, the New Zealand Police Sexual Assault Investigation Policy appears to have changed little in practice, apart from promoting opposition in some quarters to the way it has been developed and introduced. The results of the current research provide a clear demonstration of the urgent need for the New Zealand Police to ensure this policy undergoes no further dilution and is fully implemented. Along with the training and procedures recommended,[64] resources must be spent on monitoring and evaluating the effectiveness of this policy in addressing the concerns raised by rape victims, support agencies, doctors, researchers and detectives themselves.

Staff deployment and specialist units

The question of officers' deployment can be a vexed one for police. Despite the opposition of some police officers in New Zealand, the merits of having dedicated squads have been well established overseas (Epstein and Langenbahn, 1994; LaFree, 1981). As noted earlier in this chapter, however, police officers in New Zealand typically oppose selective deployment in relation to rape investigations, despite recognising their effectiveness for responding to other kinds of offences. The research results presented here point emphatically to the conclusion that adult sexual assault demands a specialised response. Accounts provided by both detectives and complainants clearly suggest that not all officers are equally able to manage sexual assault investigations in ways which reflect well on the police as an organisation. Whether disrespectful and insensitive treatment of victims results from personal style, past experience, inadequate training or some other factor is irrelevant to victims who are at the receiving end of such treatment. At the end of the day, poor police conduct alienates rape victims and their friends/family as witnesses and informants, whilst potentially aiding sexual offenders to evade arrest and prosecution. A strong case can be made for selective deployment to ensure satisfactory outcomes for both victims and the police. To continue to desist from prioritising rape investigations in this way will perpetuate high levels of dissatisfaction in complainants, and will work against the successful apprehension and prosecution of offenders by the police.

Delayed statement-taking

The issue of delaying statement-taking appears to be somewhat controversial amongst New Zealand detectives, despite support for it overseas (Blair, 1985; Epstein and Langenbahn, 1994) and by some experienced local sexual assault detectives (Pers. comm., 2000). Views expressed by complainants, however, and the harsh experiences recounted by some, strongly indicate a preference to be interviewed when they are not as shocked and exhausted as they are immediately post-rape.

From a police perspective also, it is advantageous to conduct interviews when complainants have had at least a little time to recover, when they tend to have clearer recall and be more prepared and physically able to provide full responses to police questions. Taking statements from women when they are in shock and exhausted not only compromises the quality of information which the police will obtain, but can also compromise perceptions of her credibility. This is likely to occur if the complainant is still feeling hazy, has dissociated, or is simply so tired that she gives perfunctory answers to questions asked by the police. The unfortunate possibility exists that a statement obtained under such conditions can later be presented in a court case and used against the complainant. The option of delayed statement-taking in such situations would be to the benefit of both parties.

Responding to false complaints

The basic tenet of this book is that the proportion of allegedly false rape complaints has been greatly overestimated by many police officers, in part because of a wider societal reluctance to acknowledge the extent of sexual victimisation against women and children, particularly within the traditionally private sphere of the home. However, it must also be acknowledged that complaints of rape are sometimes made which are subsequently proven to be false (Aiken *et al.*, 1999; Kelly, 2002; O'Reilly, 1984). Police understanding of the reasons underlying such false complaints appears to be minimal, and this is reflected in limited and often inappropriate responses to such complainants. Greater training and awareness of the issues which may be associated with such cases needs to be fostered within the police. One possibility, for example, is that in some cases unresolved issues arising from previous rape or trauma incidents may underlie false complaints. As examples considered in Chapter 4 showed, complainants may feel trapped in untenable situations which they are trying to draw attention to, or may have psychiatric difficulties that require attention and treatment. Whilst not necessarily victims of what they initially claimed, many of these individuals have been victimised in other ways and/or require understanding and assistance. Thus, Eugene Kanin has urged:

> ... false accusations can be viewed as the impulsive and desperate gestures of women simply attempting to alleviate understandable conditions of personal and social distress. (Kanin, 1994, p. 88)

Seen from this perspective, the approach of such women to the police is often an attempt to obtain the help they need. Attention-seeking for its own sake has been argued to be relatively rare (McDowell and Hibler, in Aiken *et al.*, 1999), with the suggestion being made that these women may be trying to use and manipulate the police to access ways of resolving psychological difficulties.

> In much the same way that Munchausen patients manipulate hospitals and doctors, a fraudulent claim of rape might be interpreted as a form of manipulation directed at the criminal justice system. (McDowell and Hibler, in Aiken *et al.*, 1999, p. 233)

Those experienced in the area of false allegations contend that, although numerically very rare, some women may self-injure in an attempt to meet overwhelming emotional needs (Aiken *et al.*, 1999). Thus whilst 'truly' false complaints are uncommon, they require skilled and professional intervention. The context within which the allegation occurs often provides the key to interpretation and understanding of what the complainant is trying to manage or resolve (ibid.). To prevent these women from growing increasingly desperate, and possibly becoming a constant irritant to the police, or engaging in further self-destructive behaviour, it is important that they be responded to with great care. Such individuals are still police clients looking for a service, and whilst their chosen method of approaching the police may not be appropriate, nevertheless their situation requires a professional and supportive response. Those attempting to shed light on this phenomenon also offer:

> A final word of caution: it must be remembered that even those who are emotionally prone to make a false allegation can be raped. Basic principles of police professionalism require that officers who investigate rapes remain objective and compassionate. If they do not, the veracity of the allegation may never be known, and the victim, for she is a victim in either case, may never receive the help and support she needs. (Aiken *et al.*, 1999, p. 238)

An American police manual highlights the difficulties of addressing false rape allegations within police training by likening these to 'the elephant in the living room' conundrum (National Center for Women and Policing, 2001, p. 1). While instructors present material on victim sensitivity, rape myths, and trauma effects, all those taking notes and nodding assent are doing so from a position of tacit acknowledgement that such issues are applicable only to dealing with 'real' rapes. The underlying assumptions and stereotypes are never directly challenged, and are thereby perpetuated from class to class of trainee investigators (ibid.).

Victims with intellectual disabilities

Similar comments as those made in the above section can be made about persons with intellectual disability who report sexual assault to the police. No existing mechanism exists to ensure such individuals receive an educated and trained professional response. The enhanced vulnerability of these persons to sexual assault is ignored in favour of stressing their diminished competency as witnesses. The increased trust that those with intellectual disabilities may place in others is compounded by their structural dependency on others, their social powerlessness, and their own emotional and social insecurities (Hayes, 1993; McCarthy, 1996; Tharinger *et al.*, 1990, cited in Brook, 1997). Cases examined in the police file analysis suggested a strong chance of complaints of sexual assault from persons with intellectual disability being dismissed as probably false, whilst caregivers were lone voices calling for specialised interviewing in such cases. Gross injustices will continue to be perpetrated in this area until the issue is addressed directly and responded to positively. The current inadequacies of the system virtually present persons with intellectual disability on a platter for sexual predators and opportunists.

Capacity for the police to reflect on the effect they have on victims

Greater awareness needs to be fostered in training courses at all levels, as well as through regular supervision, to equip police officers to be self-reflective concerning how they are perceived by the public and how they impact on those around them. The position and power of the police in society can make them formidable for citizens to approach, and many victims and witnesses fear they will be judged negatively if minor law-breaking becomes apparent in the course of other investigations. Attention needs to be given to encouraging police officers to engage in greater self-reflection regarding how their symbolic status as authority figures can impact on relationships with those with whom they come in contact. Many of the women who reported sexual assaults tried initially to conceal or minimise behaviours which they feared the police would condemn, only to find that the fact of concealment often irreversibly damaged their credibility in the eyes of the police. In such situations, the chances of the investigation proceeding may be substantially reduced, and there is no guarantee as to whether the complainants will be dealt with hostilely or given clear reasons as to why their case has been dismissed. The frequency with which such situations can arise suggests it may be useful for this issue to be raised with complainants prior to interviewing, a practice which individual detectives may adhere to but which does not appear to be routinely encouraged.

Increasing recognition is being given to the significance of the police–victim relationship in relation to either enhancing or minimising the risks of secondary victimisation (Winkel *et al.*, 1991). Specialist training is required to equip police officers with the skills and understanding necessary to manage the interviewing of victims sensitively and professionally, and to foster awareness of the possible effects of both their verbal and non-verbal communication on complainants. Greater awareness and overall reflection on the psychological roles that police officers may adopt should also be encouraged. The 'Karpman triangle', for example, may be a useful tool in this regard (Stewart and Joines, 1987). This model suggests that certain interactions between individuals can be interpreted within the context of a triangle of dynamics as the players move between the roles of 'Persecutor', 'Victim' and 'Rescuer'. All three roles are described as 'inauthentic' to the extent that when people are in them, they are responding more to scripts and messages learned in the past than they are to what is happening in the present (ibid., p. 237). Police officers who take up the position of Rescuer may be in danger of assuming excessive responsibility for protecting and supporting a rape victim, but only to the extent that she is perceived as a Victim. An officer's doubts regarding her credibility, however, might place the officer in the role of Persecutor. Either way, whilst in the role of Victim, the woman is likely to discount herself and her experience, accepting either the Rescuer's view of her as needy or the Persecutor's view that she is blameworthy. Police awareness of such issues may help to inform the stances they adopt in relation to complainants, as well as enhancing the conditions within which women can make the transition from victim to survivor.

A related issue of responsibility for the police pertains to the need for training regarding boundary setting in professional relationships. Although this could be advantageous with regards to male officers working with female officers, it is particularly needed in relation to the police–complainant relationship in rape cases. In Chapter 5, the possible dangers associated with having young, good-looking male detectives spending long hours with young, needy, female rape victims were canvassed. In such a scenario, it is easy for the detective to become the knight on the white charger who rescues the damsel in distress and carries her off into the sunset. Except, of course, that training and good supervision should help to ensure that no such 'romantic' and potentially abusive outcomes result.[65] The responsibility lies with the police organisation to sensitise officers to the possibilities and to equip them to manage such situations sensitively and with ethical integrity. Issues such as this may be delicate to address, but need to be tackled directly if they are to be managed professionally.

Implications for victims and victims' advocates

The research findings presented here have implications not only for the police but also for victims and victims' advocates.

Advice to victims

Approaching the police with a sexual assault complaint is a scary undertaking, and victims may need not only support but also guidance on how best to do so. While some very good publications have been produced offering legal advice to victims (for examples, see *Rape Survivors' Legal Guide*, 1993, and Sullivan, 1986), these are not generally available when the victim first reports the offence. At this time, complainants may need information tailored specifically to their rights as crime victims, and on police responsibilities towards them. This includes such issues as those raised in the New Zealand Police Sexual Assault Investigation Policy regarding the presence of a support person for the complainant, and the option of delayed statement-taking.

Given the results of the research presented here, it may also be advantageous to offer complainants advice on such matters as not concealing drug and alcohol use or previous consensual sex with the accused, and other factors which they consider could influence police perceptions of their credibility. As these data show, any attempts at concealment are likely to irretrievably damage a victim's case.

Agencies working with victims

The effects of rape trauma on victims may diminish their capacity to assert their own needs or to be fully cognisant of their mental state (Burgess and

Hazelwood, 1999; Kelly, 1988). They are also unlikely to have advance knowledge of investigation and medical procedures. The police have a responsibility to provide complainants with the necessary information and options available, with support agencies being available to ensure this happens and to provide emotional support and guidance to victims. The results of this research suggest that currently there is widespread inconsistency in police responses to rape complainants, including differential perceptions of the degree to which support agency involvement should be encouraged. Specialist agencies tend to be regarded suspiciously by some police, who perceive them as rabidly feminist and, as one detective said, 'full of hairy-legged lesbians'. Police antipathy to such agencies has been noted also in the English context (Foley, 1996). The effects of rape, however, reinforce the need for complainants to at least be offered the choice of having an advocate present to oversee reporting and interview processes. Family members and friends may inhibit the complainant's willingness to divulge details of the attack fully, while an unknown but informed and sympathetic support person may be a safer and more reliable option (Epstein and Langenbahn, 1994; Jordan, 1998a).

Issues such as the damaging effects of concealment and the need for specialist oversight for complainants with intellectual disability are two specific areas which support agencies might find of interest in this research. Attention also needs to be given to the very mixed findings emerging regarding how complainants rated support and counselling assistance. Significant levels of dissatisfaction were voiced by some women whom Malcolm Rewa attacked, for instance, regarding their treatment by support agency workers. Specific criticisms included the women feeling that assumptions had been made that they would/should hate all men now, or would cooperate in what some of them felt to be inappropriate counselling techniques. The women's concerns usually seemed to result from their feeling disregarded as individuals and expected to fit some predetermined pattern of response. Similar concerns were raised by complainants interviewed in my earlier research (Jordan, 1998a). These suggest a need for more intensive training and an awareness of the diversity in women's responses to rape, and in some cases more careful selection and screening of support workers. A major obstacle to achieving consistency in this area, however, relates to the grossly inadequate levels of funding given to support agencies (Crawshaw, 1998; Foley, 1996; Stirling, 1997). Victims of rape and sexual assault have a right to expert high quality, educated, and professional treatment from all of those with whom they interact; support agencies cannot be expected to provide such professional expertise, however, when they are not funded or resourced as professional agencies.

Implications for researchers

The experience of conducting the various studies presented here was useful not only in terms of the results obtained but also with regard to the processes involved. Research is not simply a means to an end, but a journey in its own right. My own learning from engagement in this research was extensive, prompting the raising of issues here which I consider it would be valuable to acknowledge and to debate more fully in the literature.

Effects of rape research on researchers

Being raped is obviously traumatic; hearing women speak about being raped is also traumatic. Researching rape is not the same as researching coastal erosion or the breeding patterns of the paradise duck. Having experienced my own forms of sexual victimisation and, I believed, come to terms with them, I did not expect to experience vicarious victimisation whilst undertaking this research. I was wrong. The worst effects arose during the first rape research I conducted, when I was at home, alone, for days on end, transcribing the women's accounts. This, I discovered, was not a good arrangement. It prompted the return of some post-traumatic stress disorder symptoms, and I became jumpy, nervous, slept poorly, suffered from nightmares and had flashbacks to my own experiences. To manage this, I sought several sessions of professional supervision and altered my working arrangements to reduce the length of time I spent each day on the tapes, and to avoid listening to them in situations where I felt isolated and vulnerable. My partner and I also decided to have a burglar alarm fitted in our home, which we set every night during the periods when I felt the most anxious and fearful of intruders.

Studying the police files I thought would be easier. These are somewhat removed accounts, different from hearing the pain in a woman's voice as she speaks and cries on tape. Again, I was wrong. To begin with, I was going in to Police Headquarters after hours, and became increasingly aware that I was sitting alone, in a dark, mostly deserted city high-rise building at night, reading accounts of rape and violence, and sensing in some offenders' accounts (and in a few police officers' as well) a deep hatred for women. Leaving the building and walking to my car became an ordeal. Again, I had to change my working patterns and negotiate desk space so that I could read the files in daylight hours with 'normal' office routines going on around me.

Interviewing the women attacked by Malcolm Rewa was also hard at times. The actual time spent with the women themselves was generally fine, because I was so heavily focussed on them and how they were feeling. It was after they had left, and I was on my own, at night, away from home in someone else's apartment, that my own emotions were unleashed. Sometimes a vast sense of fear would engulf me as I tried to sleep, and I would feel passive and in victim-mode. Other times I would rage in anger at the degradation Rewa perpetrated. These feelings sometimes accompanied me when I returned home, as the following thoughts penned in February, 1999 indicate:

I've been back in Wellington several days now and can't get these women's stories out of my head. I do so much think they need to be told

.... I had a hard time in Auckland, though. Hearing so much talk of the fear this man generated and the way it oozed throughout these women's lives got to me. That same fear oozed its way into me after a while so that I was feeling paralysed about going into dark rooms, or being jolted out of semi-sleep into an urgent, heart-thumping watchful alertness, convinced Rewa's 'brother' was lurking in a dark corner of the bedroom. At least I could fly back to Wellington and leave it all behind, but these women had to manage this fear for years, and will do to some extent for the rest of their lives.

Partly this situation arose because I was trying to maximise what I achieved during my short stays in Auckland. Once again, though, I needed to change my work routine so that I was not interviewing continually for days on end, but took a few hours or even a day out at times, for the sake of my emotional sanity.

In contrast to the extensive literature on rape and sexual abuse that now exists, recognition of the emotional dimensions involved in sexual violence research happens rarely. I know I felt intense relief when I discovered that feminist writers such as Liz Kelly (1988) and Betsy Stanko (1997) were willing to share publicly some of the ways in which researching sexual violence impacted on them emotionally. From my experiences, and those of others (e.g. Gordon and Riger, 1991; Kelly, 1988; Stanko, 1997), I consider it is important for researchers working in areas such as rape to establish good safeguards to prevent vicarious victimisation. This will vary for different individuals and projects, but might involve careful scheduling, professional supervision, self-care and a little pampering! It is important for us as researchers to find our own ways of debriefing and strengthening our sense of self and safety in the world. Promoting greater discussion and reflection on the ways in which research with victims of violence can impact on the researcher is an important, but often neglected, issue. It may be easier to minimise the stressful aspects of research rather than fear being criticised for loss of perspective or over-identification with the research subject. In this respect, we may still need to shake ourselves free of the shackles of positivism and acknowledge the subjectivities of all those involved in the research process. Fuller sharing about these issues with other researchers may help in accepting and dealing with the effects of exposure to such deep levels of pain, fear and anguish in women's lives. It may also promote greater sharing of the positive and often inspirational aspects of research with the survivors of sexual violence.[66]

Future research

The police response to sexual assault has been a largely neglected research arena. Compared with the areas of family violence and child abuse, scant regard has been paid to victims of sexual violence. Even the coerced sex which is typically associated with family violence has tended to be ignored, reinforcing prevalent views that 'real' violence leaves visible physical injuries. In the case of children, physical abuse and the battered child syndrome began to be more widely acknowledged in the 1960s, while child sexual abuse remained virtually invisible for a further 20–30 years. The sexual assault of adults still awaits our attention. If a similar pattern occurs in relation to adults as it did for children, it may be a further ten years or so before that acknowledgement comes. It is possible that increased understanding in related areas may speed up the process; what counts against this, however, is the tenacious hold of negative stereotypes regarding both the nature of rape and the nature of women. While sexual coercion remains so little understood, and women continue to be regarded as liars, concealers and deceivers, advances in this area are likely to be minimal.

In the meantime, it is imperative that ongoing research is undertaken for several major reasons:

- to increase our knowledge base concerning the effects of sexual assault and how these impact on the demeanour and presentation of victims;
- to continue to document the ways in which police attitudes and behaviours impact on crime victims;
- to monitor the implementation process as police training and policies on sexual assault investigations are introduced, and evaluate the effectiveness of such developments.

The research conducted here hopefully provides benchmarks against which the results of subsequent studies can be assessed and compared. It also highlights key areas which should be prioritised for future research. These include:

- evaluation of police interactions with victims of sexual assault who are intellectually impaired;
- assessment of police interactions with victims of sexual assault who are psychiatrically impaired;
- an international study assessing the specialist deployment of detectives to sexual assault investigations;
- analysis of sexual assault cases referred by dissatisfied complainants to the Police Complaints Authority; and
- comparative, international research on police training in relation to rape and sexual assault, with an emphasis on police–victim interaction.

An encouraging development was evident in Britain with the recent inspection of rape investigations and prosecutions conducted jointly by Her Majesty's Inspectorate of Constabulary and Her Majesty's Crown Prosecution Service Inspectorate (2002). Prompted by concern over high attrition rates, the study aimed in part to assess the quality of investigations and the treatment of victims and witnesses. The good practice guidelines and recommendations which resulted provide the rationale for substantial improvements which, if implemented and monitored effectively, could inform international developments in this area. Before rape investigations can be improved, however, two things need to happen: first, they must be acknowledged as flawed, and second, they must be perceived and treated as an area of priority. The stigma of rape, and the question marks over women's testimony, mean it may be some considerable time before such changes eventuate.

8
Conclusion: True 'lies' and 'false' Truths

> Man is a credulous animal, and must believe *something*; in the
> absence of good grounds for belief, he will be satisfied with bad ones.
>
> (Bertrand Russell, 1950, p. 130)

What worth the word of a woman? This book has considered this question
through an examination of police responses to rape complainants, analysing
these within the social and historical contexts of ideologies pertaining both
to the nature of women and the nature of rape. The results of the police file
analysis, presented in Chapter 4, provided insights into police decision-
making, which were expanded upon in the material obtained from interviews
with detectives (presented in Chapter 5). These data were examined and
analysed against the backdrop of the historical legacy of patriarchal thinking about women and rape, outlined in Chapter 2. High levels of belief in
women lying about rape have their origins in these myths and assumptions,
and are enhanced further within a male-dominated police culture characterised by sexism and suspiciousness. The strain that such mistrust can place
on police–complainant relationships became apparent when the victims of
a serial rapist, who seldom face difficulties in establishing their credibility
with the police, appraised their experiences of policing (Chapter 6). A fundamentally positive and trusting relationship between police officers and a
rape complainant will provide a solid base to ensure ongoing victim cooperation, even if individual police officers do not always deliver 'perfect'
policing in the victim's eyes.

Overall, the research suggests that there is no single factor underlying
police responses to women rape complainants. Instead, combinations of factors appear to interact within a particular social context in ways which
reproduce existing power and gender relations. Any explanatory model
must, therefore, be developed in ways which take account of this broader
context and the factors that shape it. Such a model is proposed here.

At its heart is the police–complainant relationship. Influencing and
surrounding this dynamic are the key factors which affect each party. For the

police, these include evidential concerns, practical realities and legal considerations, all of which produce a suspicious, evidence and offender-oriented mindset. The 'cues' they notice, and the meanings they ascribe to such cues, are essentially developed within a crime-fighting and offender-focussed framework. Such suspicious, aggressive styles of interviewing are not easily transferable to police interactions with victims of sexual violence. For the rape victim, the likely factors affecting presentation may relate to trauma impact, fear of the repercussions of reporting, confusion regarding desired outcomes (since, in many cases, the offender is someone well known to her), as well as shame and self-blame. She may be tentative while the police demand clarity; she may show inconsistent and flawed recall when they expect accuracy and consistency; she may appear emotional in the face of their detached rationality; and she may seem ambivalent when they expect cooperation and commitment.

Surrounding the police–complainant relationship is the police organisation, the dominant beliefs of the occupational culture, and wider societal ideologies. The beliefs of the police occupational culture have been shaped by its origins as a male-dominated organisation enforcing laws designed to protect male property owners, with women being construed as part of men's property. Police investigations require certain procedures to be adhered to and, while these will be routine to the police, they may feel arbitrary and intrusive for complainants. Greater communication, information provision and flexibility would all be advantageous from the complainant's perspective. The positioning of the police organisation itself within the wider societal framework poses a more entrenched difficulty, necessitating challenges to a legacy of patriarchal thinking about both the nature of rape and the nature of women.

The key question raised by the studies presented here relates to the need to understand why the issue of belief continues to be such a vexed and controversial issue. Beliefs in women's inherent deceitfulness appear to have existed almost as long as women themselves have trodden the earth, and show little sign of abating. Given the long history of patriarchy, the entrenchment of such beliefs is scarcely surprising given the role they have played in regulating sexual relations and maintaining men's social dominance.

A curious paradox emerges. When women accuse men of wrongdoing, they are doubted; when they retract, they are believed. If they allege abuse, their word is suspect; if they retract an abuse allegation, their word suddenly becomes credible. One is prompted to ask: Why is women's word to be trusted only when it excuses and absolves men of responsibility for their violence against women? What makes the voice of retraction more credible than the voice of accusation? Is women's word primarily believed when it says what men want to hear and doubted when it challenges? This appears to be the very crux of the matter.

To conceal the truth of their behaviour, men have resorted to lying about women, with one of the most prevalent and destructive lies being that *women* lie. Men have made preposterous claims about women in the past, and have been believed; women have tried to reveal the truth about men, and have been disbelieved. Justice Hale, for example, believed some women were witches who could fly and cast spells on men, and when he condemned them to death, his word was believed and they were killed (Scutt, 1997); such views no longer have currency. When, as we saw in Chapter 2, this same man said women's allegations about men raping them were suspect and hard to prove, however, his word was believed and has been enshrined in legal texts ever since. Why? The particular social control mechanism of the witch-hunts depended on an ideological environment infused with beliefs concerning God, the devil, magic and superstition. Torturing and burning women for being witches could not occur once these ideas waned in popularity and power. Expressing doubts about the credibility of women's word, especially when accusing men of sexual violence towards them, is an ideological notion supported by a more universal and enduring belief system. As Chapter 2 showed, there have been centuries of history characterised by depictions of women as fickle, untrustworthy, vengeful and lying. Hale's dictum reflected this legacy and, in turn, was adopted and enshrined in legal thinking in a way which reinforced such misogynist beliefs. The view of women presented is so consistent with centuries of patriarchal thought that it is barely recognisable to some as misogyny (Johnson, 1997; Jukes, 1993). Little of substance can change while such notions continue to be one design on the ideological wallpaper against which both men and women live their lives.

In the crime of rape, we have often simply the word of a woman against the word of a man. Yet there is nothing 'simple' when it comes to assessing whether or not the woman is telling the 'truth'. Writing about rape trials within the court system, Andrew Taslitz has pointed out that

> ... 'truth' is sometimes a social notion. When a jury judges an act 'consensual', it does not discover some independent, objectively verifiable truth. Rather, it creates an interpretive truth based on its notions of worthy, coherent narratives and its moral judgment about the gendered meaning to be ascribed to the man's and woman's social behavior. (Taslitz, 1999, p. 141)

As the findings of this book demonstrate, similar processes of social construction are evident within the police. Investigative officers approach rape complainants with particular cultural narratives in mind, narratives which have been shaped within a social environment characterised by stereotypical and judgmental views of women. Against such a backdrop it becomes disturbingly easy to dismiss a rape complaint as false. Judge a victim for not coming forward sooner, for drinking too much, for trusting too readily.

Blame her for how she dresses, acts, behaves. Expect her to give a completely full and consistent statement when she's exhausted, hung-over, terrified or in shock. Write off her complaint if it later emerges that she tried to conceal having smoked a joint with the alleged offender earlier in the evening. And if the accused is ever interviewed, believe him when he says she's a 'vindictive little bitch' or that it was all just 'a bit of rough'.

The legacy of centuries of misogynist pronouncements about women has not been erased by 30 years of feminists challenging such thinking. Instead of eliminating beliefs about women which saw witches burned at the stake, feminists themselves have been hailed as the new 'witches' (Faith, 1993; Faludi, 1991). While they may not be accused of removing men's 'virile members' in quite the same way, nevertheless men fear the limitations to their sexual 'freedom' posed by these new harridans.

In a society which has historically empowered men over women, and where those in charge of law making and judicial processes have traditionally been male, it is hardly surprising that the criminal justice system has operated in ways which benefit men to the detriment of women. Trying to convict a man of rape involves swimming upstream, against the strong currents of patriarchal thought and belief. While patriarchal privilege has traditionally provided men with protection from the law, women have had to rely, in turn, on these same men for their protection. Patriarchy, in effect, removed power from women and made them dependent upon men. If these same men abused their power, through the crime of rape, for example, the legal system was designed to operate in men's favour. In such an environment, it is scarcely surprising that the conviction rate for rape is so low (Harris and Grace, 1999; Her Majesty's Inspectorate of Constabulary and Her Majesty's Crown Prosecution Service Inspectorate, 2002; Kelly, 1999, 2002; Lees and Gregory, 1993; Temkin, 2002).[67]

Until very recently, marriage contracts guaranteed men unlimited sexual access to their wives (Bergen, 1996; Peacock, 1995; Russell, 1991; Temkin, 2002). Historically, wives were construed as the legal property of men, with few rights of their own. Significant changes have occurred since the late nineteenth century, ensuring that women now are able to own property themselves rather than simply be owned as part of men's property. From 1986 onwards in New Zealand, a wife's rights have been extended to give her sexual autonomy legally. In fact, the right of a woman to say no to the sexual demands of a man, even if he is her husband, has never been so completely written into law. Yet research indicates that marital rape continues, seemingly little abated by such legal changes (Easteal, 1998b; Lees, 1997; Russell, 1991). Few charges of rape within marriage have been laid since the law changes, and even fewer proceeded with through the legal system. In effect, the unprotected property status of women continues.

The position of women within marriage exists at the end of a continuum of ownership along which all women's lives are placed. The lack of protection offered to wives highlights the relative social vulnerability of all women in their relationships with men. While women's status has increased markedly in many ways over the last hundred years, fundamental gender inequalities remain. These continue to prioritise men's rights to sexual access to women over women's rights of refusal. While much of the rhetoric talks about what women want, in reality what dominates is what men want. One recent example of this is evident in research indicating that the quest for drugs to enhance men's sexual virility has completely ignored the effects on their female partners (Potts *et al.*, 2003). It seems self-evident that if men want more sex, and longer sex, we simply develop a drug like Viagra so they can have it. For women, the right to say no may exist legally but is limited socially and structurally. Men who force sexual relations on women who are strangers are condemned, since the rape of the unknown woman may mean raping a woman who belongs to another man, a crime recognised for centuries as heinous. Raping one's 'own' woman is, by comparison, a mere technicality.

Continuing to minimise the extent of sexual abuse and violence in homes and families is important if the traditional structures that have served patriarchy so well are to be upheld. Resisting recognition of fathers as abusers and husbands as rapists is one way of ensuring the continuing dominance of the family as a social unit, and of men's power within this unit. When rape was initially highlighted by feminists, women's vulnerability to sexual attack was acknowledged in the context of stranger danger (Gordon and Riger, 1991; Scully, 1990; Stanko, 1985). As long as the offender was clearly aberrant and predatory, attacking women who did not belong to him, then his dangerousness was recognised and his behaviour condemned. During the 1980s, women's fear of rape gradually began to be acknowledged, and small amounts of public funding were made available for rape prevention campaigns. Research into rape began, however, to identify women as being at greater risk of sexual violence from men they knew and may already be in relationships with (Gavey, 1991; Kelly, 1988; Koss *et al.*, 1987; Russell, 1990; Stanko, 1985; Warshaw, 1988; Wiehe and Richards, 1995). Over the last few years, women's fear of rape seems to have slipped from public and media consciousness, to be largely replaced by men's fear of false accusations. While once it was women who constituted the 'at risk' group, now men are seen as being at risk. In a climate where 'stranger danger' has been replaced by 'woman danger', access to justice for rape victims is destined to remain elusive.

The current environment does show small signs of promise, evident in greater diversity in police recruiting practices, and the introduction of policy initiatives which specifically address police interaction with sexual assault victims. The translation of policy into practice, however, seems not so assured. Whilst the crime-fighting, offender-oriented ethos of the police reigns supreme, and sceptical attitudes towards women complainants of sexual assaults remain unchallenged, significant progress in this area is unlikely. For any rape law or policy reform initiatives to be effective, significant changes in beliefs and attitudes need to occur throughout every aspect of the model outlined here. It will be impossible to fully attain women's rights in an environment which continues to credit rape myths with 'truth' status. Whilst gender inequality persists within society, the attainment of gender equity is unlikely to be achieved within the police organisation nor evident in interactions with complainants. Feminism may have impacted on the law and social conscience of society, but it has not yet managed to supplant the underlying beliefs.

The politics of silence and denial operate to conceal the truths and realities of rape. A woman's word is not to be trusted in part because the very act of her speaking may be considered offensive. A silent woman has long been held up as a model of virtuous femininity, while negative connotations associated with a woman's voice have resulted in her speech being dismissed as gossip, nagging and lying (Faith, 1993). Thus, as Taslitz has recently observed, the woman who speaks of her experience of rape 'breaks the rule of silence' (Taslitz, 1999, p. 20); in so doing, she risks either being blamed for what happened, or being disbelieved for saying what happened.

Against this backdrop the police, as part of the criminal justice system, will continue to reflect dominant cultural narratives and stereotypes unless these are consciously identified, challenged and changed. While such a process may sound reasonable and straightforward, in practice it may be near to impossible because what holds such beliefs in place is neither reasonable nor straightforward. Centuries of negative attitudes towards women, combined with justice systems designed primarily around men's interests, have resulted in the crime of rape being one of the most concealed, minimised and misunderstood offences that we have on the statute books. Whilst laws and policies may verbally acknowledge the seriousness of rape, police practices and procedures continue to perpetuate distinctions between 'rape' and 'real' rape, and to reflect adherence to negative and misogynistic views of women.[68]

This book has examined two conceptually related phenomena – 'true lies' and 'false truths'. Police officers, as members of a conservatively positioned and authoritarian social organisation, have traditionally adhered to beliefs that reflect both the masculinity and suspiciousness of their occupational culture (Gregory and Lees, 1999; Reiner, 1994; Smith and Gray, 1985). Within this culture, adherence to certain 'truths' is taken for granted. Amongst such 'truths' is the perception that women routinely lie about 'sex', fuelling a belief in high numbers of rape complaints being false. What the research results presented here demonstrate, however, is that these are 'false truths', myths perpetrated about women which have achieved a form of truth status. With reference to rape, for example, a delay by the victim in reporting the offence may be construed as indicative of a complainant's lack of credibility, reflecting a dominant mindset which assumes immediate reporting to be a 'natural' response. As this and other research has demonstrated, there is nothing 'natural' about prompt reporting nor inherently 'false' about delayed reporting. The material presented in this book illustrates a long legacy of thinking based on masculinist, and often misogynist, assumptions about women, which has infused the male-dominated culture of the police organisation. The distorted lenses through which police officers view the social world skews their slant on 'reality', and their gaze is shaped and informed by a narrow set of 'understandings' and conventions that have been constructed on mythical foundations. Police 'truths' about rape reflect myth and misogyny more than they do the actualities of women's experience.

If the police had a fuller and better informed understanding of the trauma induced by rape, they would recognise that victims routinely engage in minimising behaviour and will often try to avoid disclosing sexual violation. If the police understood the difficulties associated with approaching them to report a sexual assault, they would appreciate why some women tell 'lies' to conceal aspects of the offence. They would appreciate how humiliating the process can feel for complainants, and how shame can be a silencing mechanism. If the police knew the extent to which victims feared being blamed for what happened, they would not be surprised when complainants did things to try and bolster their credibility in the police's eyes. As this research showed, such concealment by victims typically results in their entire allegation being questioned and often rejected. Yet these may be 'true lies', lies which are told when women fear that the 'truth' of their experience will be ignored. Many women, having internalised the negativity of men's thinking towards them, can anticipate how others will view, judge, blame and condemn them. Women's own feelings towards themselves will reflect aspects of men's hatred, blame and revilement of them. Victims of rape who approach the police must walk the credibility tightrope and take their chances. To disclose and be discredited, because what was disclosed was discrediting; or to conceal and be discredited, because concealment itself is discrediting. Historically, rape discredited a woman and her family like no other crime; today, women must still fight to be seen as credible. Women's voices and women's words still struggle to be heard; if heard, to be believed; and if believed, to be understood. If the police subscribed to fewer 'false truths', they would be better able to recognise the 'true lies'.

End Poem

And She Has been Raped

Rape is a plain word. But it is so hard to know
that she has been raped. How bearably hard
it is for her and how bearably hard it is
for you. In the gentleness

that will heal her

you will be fluent
in her, not your own, intentions
                              (Dinah Hawken, 1991)

Thanks to Dinah Hawken and Victoria University Press for copyright permission to reprint this poem from Dinah Hawken, *Small Stories of Devotion*, Victoria University Press, Wellington, 1991.

Notes

'She stings while she delights': Rape Definitions and Representations

1. For an overview of rape law reforms in Australia, see Heath (1998); and see Temkin (2002, chapter 2) for commentary on the debate over widened definitions of rape within English law.

2. In the United States of America, despite marital rape becoming a crime in all 50 states under at least one section of the sexual offence codes, in many states some exemptions are still available to protect husbands from rape prosecution (e.g., where a wife is asleep or unconscious, or physically or mentally impaired) (Bergen, 1996).

3. 'Riding the bull at Gilleys' refers to a mechanical bull in a bar, which patrons take turns riding in bucking bronco fashion (Scully and Marolla, 1993, p. 41).

4. In this example, the defence lawyer passes the coke bottle to a jury member, asking him or her to move it round while the lawyer tries to insert the pencil into the bottle. The difficulty of achieving entry is likened to the apparent impossibility of sexual penetration occurring without a woman's cooperation (Shapcott, 1988, p. 185).

5. The legislation enacted in New Zealand in 1986 acknowledged to some extent the role of threat, and included the offence of Inducing Sexual Connection by Coercion, in which persons might abuse their authority to have sexual relations with another party (Sullivan, 1986).

6. 'Dissociation' refers to the psychological distress symptom evident in trauma survivors when they distance themselves by temporarily separating, or splitting themselves off, from the pain (Herman, 1992). This can induce a sense of numbness, and a feeling of not being in one's body.

7. In some societies, such as Peru, the penalty for rape decreases with the age of the victim, dropping to virtually no punishment in cases involving the rape of a mature woman (cited in Koss et al., 1994).

8. Highwater refers to this Goddess by the name 'Gaia'; other terms used include Triple Goddess, Hera, Great Goddess, the Creatrix, and some refer to the Ten Thousand Names of the Great Mother Goddess (Gimbutas, 1989; Wilshire, 1994).

9. For example, Deuteronomy, Chapter XXI, verses 10–15 spells out that in warfare a man take possession of a beautiful woman prisoner as his wife, until she ceases to please him, when he can discard her as he wishes.

10. The 'Sirens' were mythological women nymphs of the sea '... who had the power of charming by their songs all who heard them, so that the unhappy mariners were irresistibly impelled to cast themselves into the sea to their destruction' (Bulfinch, 1965).

11. Jean Jacques Rousseau (1712–78), a French deistic philosopher and author (Honderich, 1995).

12. Honoré de Balzac (1799–1850), who trained as a lawyer and went on to become one of France's most celebrated novelists (Lagasse, 2000).

13. Arthur Schopenhauer (1788–1860), a German philosopher renowned for his pessimism (Honderich, 1995).

14. Friedrich Nietzsche (1844–1900), German existentialist philosopher (Honderich, 1995).
15. This book was originally published in the United States of America in 1950.
16. The fact that New Zealand doctor, Morgan Fahey, could sexually assault his patients without detection for so many years, trading on his credibility and their lack of it, exemplifies this point (*The Dominion*, 26 May 2000; *The New Zealand Herald*, 2 June 2000). As well as being a respected Christchurch medical practitioner, Fahey was Deputy Mayor and had been awarded the OBE by the Queen – initially few citizens believed his women patients' allegations. His eventual conviction in June, 2000 for rape and other sexual offending provoked both national outrage and bewilderment.
17. This is common practice for COSA (Casualties of [*false*] Sexual Allegations), as evidenced in their organisation's newsletters (e.g., Issue 6, October 2000 contained such clippings as 'Girls fail to appear in court to back sex allegations in residential case: acquittal' and 'Patea High School teacher cleared: false sex allegations').

'Have you really been raped?' Criminal Justice System Responses

18. When I visited Thames Valley Police in 1996, two young officers, who would have been at school when the documentary was first screened in 1983, greeted me proclaiming that things were no longer like they had been on 'that programme'. The power of this incident probably lives on in the cultural memory of not only Thames Valley, but British police forces generally.
19. COSA is an advocates' group for men who believe they have been falsely accused of sexual assault.
20. The 48 women had reported a total of 50 incidents of rape or sexual assault to the police in the period 1990–93 – two women had been raped on two separate occasions by the same perpetrator.
21. Details of the women's experiences of the medical examination and support agency services are contained in the full 1998 report (Jordan, 1998a).
22. Further discussion of the gender variable in relation to police interviewing is contained in Jordan, 2002.
23. Further detail concerning each of these themes is available in Jordan (1998a).
24. Relevant literature on this distinction includes Kerstetter, 1990; LaFree, 1981; Shapcott, 1988; Warshaw, 1988; Weis and Borges, 1975.

Beyond Belief: Police Files on Rape

25. It should be noted that, in 1998, the police instituted major changes to their method of recording offences, in effect doing away with the statistics for reported offences and replacing these with recorded and resolved categories. Cases where the offence was declared to be 'no offence disclosed' are no longer being recorded as such, and the proportion of such cases is now extremely difficult to determine.
26. The figures in this row include all offences within the Sexual Violation category, including complainants over 16 years.
27. New Zealand has a national, centralised police agency, with headquarters based in Wellington.

28. Under New Zealand law, the term sexual violation covers the offence categories of both rape and unlawful sexual connection, with the latter category applied to incidents involving non-penile violation such as forced oral sex, and rape with an object.
29. Cases were filed as involving intellectual impairment when the police described the complainant as being intellectually handicapped, simple, or having a mental age well below their chronological years.
30. The category of psychiatric disturbance was applied to cases described as involving current or former mental or psychiatric patients, persons with personality disorders, or those with histories of depression or self-mutilation (or anybody else categorised in police shorthand as a '1M').
31. Hospital-based psychiatric teams are notified of patients who may require mental health assessment and treatment.
32. It should be noted that the latter involved a young woman of 17 years making a charge against the man who was now her ex-partner, and who had been her de facto partner – the use of the Husband Rapes Wife offence category on the files suggested there was no consistency in the use of this term whatsoever. Current husbands were not necessarily charged under this category, while ex-de facto partners sometimes were.
33. In 1997 the minimum age for admission to licensed premises was 20 years of age – this was reduced to 18 in 1999.
34. NIS refers to a New Zealand police national database, known as the National Intelligence System. These records are separate from the main police computer, and are used to store information on persons who have been in police contact for various reasons deemed noteworthy, whether or not these resulted in their arrest. Should, for example, this complainant have subsequent police contact, information will be available to police showing that she has a previous record for making a false complaint.
35. New Zealand does not have a separate, independent prosecutions service.

Having 'a nose for it': How Investigators Investigate

36. The specific areas are not identified, to provide some anonymity for the participants.
37. Each detective was given a numerical code (e.g. D1, D2) to assist in distinguishing his/her comments from others interviewed.
38. For brief background notes on Fahey, see Chapter 2, note 16.
39. At the discretion of the police, who make prosecutorial decisions in New Zealand, the option of having a case 'diverted' from the formal criminal justice system is offered to offenders on the basis that they admit guilt, and agree to the payment of fines or reparation, undertake community service, or fulfil other specified conditions.
40. A reference to Operation Park, one of the biggest investigations held in New Zealand to identify a serial rapist in Auckland.
41. Three major serial rape investigations were conducted in Auckland, New Zealand's largest city, in the 1990s, referred to by the police as Operation Park, Operation Harvey and Operation Atlas. Operation Park resulted in the arrest of Joseph Thompson, who pleaded guilty in 1995 to 46 counts of Sexual Violation by Rape and 15 counts of sexual violation by Unlawful Sexual Connection, as well as multiple counts of burglary related offences (Williams, 1998, p. 237). Operations

Harvey and Atlas were merged when it became clear that these investigations involved the same offender, the person later identified as Malcolm Rewa.

42. 'Michelle' was the name used to refer to this woman in an article published in the *New Zealand Woman's Weekly*, 15 June 1998.

43. 'Hammer' was Malcolm Rewa's nickname, given to him by Highway 61 members after he became known for strapping a hammer to his motorcycle 'to sort out any trouble' (Williams, 1998, p. 219).

44. K3 refers to the New Zealand Police's code for cases filed as 'no offence disclosed'.

45. Progress is being made in this area – in 2003 the New Zealand Police offered three-week long courses, each attended by approximately 20 detectives, on adult sexual assault investigations.

Perfect Victims/Perfect Policing? In the Words of the Women

46. A full account of this research process is contained in Jordan (2001b).

47. The 1998 trial included also charges against Rewa relating to the rape and murder of Susan Burdett in 1992. Rewa was initially acquitted on both counts but at a retrial in December 1998 he was convicted of the rape of Susan Burdett, but not of her murder.

48. A detective who interviewed both rapists commented that Thompson began confessing as soon as he was arrested, even to rapes that the police did not know about, whereas Rewa remained mute and hostile.

49. Only one of the women I interviewed was attacked away from her home, when Rewa abducted her as she returned to her car late at night.

50. Figures presented here refer primarily to the 14 women interviewed whose cases were tried for the first time in the 1998 court case and exclude the experiences of the woman attacked in 1975 unless otherwise stated.

51. Each woman decided how she wanted to be referred to in the research, usually by choosing her own pseudonym.

52. Detective Sergeant Dave Henwood, commonly known as Chook, a senior member of both the Malcolm Rewa and Joseph Thompson investigation teams.

53. Detective Inspector Steve Rutherford, who headed the Rewa investigation.

54. My questions are included where I consider these a useful preface to the women's responses.

55. One of the first women detectives assigned as a dedicated complainant officer left the police and was replaced during the trial preparation period.

56. Although I spoke with this woman several times by phone, during which she shared details of her experience, she decided not to be formally interviewed because of her current life circumstances and desire to move on emotionally after the trial.

57. The issues of complainant credibility evident here are strongly reminiscent of the factors identified earlier in this book as being linked to police perceptions and judgements concerning victim veracity.

58. Whilst the police were confident that Rewa was the offender in both these incidents, the jury acquitted him on all counts derived from these two attacks. The jury's decision appears to have been related to an absence of corroborative evidence that Rewa had intended raping these women when he attacked them (he was charged with Assault with Intent to Commit Rape).

59. Several of the women interviewed indicated that they chose to spend considerable periods of time at the court after they gave evidence. Some were keen to see

Rewa take the stand, and/or be present for the judge's summing up, jury verdict, and sentencing.

60. A computer-assisted sketch to aid in offender identification.
61. It is also possible that other mistakes and errors were made which were not detected by the women and which the police managed to keep concealed.

'Getting it right': Reviewing Police Responses to Rape

62. Strident opposition to the concept of specialist squads has been voiced at recent training sessions for police detectives that I have participated in, as well as in debate over the content of the New Zealand Police Sexual Assault Investigation Policy.
63. When the New Zealand Police introduced a specific policy on family violence in 1994, a Police Family Violence Coordinator was appointed; however, that individual left the police in 2000 and, as yet, no one has been appointed to assume specialist responsibility in this area.
64. The national police training college in New Zealand has recently incorporated some of the suggestions made on pages 228–229 into an expanded adult sexual assault investigators' course.
65. In my earlier research (Jordan, 1998a), two women rape complainants were sexually propositioned by officers involved in their cases.
66. My attention has been drawn recently to a reflective and challenging book by Rebecca Campbell, in which she researches the impacts experienced by those involved in interviewing rape survivors (Campbell, 2002).

Conclusion: True 'lies' and 'false' Truths

67. A British Home Office study revealed that, of all cases recorded as rape by the police, only 6 per cent resulted in conviction; this represents 9 per cent of 'crimed' rapes (Harris and Grace, 1999).
68. In early 2004, as this book was nearing completion, media investigations prompted the re-opening of a rape complaint originating in 1986 (*The Dominion Post*, 31 January 2004, *Sunday Star Times*, 1 February 2004). The case involved a teenage woman allegedly raped by three policemen, including the forcible use of a police baton. The failure of senior police to investigate this matter fully, and statements from detectives implying that many in the organisation closed rank to protect their own, has now resulted in the New Zealand Government ordering a Commission of Inquiry into this case, as well as suggesting the need for a re-examination of police culture and investigation procedures. The fact that one of the accused officers is currently an Assistant Commissioner, and in the running to be the next Commissioner (the highest ranking officer in the land), has further enhanced public interest in this case. The Commission of Inquiry is not expected to complete its report until late 2004.

References

Abbey, Antonia, Zawacki, Tina, Buck, Philip O., Clinton, A. Monique and McAuslan, Pam (2001). 'Alcohol and sexual assault'. *Alcohol Research and Health*, 25 (1): 43–51.

Adler, Zsuszanna (1987). *Rape on Trial*. London: Routledge and Kegan Paul.

Adler, Zsuzsanna (1991). 'Picking up the pieces'. *Police Review*, 31 May: 1114–15.

Agonito, Rosemary (1977). *History of Ideas on Women: A Source Book*. New York: Paragon.

Aiken, Margaret, Burgess, Ann Wolbert and Hazelwood, Robert R. (1999). 'False rape allegations'. In Robert R. Hazelwood and Ann W. Burgess (eds), *Practical Aspects of Rape Investigation: A Multidisciplinary Approach*, 2nd edition. Boca Raton: CRC Press.

Allison, Julie A. and Wrightsman, Lawrence S. (1993). *Rape: The Misunderstood Crime*. Newbury Park, California: Sage.

Amir, Menachem (1967). 'Victim precipitated forcible rape'. *Journal of Criminology, Criminal Law and Police*, 58 (4): 493–502.

Amir, Menachem (1971). *Patterns in Forcible Rape*. Chicago: University of Chicago Press.

Anstiss, Vivienne (1995). 'Police Officers and Rape Victims: Attitudes and Interface'. MSc Psychology thesis. Christchurch: University of Canterbury.

Bachman, Ronet (1993). 'Predicting the reporting of rape victimizations: Have rape reforms made a difference?' *Criminal Justice and Behavior*, 20 (3): 254–70.

Baker, Katharine (1999). 'Sex, rape, and shame'. *Boston University Law Review*, 79 (3): 663–716.

Barak, G. (1994). 'Between the waves: Mass-mediated themes of crime and justice'. *Social Justice*, 21 (3): 133–47.

Bargen, Jenny and Fishwick, Elaine (1995). *Sexual Assault Law Reform: A National Perspective*. Canberra: Office of the Status of Women.

Barry, Kathleen (1979). *Female Sexual Slavery*. New York: Avon Books.

Bart, Pauline B. (1979). 'Rape as a paradigm of sexism in society: Victimization and its discontents'. *Women's Studies International Quarterly*, 2: 347–57.

Basile, Kathleen C. (1999). 'Rape by acquiescence: The ways in which women "give in" to unwanted sex with their husbands'. *Violence Against Women*, 5 (9): 1036–58.

Bayley, David (1994). *Police for the Future*. New York: Oxford University Press.

Beckett, Linda (2000). 'Preventing Secondary Victimisation: An Analysis of the New Zealand Police Training for Investigating Sexual Assault'. MA Education thesis. Auckland: University of Auckland.

Bell, C. and Roberts, H. (eds) (1984). *Social Researching: Politics, Problems, Practice*. London: Routledge.

Bell, Diane (1991). 'Intraracial rape revisited: On forging a feminist future beyond factions and frightening politics'. *Women's Studies International Forum*, 14 (5): 385–412.

Bell, Vikki (1993). *Interrogating Incest: Feminism, Foucault and the Law*. London: Routledge.

Bergen, R. K. (1996). *Wife Rape: Understanding the Response of Survivors and Service Providers*. Thousand Oaks, CA: Sage.

Berger, John (1977). *Ways of Seeing*. London: British Broadcasting Corporation and Penguin Books.

Blair, Ian (1985). *Investigating Rape: A New Approach for Police*. London: Croom Helm/The Police Foundation.

Bohmer, Carole (1991). 'Acquaintance rape and the law'. In Andrea Parrot and Laurie Bechhofer (eds), *Acquaintance Rape: The Hidden Crime*. New York: John Wiley.

Bottomley, A. K. and Coleman, C. A. (1981). *Understanding Crime Rates*. Farnborough: Saxon House.

Bouffard, Jeffrey A. (2000). 'Predicting type of sexual assault case closure from victim, suspect, and case characteristics'. *Journal of Criminal Justice*, 28 (6): 527–42.

Bourque, Linda Brookover (1989). *Defining Rape*. Durham and London: Duke University Press.

Box, Steven (1983). *Power, Crime, and Mystification*. London: Tavistock.

Bronitt, Simon (1998). 'The rules of recent complaint: rape myths and the legal construction of the "reasonable" rape victim'. In Patricia, Easteal (ed.) *Balancing the Scales: Rape, Law Reform and Australian Culture*. Leichhardt, Sydney: The Federation Press.

Bronson, Dr F. R. (1918). 'False accusations of rape'. *American Journal of Urology and Sexology*, 14 (12): 539–52.

Brook, Jane (1997). 'Sexual abuse and people with intellectual disabilities'. *Social Work Review*, New Zealand Association of Social Workers, 9 (3): 16–17.

Brown, Jennifer (1997). 'Women in policing: A comparative research perspective'. *International Journal of the Sociology of Law*, 25: 1–19.

Brown, Jennifer (1998). 'Aspects of discriminatory treatment of women police officers serving in forces in England and Wales'. *British Journal of Criminology*, 38 (2): 265–82.

Brown, Jennifer, Burman, Michele and Jamieson, Lynn (1993a). *Sex Crimes on Trial*. Edinburgh: Edinburgh University Press.

Brown, J., Maidment, A. and Bull, R. (1993b). 'Appropriate skill-task matching or gender bias in deployment of male and female police officers?' *Policing and Society*, 3: 121–36.

Brown, Jennifer and Heidensohn, Frances (2000). *Gender and Policing: Comparative Perspectives*. Basingstoke: Macmillan.

Brownmiller, Susan (1975). *Against Our Will: Men, Women and Rape*. Harmondsworth: Penguin.

Buckingham, Judith I. (2004). '"Newsmaking Criminology" or "Info-Tainment" Criminology: The Case for Drawing Distinctions'. *Australian and New Zealand Journal of Criminology*, 37 (2): 253–75.

Buerger, Michael (1993). 'The challenge of reinventing police and community'. In David Weisburd and Craig Uchida (eds), *Police Innovation and Control of the Police: Problems of Law, Order and Community*. New York: Springer-Verlag.

Bulfinch, Thomas (1965). *Bulfinch's Mythology: The Age of Fable*. New York: Airmont Publishing Company.

Bullough, Vern (1974). *The Subordinate Sex: A History of Attitudes Toward Women*. New York: Penguin.

Bureau of Justice Statistics (1991). *Female Victims of Violent Crime*. Washington DC: US Department of Justice.

Burgess, Ann Wolbert (1999). 'Public beliefs and attitudes toward rape'. In Robert R. Hazelwood and Ann W. Burgess (eds), *Practical Aspects of Rape Investigation: A Multidisciplinary Approach*, 2nd edition. Boca Raton: CRC Press.

Burgess, Ann Wolbert and Hazelwood, Robert R. (1999). 'The Victim's Perspective'. In Robert R. Hazelwood and Ann W. Burgess (eds), *Practical Aspects of Rape Investigation: A Multidisciplinary Approach*, 2nd edition. Boca Raton: CRC Press.

Burt, Martha (1980). 'Cultural myths and supports for rape'. *Journal of Personality and Social Psychology*, 38 (2): 217–30.

Burt, Martha (1991). 'Rape myths'. In Andrea Parrot and Laurie Bechhofer (eds) *Acquaintance Rape: The Hidden Crime*. New York: John Wiley and Sons.

Burt, M. R. and Katz, B. L. (1985). 'Rape, robbery, and burglary: responses to actual and feared victimization, with special focus on women and the elderly'. *Victimology: An International Journal*, 10: 325–58.

Cahill, Ann J. (2001). *Rethinking Rape*. Ithaca: Cornell University Press.

Callihan, Jean M. (2003). 'Victim impact statements in capital trials: a selected bibliography'. *Cornell Law Review*, 88 (2): 569–82.

Cameron, Deborah and Frazer, Elizabeth (1987). *The Lust to Kill: A Feminist Investigation of Sexual Murder*. New York: New York University Press.

Cameron, Neil (1986). 'Developments and issues in policing New Zealand'. In Neil Cameron and Warren Young (eds), *Policing at the Crossroads*. Wellington: Allen and Unwin/Port Nicholson Press.

Campbell, Rebecca (2002). *Emotionally Involved: The Impact of Researching Rape*. New York: Routledge.

Campbell, Rebecca and Johnson, Camille R. (1997). 'Police officers' perceptions of rape: Is there consistency between state law and individual beliefs?' *Journal of Interpersonal Violence*, 12 (2): 255–74.

Campbell, Rebecca and Raja, Sheela (1999). 'Secondary victimization of rape victims: Insights from mental health professionals who treat survivors of violence'. *Violence and Victims*, 14 (3): 261–75.

Carrington, Kerry and Watson, Paul (1996). 'Policing sexual violence: Feminism, criminal justice and governmentality'. *International Journal of the Sociology of Law*, 24: 253–72.

Cavanagh, Barbara Kirk (1971). ' "A little dearer than his horse": Legal stereotypes and the feminine personality'. *Harvard Civil Rights – Civil Liberties Law Review*, 6 (2): 260–87.

Chambers, Gerry and Millar, Ann (1983). *Investigating Sexual Assault*. Edinburgh: Scottish Office Central Research Unit.

Chan, Janet (1996). 'Changing police culture'. *British Journal of Criminology*, 36 (1): 109–34.

Chan, Janet B. L. (2003). *Fair Cop: Learning the Art of Policing*. Toronto: University of Toronto Press.

Chappell, Duncan and Singer, Susan (1977). 'Rape in New York City: A study of material in the police files and its meaning'. In D. Chappell, R. Geis and G. Geis (eds), *Forcible Rape: The Crime, the Victim and the Offender*. New York: Columbia University Press.

Clark, L. and Lewis, D. (1977). *Rape: The Price of Coercive Sexuality*. Toronto: The Women's Press.

Cossins, Annie (1998). 'Tipping the scales in her favour: The need to protect counselling records in sexual assault trials'. In Patricia, Easteal (ed.), *Balancing the Scales: Rape, Law Reform and Australian Culture*. Leichhardt, Sydney: The Federation Press.

Crawshaw, Michele (1998). 'The second rape'. *Metro*, September, 207: 60–5.

Crowell, Nancy A. and Burgess, Ann W. (eds) (1996). *Understanding Violence Against Women*. Washington, DC: National Academy Press.

Culbertson, R. (1995). 'Embodied memory, transcendence, and telling: Recounting trauma, re-establishing the self'. *New Literary History*, 26 (1): 169–96.

Dacre, Paul (1996). 'Defence counsel's perspective'. In Juliet Broadmore, Carol Shand and Tania Warburton (eds) *The Proceedings of Rape: Ten Years' Progress? An Interdisciplinary Conference*. Wellington, New Zealand: Doctors for Sexual Abuse Care (DSAC).

Daly, Mary (1979). *Gyn/Ecology: The Metaethics of Radical Feminism.* London: Women's Press.

Dann, Christine (1985). *Up From Under: Women and Liberation in New Zealand 1970–1985.* Wellington: Allen and Unwin/Port Nicholson Press.

Dershowitz, Alan M. (1994). *The Abuse Excuse: And Other Cop-outs, Sob Stories and Evasions of Responsibility.* Boston: Little, Brown and Company.

Deutsch, Helene (1944). *The Psychology of Women.* London: Grune and Stratton.

Doerner, William G. and Lab, Steven P. (1998). *Victimology.* 2nd edition. Cincinnati, OH: Anderson Publishing.

Donat, Patricia and D'Emilio, John (1992). 'A feminist redefinition of rape and sexual assault: Historical foundations and change'. *Journal of Social Issues,* 48 (1): 9–22.

Doran, Sally and Chan, Janet (2003). 'Doing Gender'. In Janet B. L. Chan, *Fair Cop: Learning the Art of Policing.* Toronto: University of Toronto Press.

Dowdeswell, Jane (1986). *Women On Rape: Firsthand Feelings, Attitudes and Experiences from the Women Involved, Backed up by the Facts.* Wellingborough: Thorsons Publishing Group.

Du Chateau, Carroll (1993). 'Is the child sex abuse industry telling the truth?' *Metro,* Auckland, March: 72–8.

Du Mont, Janice, Miller, Karen-Lee and Myhr, Terri L. (2003). 'The role of "real rape" and "real victim" stereotypes in the police reporting practices of sexually assaulted women'. *Violence Against Women,* 9 (4): 466–86.

Dworkin, Andrea (1982). *Our Blood: Prophecies and Discourses on Sexual Politics.* London: The Women's Press.

Easteal, Patricia (ed.) (1993). *Without Consent: Confronting Adult Sexual Violence: Proceedings of a Conference.* Canberra, Australia: Australian Institute of Criminology.

Easteal, Patricia (1998a). 'The cultural context of rape and reform'. In Patricia Easteal (ed.), *Balancing the Scales: Rape, Law Reform and Australian Culture.* Leichhardt, Sydney: The Federation Press.

Easteal, Patricia (1998b). 'Rape in marriage: Has the licence lapsed?' In Patricia Easteal (ed.), *Balancing the Scales: Rape, Law Reform and Australian Culture.* Leichhardt, Sydney: The Federation Press.

Edwards, Anne and Heenan, Melanie (1994). 'Rape trials in Victoria: Gender, socio-cultural factors and justice'. *Australian and New Zealand Journal of Criminology,* 27 (3): 213–36.

Edwards, R. (1993). 'An education in interviewing: Placing the researcher and the research'. In C. M. Renzetti and R. M. Lee (eds), *Researching Sensitive Topics.* Newbury Park: Sage.

Edwards, Susan M. (1981). *Female Sexuality and the Law.* Oxford: Martin Robertson.

Ehrlich, Susan (2001). *Representing Rape: Language and Sexual Consent.* London: Routledge.

Eisler, Riane (1987). *The Chalice and the Blade: Our History, Our Future.* New York: HarperCollins.

English Collective of Prostitutes (1997). 'Campaigning for Legal Change'. In Graham Scambler and Annette Scambler (eds), *Rethinking Prostitution: Purchasing Sex in the 1990s.* London: Routledge.

Enns, Carolyn Zerbe (1996). 'Counselors and the backlash: "Rape hype" and "false-memory syndrome".' *Journal of Counseling and Development,* 76: 358–67.

Epstein, Joel and Langenbahn, Stacia (1994). *The Criminal Justice and Community Response to Rape.* Issues and Practices in Criminal Justice series, National Institute of Justice. Washington: US Department of Justice.

Estrich, Susan (1987). *Real Rape*. Cambridge, MA: Harvard University Press.

Ettorre, Elizabeth (1992). *Women and Substance Use*. London: Macmillan.

Fairstein, Linda A. (1993). *Sexual Violence: Our War Against Rape*. New York: William Morrow and Company.

Faith, Karlene (1993). *Unruly Women: The Politics of Confinement and Resistance*. Vancouver: Press Gang Publishers.

Faludi, Susan (1991). *Backlash: The Undeclared War Against Women*. London: Chatto and Windus.

Fancourt, R., Shand, C., Broadmore, J. and Milford, R. (1994). *The Medical Management of Sexual Abuse*, 4th edition. Auckland: Doctors for Sexual Abuse Care (DSAC).

Feild, H. S. (1978). 'Attitudes towards rape: A comparative analysis of police, rapists, crisis counsellors, and citizens'. *Journal of Personality and Social Psychology*, 36: 156–79.

Feldman-Summers, Shirley and Palmer, Gayle C. (1980). 'Rape as viewed by judges, prosecutors, and police officers'. *Criminal Justice and Behavior*, 7 (1): 19–40.

Feldman-Summers, S. and Norris, H. (1984). 'Differences between rape victims who report and those who do not report to a public agency'. *Journal of Applied Social Psychology*, 14: 562–73.

Fielding, Nigel (1995). 'Cop canteen culture'. In Tim Newburn and Elizabeth A. Stanko (eds), *Just Boys doing Business? Men, Masculinities and Crime*. London: Routledge.

Finch, J. (1984). ' "It's great to have someone to talk to": The ethics and politics of interviewing women'. In C. Bell and H. Roberts (eds), *Social Researching: Politics, Problems, Practice*. London: Routledge.

Firth, Alan (1975). 'Interrogation'. *Police Review*, 28 November: 1507.

Fleming, Donna (1998). ' "Police wouldn't believe me".' *New Zealand Woman's Weekly*, 15 June: 20–3.

Foley, Marian. (1996). 'Who is in control?: Changing responses to women who have been raped and sexually abused'. In Marianne Hester, Liz Kelly and Jill Radford (eds), *Women, Violence and Male Power: Feminist Activism, Research and Practice*. Buckingham: Open University Press.

Ford, L. A. and Crabtree, R. D. (2002). 'Telling, re-telling and talking about telling: Disclosure and/as surviving incest'. *Women's Studies in Communication*, 25 (1) 53–87.

Foucault, Michel (1981). *The History of Sexuality, Vol. 1*. Harmondsworth: Pelican Books.

Frazier, P. A. and Borgida, E. (1999). 'Rape trauma syndrome: A review of case law and psychological research'. In Robert R. Hazelwood and Ann W. Burgess (eds), *Practical Aspects of Rape Investigation: A Multidisciplinary Approach*, 2nd edition. Boca Raton: CRC Press.

Frazier, Patricia A. and Haney, Beth (1996). 'Sexual assault cases in the legal system: Police, prosecutor, and victim perspectives'. *Law and Human Behavior*, 20: 607–28.

Frazier, P. and Seales, L. (1997). 'Acquaintance rape is real rape'. In Martin Schwartz (ed.), *Researching Sexual Violence Against Women*. Newbury Park: Sage.

Freckelton, Ian (1998). 'Sexual offence prosecutions: A barrister's perspective'. In Patricia Easteal (ed.), *Balancing the Scales: Rape, Law Reform and Australian Culture*. Leichhardt, Sydney: The Federation Press.

French, Marilyn (1992). *The War Against Women*. London: Hamish Hamilton.

Frohmann, Lisa (1995). 'Discrediting victims' allegations of sexual assault: prosecutorial accounts of case rejections'. In Patricia Searles and Ronald J. Berger (eds), *Rape and Society: Readings on the Problem of Sexual Assault*. Boulder, CO: Westview Press.

Frohmann, Lisa (1998). 'Constituting power in sexual assault cases: Prosecutorial strategies for victim management'. *Social Problems*, 45 (3): 393–407.

Galliano, Grace, Noble, Linda M., Travis, Linda A. and Puechl, Carol (1993). 'Victim reactions during rape/sexual assault'. *Journal of Interpersonal Violence*, 8 (1): 109–14.

Gartner, R. and McMillan, R. (1995). 'The effect of victim–offender relationship on reporting crimes of violence against women'. *Canadian Journal of Criminology*, 37 (3): 393–429.

Gavey, Nicola (1991). 'Sexual victimization prevalence among New Zealand university students'. *Journal of Consulting and Clinical Psychology*, 59 (3): 464–6.

Gavey, Nicola (1999). ' "I wasn't raped, but" ... : Revisiting definitional problems in sexual victimization'. In Sharon Lamb (ed.), *New Versions of Victims: Feminists Struggle with the Concept*. New York: New York University Press.

Gavey, Nicola and Gow, Virginia (2001). ' "Cry Wolf", cried the wolf: Constructing the issue of false rape allegations in New Zealand media texts'. *Feminism and Psychology*, 11 (3): 341–60.

Gilbert, Keith (1993). 'Rape and the sex industry'. In Patricia Easteal (ed.), *Without Consent: Confronting Adult Sexual Violence: Proceedings of a Conference*. Canberra, Australia: Australian Institute of Criminology.

Gillespie, Terry (1996). 'Rape crisis centres and "male rape": A face of the backlash'. In Marianne Hester, Liz Kelly and Jill Radford (eds), *Women, Violence and Male Power: Feminist Activism, Research and Practice*. Buckingham: Open University Press.

Gilmore, K. and Pittman, L. (1993). *To Report or Not to Report: A Study of Victim/Survivors of Sexual Assault and Their Experience of Making an Initial Report to the Police*. Melbourne: Centre Against Sexual Assault (CASA House) and Royal Women's Hospital.

Gimbutas, Marija (1989). *The Language of the Goddess*. San Francisco: Harper and Row.

Glaser, B. and Strauss, A. L. (1967). *The Discovery of Grounded Theory*. Chicago: Aldine.

Goldberg-Ambrose, Carole (1992). 'Unfinished business in rape law reform'. *Journal of Social Issues*, 48 (1): 173–85.

Goleman, Daniel (1985). *Vital Lies, Simple Truths: The Psychology of Self-Deception*. New York: Simon and Schuster, Inc.

Goodman, Lisa A., Koss, Mary P. and Russo, Nancy Felipe (1993). 'Violence against women: Physical and mental health effects. Part I: Research findings'. *Applied and Preventive Psychology*, 2: 79–89.

Goodstein, Lynne and Lutze, Faith (1992). 'Rape and criminal justice system responses'. In Imogene Moyer (ed.), *The Changing Roles of Women in the Criminal Justice System: Offenders, Victims, and Professionals*, 2nd edition. Illinois: Waveland Press.

Goodyear-Smith, Felicity (1995). 'Review of "Was Eve merely framed; or was she forsaken?" ' *New Zealand Law Journal*, July: 230–33.

Gordon, Margaret T. and Riger, Stephanie (1991). *The Female Fear: The Social Cost of Rape*. Urbana: University of Illinois Press.

Grabosky, Peter (1995). 'Counterproductive regulation'. *International Journal of the Sociology of Law*, 23: 347–69.

Green, William M. (1988). *Rape: The Evidential Examination and Management of the Adult Female Victim*. Massachusetts: Lexington Books.

Greene, Jack R. and Mastrofski, Stephen D. (1988). *Community Policing*. New York: Praeger.

Gregory, Jeanne and Lees, Sue (1996). 'Attrition in rape and sexual assault cases'. *British Journal of Criminology*, 36 (1): 1–17.

Gregory, Jeanne and Lees, Sue (1999). *Policing Sexual Assault*. London: Routledge.

Griffin, Susan (1975). 'Rape: The all-American crime'. In Leroy G. Schultz, *Rape Victimology*. Springfield, Illinois: Charles C. Thomas.

Hale, Donna C. and Bennett, C. Lee (1995). 'Realities of Women in Policing: An Organizational Cultural Perspective'. In Alida V. Merlo and Joycelyn M. Pollock (eds), *Women, Law, and Social Control*. Boston: Allyn and Bacon.

Halford, Alison (1993). *No Way Up the Greasy Pole*. London: Constable.

Hall, Ruth E. (1985). *Ask Any Woman: A London Inquiry into Rape and Sexual Assault*. Bristol: Falling Wall Press.

Hamlin, John E. (1988). 'Who's the victim? Women, control, and consciousness'. *Women's Studies International Forum*, 11 (3): 223–33.

Harrington, Nicole Turillon and Leitenberg, Harold (1994). 'Relationship between alcohol consumption and victim behaviors immediately preceding sexual aggression by an acquaintance'. *Violence and Victims*, 9 (4): 315–24.

Harris, Jessica and Grace, Sharon (1999). *A Question of Evidence? Investigating and Prosecuting Rape in the 1990s*. London: Home Office.

Hawken, Dinah (1991). *Small Stories of Devotion*. Wellington: Victoria University Press.

Hayes, Susan (1993). 'Sexual violence against intellectually disabled victims'. In Patricia Easteal (ed.), *Without Consent: Confronting Adult Sexual Violence: Proceedings of a Conference*. Canberra, Australia: Australian Institute of Criminology.

Hazelwood, Robert R. and Burgess, Ann Wolbert (1999). 'The behavioral-oriented interview of rape victims: The key to profiling'. In Robert R. Hazelwood and Ann W. Burgess (eds), *Practical Aspects of Rape Investigation: A Multidisciplinary Approach*, 2nd edition. Boca Raton: CRC Press.

Heath, Mary (1998). 'Disputed truths: Australian reform of the sexual conduct elements of common law rape'. In Patricia Easteal (ed.), *Balancing the Scales: Rape, Law Reform and Australian Culture*. Leichhardt, Sydney: The Federation Press.

Heidensohn, Frances (1992). *Women in Control? The Role of Women in Law Enforcement*. Oxford: Clarendon.

Henning, Terese and Bronitt, Simon (1998). 'Rape victims on trial: Regulating the use and abuse of sexual history evidence'. In Patricia Easteal (ed.), *Balancing the Scales: Rape, Law Reform and Australian Culture*. Leichhardt, Sydney: The Federation Press.

Her Majesty's Inspectorate of Constabulary and Her Majesty's Crown Prosecution Service Inspectorate (2002). *A Report on the Joint Investigation into the Investigation and Prosecution of Cases Involving Allegations of Rape*. London: Her Majesty's Inspectorate of Constabulary and Her Majesty's Crown Prosecution Service Inspectorate.

Herman, Judith (1992). *Trauma and Recovery*. New York: Basic Books.

Herman, J. L. and Harvey, M. (1993). 'The false memory debate: Social science or social backlash?' *Just Us*, May/June: 5–8.

Hester, Marianne (1992). *Lewd Women and Wicked Witches: A Study of the Dynamics of Male Domination*. London: Routledge.

Highwater, Jamake (1990). *Myth and Sexuality*. New York: NAL Books.

Hinck, Shelly Schaefer and Thomas, Richard W. (1999). 'Rape myth acceptance in college students: How far have we come?' *Sex Roles*, 40 (9/10): 815–32.

Holdaway, S. (1983). *Inside British Police: A Force at Work*. Oxford: Basil Blackwell.

Holmstrom, Lynda Lytle and Burgess, Ann Wolbert (1974). 'Rape trauma syndrome'. *American Journal of Psychiatry*, 121 (9).

Holmstrom, Lynda Lytle and Burgess, Ann Wolbert (1978). *The Victim of Rape: Institutional Reactions*. New York: Wiley.

Holmstrom, Lynda Lytle and Burgess, Ann Wolbert (1991). *The Victim of Rape*. New Brunswick, NJ: Transaction Publishers.

Honderich, Ted (ed.) (1995). *The Oxford Companion to Philosophy*. New York: Oxford University Press.

Horn, Rebecca (1995). 'Reflexivity in placement: Women interviewing women'. *Feminism and Psychology*, 5 (1): 94–8.

Hough, Mike (1987). 'Thinking about effectiveness'. *British Journal of Criminology*, 27 (1): 70–9.

Howe, Adrian (1998). 'Introduction: Sex, sex ... sexed crime in the news'. In Howe, Adrian (ed.), *Sexed Crime in the News*. Leichhardt, NSW: The Federation Press.

Hyman, Prue (2000). *Women in the CIB: Opportunities and Barriers to the Recruitment, Progress, and Retention of Women in the Criminal Investigation Branch (CIB)*. Wellington: New Zealand Police.

Jackson, Stevi (1978). 'The social context of rape: Sexual scripts and motivation'. *Women's Studies International Quarterly*, 1: 27–38.

Jackson, Stevi (1996). 'Heterosexuality, power and pleasure'. In Stevi Jackson and Sue Scott (eds), *Feminism and Sexuality: A Reader*. Edinburgh: Edinburgh University Press. pp. 175–79.

Jefferson, Tony (1997). 'The Tyson rape trial: The law, feminism and emotional "truth"'. *Social and Legal Studies*, 6 (2): 281–301.

Johnson, Allan G. (1997). *The Gender Knot: Unraveling our Patriarchal Legacy*. Philadelphia: Temple University Press.

Jones, Sandra (1986). *Policewomen and Equality*. Basingstoke: Macmillan.

Jordan, Jan (1996). 'Women, rape and the reporting process'. In Juliet Broadmore, Carol Shand and Tania Warburton (eds), *The Proceedings of Rape: Ten Years' Progress? An Interdisciplinary Conference*. Wellington, New Zealand: Doctors for Sexual Abuse Care (DSAC).

Jordan, Jan (1998a). *Reporting Rape: Women's Experiences with the Police, Doctors and Support Agencies*. Wellington: Institute of Criminology.

Jordan, Jan (1998b). ''There's not a lot of Justice in the System': Rape victims' views and the police response'. In Rosemary Du Plessis and Geoff Fougere (eds) *Politics, Policy & Practice: Essays in Honour of Bill Willmott*. Christchurch, New Zealand: University of Canterbury.

Jordan, Jan (2001a). 'Worlds apart? Women, rape and the reporting process'. *British Journal of Criminology*, 41 (4), 679–706.

Jordan, Jan (2001b). 'True "Lies" and False "Truths": Women, Rape and the Police'. PhD thesis, Criminology. Wellington: Victoria University of Wellington.

Jordan, Jan (2002). 'Will any woman do? Police, gender and rape victims'. *Policing: An International Journal of Police Strategies and Management*, 25 (2): 319–44.

Jordan, Jan (2004). 'Beyond belief: Police, rape and women's credibility'. *Criminal Justice*, 4 (1): 29–59.

Jukes, Adam (1993). *Why Men Hate Women*. London: Free Association Books.

Kalven, H. and Zeisel, H. (1966). *The American Jury*. Boston, MA: Little, Brown and Company.

Kanin, Eugene J. (1994). 'False rape allegations'. *Archives of Sexual Behavior*, 23 (1): 81–92.

Kassin, Saul M. and Fong, Christina T. (1999). '"I'm innocent!": Effects of training on judgments of truth and deception in the interrogation room'. *Law and Human Behavior*, 23 (5): 499–516.

Katz, Sedelle and Mazur, Mary Ann (1979). *Understanding the Rape Victim: A Synthesis of Research Findings*. New York: John Wiley and Sons.

Kelly, Liz (1988). *Surviving Sexual Violence*. Cambridge: Polity Press.

Kelly, Liz (1996). 'When does the speaking profit us?: Reflections on the challenges of developing feminist perspectives on abuse and violence by women'. In Marianne

Hester, Liz Kelly and Jill Radford (eds), *Women, Violence and Male Power: Feminist Activism, Research and Practice*. Buckingham: Open University Press.

Kelly, Liz (1999). 'A War of Attrition: Recent Research on Rape'. *Trouble and Strife*, 40: 9–16.

Kelly, Liz (2002). *A Research Review on the Reporting, Investigation and Prosecution of Rape Cases*. London: Her Majesty's Crown Prosecution Service Inspectorate.

Kelly, Liz and Radford, Jill (1996). ' "Nothing really happened": The invalidation of women's experiences of sexual violence'. In Marianne Hester, Liz Kelly and Jill Radford (eds), *Women, Violence and Male Power: Feminist Activism, Research and Practice*. Buckingham: Open University Press.

Kemmer, Elizabeth Jane (1977). *Rape and Rape-related Issues: An Annotated Bibliography*, New York: Garland Publishing.

Kennedy, Helena (1992). *Eve Was Framed: Women and British Justice*. London: Vintage.

Kerstetter, Wayne (1990). 'Gateway to justice: Police and prosecutorial response to sexual assaults against women'. *Journal of Criminal Law and Criminology*, 81 (2): 267–313.

Kerstetter, W. A. and van Winkle, B. (1990). 'Who decides?: A study of the complainant's decision to prosecute in rape cases'. *Criminal Justice and Behaviour*, 17 (3): 268–83.

Kilpatrick, D. G., Saunders, B. E., Veronen, L. J., Best, C. L. and Von, J. M. (1987). 'Criminal Victimization: Lifetime prevalence, reporting to police, and psychological impact'. *Crime and Delinquency*, 33: 479–89.

Kohut, Heinz (1977). *The Restoration of the Self*. Madison, CT: International Universities Press.

Koss, Mary P. (1990). 'The women's mental health research agenda: Violence against women'. *American Psychologist*, 45, 3: 374–80.

Koss, Mary P. (2000). 'Blame, shame and community'. *American Psychologist*, 55 (11): 1332–43.

Koss, Mary P., Dinero, Thomas E., Seibel, Cynthia A. and Cox, Susan L. (1988). 'Stranger and acquaintance rape: Are there differences in the victim's experience?' *Psychology of Women Quarterly*, 12: 1–24.

Koss, M. P., Gidycz, C. A. and Wisniewski, N. (1987). 'The scope of rape: Incidence and prevalence of sexual aggression and victimization in a national sample of higher education students'. *Journal of Consulting and Clinical Psychology*, 55 (2): 162–70.

Koss, Mary P., Heise, Lori and Russo, Nancy Felipe (1994). 'The global health burden of rape'. *Psychology of Women Quarterly*, 18: 509–37.

LaFree, Gary (1980). 'Variables affecting guilty pleas and convictions in rape cases: Toward a social theory of rape processing'. *Social Forces*, 58 (3): 833–50.

LaFree, Gary (1981). 'Official reactions to social problems: Police decisions in sexual assault cases'. *Social Problems*, 28 (5): 582–94.

LaFree, Gary (1989). *Rape and Criminal Justice: The Social Construction of Sexual Assault*. Belmont, CA: Wadsworth.

Lagasse, Paul (ed.) (2000). *The Columbia Encyclopedia, Sixth Edition*. New York: Columbia University Press.

Laing, Ronald David (1970). *Knots*. London: Tavistock.

Larson, John A. (1969). *Lying and its Detection: A Study of Deception and Deception Tests*. Montclair, NJ: Patterson Smith.

LeDoux, J. C. and Hazelwood, R. R. (1999). 'Police attitudes and beliefs concerning rape'. In Robert R. Hazelwood and Ann W. Burgess (eds), *Practical Aspects of Rape Investigation: A Multidisciplinary Approach*, 2nd edition. Boca Raton: CRC Press.

Lee, Angela and Searle, Wendy (1993). *Victims' Needs: An Issues Paper*. Wellington: Department of Justice.

Lee, Angela, Searle, Wendy and Atkinson, Kelly-Anne (1993). *Victims' Needs: The Results of the Survey*. Wellington: Department of Justice.

Lees, Sue (1995). 'Media reporting of rape: The 1993 British "date rape" controversy'. In D. Kidd-Hewitt and R. Osborne (eds), *Crime and the Media: the Post Modern Spectacle*. London: Pluto Press.

Lees, Sue (1996). *Carnal Knowledge: Rape on Trial*. London: Hamish Hamilton.

Lees, Sue (1997). *Ruling Passions: Sexual Violence, Reputation and The Law*. Buckingham: Open University Press.

Lees, Sue and Gregory, Jeanne (1993). *Rape and Sexual Assault: A Study in Attrition*. London: Islington Council Crime Prevention Unit.

Lees, Sue and Gregory, Jeanne (1997). 'In search of gender justice: sexual assault and the criminal justice system'. In Sue Lees, *Ruling Passions: Sexual Violence, Reputation and the Law*. Buckingham: Open University Press.

Lloyd, Ann (1976). *Rape: An Examination of the Crime in New Zealand: Its Social and Emotional Consequences*. Auckland: Wilson and Horton.

Loftus, Elizabeth (1992). 'When a lie becomes memory's truth: memory distortion after exposure to misinformation'. *Current Directions in Psychological Science*, 1: 121–3.

Loftus, Elizabeth, Polonsky, Sara and Fulilove, Mindy (1994). 'Memories of childhood sexual abuse: Remembering and repressing'. *Psychology of Women Quarterly*, 18: 67–84.

Lombroso, Caesar and Ferrero, William (1895). *The Female Offender*. London: T. Fisher Unwin.

London Rape Crisis Centre (1984). *Sexual Violence: The Reality for Women*. London: Women's Press.

Lonsway, K. A. and Fitzgerald, L. F. (1994). 'Rape myths: In review'. *Psychology of Women Quarterly*, 18: 133–64.

Los, Maria (1994). 'The struggle to redefine rape in the early 1980s'. In Julian V. Roberts and Renate M. Mohr (eds), *Confronting Sexual Assault: A Decade of Social and Legal Change*. Toronto: University of Toronto Press.

Luckasson, R. (1992). 'People with Mental Retardation as Victims of Crime'. In R. W. Conley, R. Luckasson and G. N. Bouthilet (eds), *The Criminal Justice System and Mental Retardation: Defendants and Victims*. Baltimore, MD: Paul Brookes.

Macdonald, John M. (1995). *Rape: Controversial Issues – Criminal Profiles, Date Rape, False Reports and False Memories*. Springfield, IL: Charles C. Thomas.

Mack, Kathy (1998). ' "You should scrutinise her evidence with great care": Corroboration of women's testimony about sexual assault'. In Patricia Easteal (ed.), *Balancing the Scales: Rape, Law Reform and Australian Culture*. Leichhardt, Sydney: The Federation Press.

MacKinnon, Catharine (1983). 'Feminism, Marxism, method and the state: Toward feminist jurisprudence'. *Signs: Journal of Women in Culture and Society*, 8 (2): 635–58.

MacKinnon, Catharine (1987). *Feminism Unmodified: Discourses on Life and Law*. Boston, MA: Harvard University Press.

MacKinnon, Catharine (1989). *Towards a Feminist Theory of the State*. Cambridge: Harvard University Press.

Maclean, Neil M. (1979). 'Rape and false accusations of rape'. *The Police Surgeon*, 15 (April): 29–40.

Madigan, Lee and Gamble, Nancy C. (1991). *The Second Rape: Society's Continued Betrayal of the Victim*. New York: Lexington Books.

Maguire, Mike (1994). 'Crime statistics, patterns and trends: Changing perceptions and their implications'. In M. Maguire, R. Morgan and R. Reiner (eds), *The Oxford Handbook of Criminology*. Oxford: Clarendon Press.

Mapes, C. C. (1906). 'A practical consideration of sexual assault'. *Medical Age*, 24: 928–39.

Mason, Gail (1995). 'Reforming the law of rape: Incursions into the masculinist sanctum'. In Diane Kirkby (ed.), *Sex, Power and Justice: Historical Perspectives of Law in Australia*. Melbourne: Oxford University Press.

Matoesian, G. (1993). *Reproducing Rape: Domination Through Talk in the Courtroom*. Chicago: University of Chicago Press.

Mawby, R. I. and Walklate, S. (1994). *Critical Victimology: International Perspectives*. London: Sage.

Maxwell, Gabrielle and Smith, Catherine (1998). *Police Perceptions of Māori*. A Report to the New Zealand Police and the Ministry of Māori Development: Te Puni Kokiri. Wellington: Victoria University of Wellington.

McCarthy, Michelle (1996). 'Sexual experiences and sexual abuse of women with learning disabilities'. In Marianne Hester, Liz Kelly and Jill Radford (eds), *Women, Violence and Male Power: Feminist Activism, Research and Practice*. Buckingham: Open University Press.

McDonald, Elisabeth (1994). 'Gender bias and the law of evidence: The link between sexuality and credibility'. *Victoria University of Wellington Law Review*, 24 (2): 175–88.

McDonald, Elisabeth (1997). ' "Real rape" in New Zealand: Women complainants' experience of the court process'. *Yearbook of New Zealand Jurisprudence*, 1 (1): 59–80.

McLoughlin, David (1997). 'To be male is to beware'. *North and South*, August: 38–53.

McNeill, Sandra (1987). 'Flashing: Its effects on women'. In Jalna Hanmer and Mary Maynard (eds), *Women, Violence and Social Control*. London: Macmillan.

McSherry, Bernadette (1998). 'Constructing lack of consent'. In Patricia Easteal (ed.), *Balancing the Scales: Rape, Law Reform and Australian Culture*. Leichhardt, Sydney: The Federation Press.

Medea, A. and Thompson, K. (1974). *Against Rape*. New York: Farrar, Straus and Giroux.

Mezey, G. and King, M. (eds) (1992). *Male Victims of Sexual Assault*. Oxford: Oxford University Press.

Mills, Elizabeth Anne (1982). 'One hundred years of fear: Rape and the medical profession'. In Nicole Hahn Rafter and Elizabeth Anne Stanko (eds), *Judge, Lawyer, Victim, Thief: Women, Gender Roles and Criminal Justice*. Boston: Northeastern University Press.

Mills, Jane (1991). *Womanwords: A Vocabulary of Culture and Patriarchal Society*. London: Virago Press.

Mintz, Betty (1973). 'Patterns in forcible rape: A review essay'. *Criminal Law Bulletin*, 9 (8): 703–10.

Mitchell, Katherine (2001). 'Rape in the News: Media Portrayals of Rapists, Victims and Rape in New Zealand'. MA Criminology thesis. Wellington: Victoria University of Wellington.

Morris, Allison (1987). *Women, Crime and Criminal Justice*. Oxford: Basil Blackwell.

Morris, Allison (1997). *Women's Safety Survey 1996*. Wellington, New Zealand: Victimisation Survey Committee.

Morris, Allison and Reilly, James (2003). *New Zealand National Survey of Crime Victims 2001*. Wellington: Ministry of Justice.

Muehlenhard, C., Powch, I., Phelps, J. L. and Giusti, L. M. (1992). 'Definitions of rape: Scientific and political implications'. *Journal of Social Issues*, 48 (4): 23–44.

Mulder, Marianne R. and Winkel, Frans Willem (1996). 'Social workers' and police officers' perceptions of victim credibility: Perspective-taking and the impact of extra-evidential factors'. *Psychology, Crime and Law*, 2: 307–19.

Myhill, Andy and Allen, Jonathan (2002). *Rape and Sexual Assault of Women: Findings from the British Crime Survey*. London: Home Office.

Naples, Nancy A. (2003). 'Deconstructing and locating survivor discourse: Dynamics of narrative, empowerment, and resistance'. *Signs: Journal of Women in Culture and Society*, 28 (4): 1151–85.

National Center for Women and Policing (2001). *Successfully Investigating Acquaintance Sexual Assault: A National Training Manual for Law Enforcement*. Violence Against Women Online Resources. http://www.vaw.umn.edu/documents/acquaintsa/acquaintsa.html

National Victim Center and Crime Victims Research and Treatment Center (1992). *Rape in America*. Fort Worth, TX: National Victim Center.

Naffine, Ngaire (1997). *Feminism and Criminology*. Cambridge: Polity Press.

New South Wales Department for Women (1996). *Heroines of Fortitude: The Experiences of Women in Court as Victims of Sexual Assault*. Canberra.

New Zealand Police (1998). 'Adult sexual assault investigation policy'. Policy Pointers 1998/1, *Ten-One: The New Zealand Police Magazine*, 159, 6 February: 11–15.

New Zealand Police (2000). *Report of the New Zealand Police for the Year Ended 30 June 2000*. Wellington: New Zealand Police.

Newbold, Greg (2000). *Crime in New Zealand*. Palmerston North: Dunmore Press.

Nixon, Christine (1992). 'A climate of change: Police responses to rape'. In Jan Breckenridge and Moira Carmody (eds), *Crimes of Violence: Australian Responses to Rape and Child Sexual Assault*. Sydney: Allen and Unwin.

Oakley, Ann (1981). 'Interviewing women: A contradiction in terms'. In Helen Roberts (ed.), *Doing Feminist Research*. London: Routledge and Kegan Paul.

Ofshe, Richard and Watters, E. (1994). *Making Monsters: False Memories, Psychotherapy, and Sexual Hysteria*. New York: Scribners.

O'Neill, Maggie (1997). 'Prostitute women now'. In Graham Scambler and Annette Scambler (eds), Rethinking Prostitution: Purchasing Sex in the 1990s. London: Routledge.

O'Reilly, Harry (1984). 'Crisis intervention with victims of forcible rape: A police perspective'. In J. Hopkins (ed.), *Perspectives on Rape and Sexual Assault*. London: Harper and Row.

Orange, Donna M. (1995). *Emotional Understanding: Studies in Psychoanalytic Epistemology*. New York: The Guilford Press.

Otto, Shirley (1981). 'Women, alcohol and social control'. In Bridget Hutter and Gillian Williams (eds), *Controlling Women: The Normal and the Deviant*. London: Croom Helm.

Paglia, Camille (1992). *Sex, Art, and American Culture*. New York: Penguin Books.

Painter, K. (1991). *Wife Rape, Marriage and the Law*. Manchester: Manchester University.

Palmiotto, M. and O'Donahue, M. (1995). 'Evaluating community policing: Problems and prospects'. *Police Studies*, 18 (2): 33–53.

Patton, Wendy and Mannison, Mary (1998). 'Beyond learning to endure: women's acknowledgement of coercive sexuality'. *Women's Studies International Forum*, 21 (1): 31–40.

Peacock, Patricia (1995). 'Marital rape'. In Vernon R. Wiehe and Ann L. Richards (eds), *Intimate Betrayal: Understanding and Responding to the Trauma of Acquaintance Rape*. Thousand Oaks, CA: Sage.

Peters, Joseph (1975). 'Social, legal and psychological effects of rape on the victim'. *Pennsylvania Medicine*, 78 (2): 34–6.

Pike, Diane Lovewell (1992). 'Women in police academy training: Some aspects of organizational response'. In Imogene Moyer (ed.), *The Changing Roles of Women in the Criminal Justice System: Offenders, Victims, and Professionals*, 2nd edition. Illinois: Waveland Press.

Pino, N. W. and Meier, R. F. (1999). 'Gender differences in rape reporting'. *Sex Roles*, 40 (11–12): 979–90.

Ploscowe, Morris (1951). *Sex and the Law*. New York: Prentice-Hall.

Polk, Kenneth (1985). 'A comparative analysis of attrition of rape cases'. *British Journal of Criminology*, 25 (2): 280–4.

Polk, Kenneth (1994). *When Men Kill: Scenarios of Masculine Violence*. Melbourne: Cambridge University Press.

Pollak, Otto (1961). *The Criminality of Women*. New York: A. S. Barnes.

Pollock, Joycelyn M. (1995) 'Gender, justice, and social control: A historical perspective'. In Alida V. Merlo and Joycelyn M. Pollock, *Women, Law, and Social Control*. Boston: Allyn and Bacon.

Porter, Stephen, Yuille, John C. and Lehman, Darrin R. (1999). 'The nature of real, implanted, and fabricated memories for emotional childhood events: Implications for the recovered memory debate'. *Law and Human Behavior*, 23 (5): 517–37.

Potts, Annie, Gavey, Nicola, Grace, Victoria M. and Vares, Tiina (2003). 'The downside of Viagra: Women's experiences and concerns'. *Sociology of Health and Illness*, 25 (7): 697–719.

Radford, Jill (1987). 'Policing male violence – Policing women'. In Jalna Hanmer and Mary Maynard (eds) *Women, Violence and Social Control*. Basingstoke, Hampshire: Macmillan.

Rape Survivors' Legal Guide Co-ordinating Group (1993). *Rape Survivors' Legal Guide: A Woman's Guide to the New Zealand Court System*. Wellington: Rape Survivors' Legal Guide Co-ordinating Group.

Reese, James (1999). 'Rape investigators: Vicarious victims'. In Robert R. Hazelwood and Ann W. Burgess (eds), *Practical Aspects of Rape Investigation: A Multidisciplinary Approach*, 2nd edition. Boca Raton: CRC Press.

Reiner, Robert (1992). *The Politics of the Police*, 2nd Edition. Hemel Hempstead: Wheatsheaf.

Reiner, Robert (1994). 'Policing and the police'. In M. Maguire, R. Morgan and R. Reiner (eds), *The Oxford Handbook of Criminology*. Oxford: Clarendon Press.

Reinharz, Shulamit (1992). *Feminist Methods in Social Research*. New York: Oxford University Press.

Resick, Patricia (1993). 'The psychological impact of rape'. *Journal of Interpersonal Violence*, 8 (2): 223–55.

Riggs, D. S., Kilpatrick, D. G. and Resnick, H. S. (1992). 'Long-term psychological distress associated with marital rape and aggravated assault: A comparison to other crime victims'. *Journal of Family Violence*, 7 (4): 283–96.

Roiphe, Katie (1993). *The Morning After: Fear and Feminism on Campus*. Little, Brown: New York.

Russell, Bertrand (1950). *Unpopular Essays*. London : George Allen and Unwin Ltd.

Russell, Diana (1984). *Sexual Exploitation: Rape, Child Sexual Abuse, and Workplace Harassment*. Beverly Hills, CA: Sage.

Russell, Diana (1990). *Rape in Marriage*, revised edition. Bloomington: Indiana University Press.

Russell, Diana (1991). 'Wife rape'. In Andrea Parrot and Laurie Bechofer (eds), *Acquaintance Rape: The Hidden Crime*. New York: John Wiley and Sons.

Saraga, Esther and MacLeod, Mary (1997). 'False Memory Syndrome: Theory or defence against reality?' *Feminism and Psychology*, 7 (1): 46–51.

Schuller, Regina and Stewart, Anna (2000). 'Police responses to sexual assault complaints: The role of perpetrator/complainant intoxication'. *Law and Human Behavior*, 24 (5): 535–51.

Schultz, Leroy G. (ed.) (1975) *Rape Victimology*. Springfield, IL: Charles C. Thomas.

Scully, Diana (1990). *Understanding Sexual Violence: A Study of Convicted Rapists*. Boston: Unwin Hyman.

Scully, Diana and Marolla, Joseph (1993). '"Riding the bull at Gilleys"': Convicted rapists describe the rewards of rape'. In Pauline B. Bart and Eileen Geil Moran (eds), *Violence Against Women: The Bloody Footprints*. London: Sage.

Scutt, Jocelynne (1993). 'Judicial vision: Rape, prostitution and the "chaste woman"'. In Patricia Easteal (ed.), *Without Consent: Confronting Adult Sexual Violence: Proceedings of a Conference*. Canberra, Australia: Australian Institute of Criminology.

Scutt, Jocelynne (1997). *The Incredible Woman: Power and Sexual Politics*. Vol. 1. Melbourne: Artemis.

Scutt, Jocelynne (1998). 'Character, credit, context: Women's lives and judicial "reality"'. In Patricia Easteal (ed.), *Balancing the Scales: Rape, Law Reform and Australian Culture*. Leichhardt, Sydney: The Federation Press.

Shapcott, David (1988). *The Face of the Rapist: Why Men Rape – The Myths Exposed*. Auckland: Penguin.

Shapland, Joanna and Cohen, David (1987). 'Facilities for victims: The role of the police and courts'. *Criminal Law Review*, 28: 28–38.

Smart, Carol (1976). *Women, Crime and Criminology: A Feminist Critique*. London: Routledge and Kegan Paul.

Smart, Carol (1989). *Feminism and the Power of Law*. London: Routledge.

Smart, Carol (1990). 'Law's Truth/women's experience'. In Regina Graycar (ed.), *Dissenting Opinions: Feminist Explorations in Law and Society*. Sydney: Allen and Unwin.

Smart, Carol (1995). *Law, Crime and Sexuality: Essays in Feminism*. London: Sage.

Smith, Cyril J. (1974). 'History of rape and rape laws'. *Women Lawyers' Journal*, 60 (Fall):188–91.

Smith, D. J. and Gray, J. (1985). *Police and People in London*. Aldershot: Gower.

Smith, Lorna (1989). *Concerns About Rape*. London: HMSO.

Snelling, H. A. (1975). 'What is rape?' In Leroy G. Schultz (ed.) *Rape Victimology*. Springfield, IL: Charles C. Thomas.

Sorenson, Susan B. and White, Jacquelyn (1992). 'Adult sexual assault: Overview of research'. *Journal of Social Issues*, 48 (4): 1–8.

Spohn, C. and Horney, J. (1992). *Rape Law Reform: A Grassroots Revolution and its Impact*. New York: Plenum.

Stace, Michael (1983). 'Rape complaints and the police'. In *Rape Study: Research Reports, Volume 2*. Wellington: Institute of Criminology and Department of Justice.

Stanko, Elizabeth A. (1982). 'Would you believe this woman? Prosecutorial screening for "credible" witnesses and a problem for justice'. In Nicole Hahn and Elizabeth Anne Stanko (eds), *Judge, Lawyer, Victim, Thief: Women, Gender Roles and Criminal Justice*. Boston: Northeastern University Press.

Stanko, Elizabeth A. (1985). *Intimate Intrusions: Women's Experience of Male Violence*. London: Unwin Hyman.

Stanko, Elizabeth A. (1988). 'Hidden violence against women'. In M. Maguire and J. Pointing (eds), *Victims of Crime: A New Deal?* Milton Keynes: Open University Press.

Stanko, Elizabeth A. (1997). ' "I second that emotion": Reflections on feminism, emotionality and research on sexual violence'. In Martin D. Schwartz (ed.), *Researching Sexual Violence Against Women: Methodological and Personal Perspectives*. Thousand Oaks, CA: Sage.

Stanley, Liz and Wise, Sue (1993). *Breaking Out Again: Feminist Ontology and Epistemology*. London: Routledge.

Stepakoff, Susan (1998). 'Effects of sexual victimization on suicidal ideation and behaviour in US college women'. *Suicide and Life-Threatening Behavior*, 28 (1): 107–26.

Stewart, Ian and Joines, Vann (1987). *TA Today: A New Introduction to Transactional Analysis*. Nottingham: Lifespace Publishing.

Stirling, Pamela (1997). 'The price of charity'. *Listener*, 8 November: 26–7.

Stone, Joan, Barrington, Rosemary and Bevan, Colin (1983), 'The victim survey'. In *Rape Study. Volume 2: Research Reports*. Wellington, New Zealand: Department of Justice and Institute of Criminology.

Stuart, Donna (1993). 'No real harm done: Sexual assault and the criminal justice system'. In Patricia Easteal (ed.), *Without Consent: Confronting Adult Sexual Violence: Proceedings of a Conference*. Canberra, Australia: Australian Institute of Criminology.

Sturman, Peter (2000). *Drug Assisted Sexual Assault*. London: Home Office and Metropolitan Police.

Sullivan, Ginette (1986). *Rape Crisis Handbook: Counselling for Sexual Abuse*. Wellington: Wellington Rape Crisis Centre.

Summers, Anne (1975). *Damned Whores and God's Police: The Colonization of Women in Australia*. Ringwood: Penguin Books.

Summers, Montague (1971). *The Malleus Maleficarum of Heinrich Kramer and James Sprenger*. New York: Dover.

Sutch, William B. (1973). *Women with a Cause*. Wellington: New Zealand University Press.

Taslitz, Andrew E. (1999). *Rape and the Culture of the Courtroom*. New York: New York University Press.

Taylor, Julie (1987). 'Rape and women's credibility: Problems of recantations and false accusations echoed in the case of Cathleen Crowell Webb and Gary Dotson'. *Harvard Women's Law Journal*, 10: 59–116.

Te Whaiti, Pania and Roguski, Michael (1998). *Māori Perceptions of the Police*. A Report to the New Zealand Police and the Ministry of Māori Development: Te Puni Kokiri. Wellington: Victoria University of Wellington.

Temkin, Jennifer (1997). 'Plus ca change: Reporting rape in the 1990s'. *British Journal of Criminology*, 37 (4): 507–28.

Temkin, Jennifer (1999). 'Reporting rape in London: A qualitative study'. *Howard Journal of Criminal Justice*, 38 (1): 17–41.

Temkin, Jennifer (2002). *Rape and the Legal Process, 2nd edition*. Oxford: Oxford University Press.

Thomas, Carol (1993). 'Sexual assault: Issues for aboriginal women'. In Patricia Easteal (ed.), *Without Consent: Confronting Adult Sexual Violence: Proceedings of a Conference*. Canberra: Australian Institute of Criminology.

Thomas, Justice E. W. (1994). 'Was Eve merely framed; Or was she forsaken?' *New Zealand Law Journal*. Part I, October: 368–73 and Part II, November: 426–32.

Tjaden, P. and Thoennes, N. (1998). *Prevalence, Incidence and Consequences of Violence Against Women: Findings from the National Violence Against Women Survey*.

Atlanta: National Institute of Justice Centers for Disease Control and Prevention, Research in Brief.

Tjaden, P. and Thoennes, N. (2000). *Extent, Nature and Consequences of Intimate Partner Violence: Findings from the National Violence Against Women Survey*. Washington: National Institute of Justice.

Toner, Barbara (1982). *The Facts of Rape*. London: Arrow Books.

Tong, Rosemarie (1984). *Women, Sex and the Law*. Savage, MD: Rowman and Littlefield.

Torrey, Morrison (1991). 'When will we be believed? Rape myths and the idea of a fair trial in rape prosecutions'. *University of California, Davis, Law Review*, 24 (4): 1013–71.

Trojanowicz, Robert, Kappeler, Victor E., Gaines, Larry K. and Bucqueroux, Bonnie (1998). *Community Policing: A Contemporary Perspective*, 2nd edition. Cincinnati: Anderson Publishing.

Tunnell, Kenneth D. (1998). 'Honesty, secrecy and deception in the sociology of crime: Confessions and reflections from the backstage'. In Ferrell, Jeff and Hamm, S. Mark (eds), *Ethnography at the Edge: Crime, Deviance and Field Research*. Boston: Northeastern University Press.

Ullman, Sarah E., Karabatsos, George and Koss, Mary P. (1999). 'Alcohol and sexual assault in a national sample of college women'. *Journal of Interpersonal Violence*, 14 (6): 603–25.

United Nations Population Fund (2000). 'Violence: One Third of Women have been Abused – John Hopkins Report'. *Populi*, 27 (1): 4.

van de Zandt, Pia (1998). 'Heroines of fortitude'. In Patricia Easteal (ed.), *Balancing the Scales: Rape, Law Reform and Australian Culture*. Leichhardt, Sydney: The Federation Press.

van der Heyden, John (1997). 'Opportunities for the New Zealand Police to Change its Occupational Culture'. MBA Business Topic. Wellington: Victoria University of Wellington.

Vigarello, Georges (2001). *A History of Rape: Sexual Violence in France from the 16th to the 20th Century*. Cambridge: Polity Press.

Vogelman, Lloyd (1990). *The Sexual Face of Violence: Rapists on Rape*. Johannesburg: Ravan Press.

Wagstaff, Graham F. (1982). 'Rape, bias and interrogation'. *Police Review*, 5 February: 224–5.

Walby, S. and Myhill, A. (2001). 'New survey methodologies in researching violence against women'. *British Journal of Criminology*, 41: 502–22.

Walklate, Sandra (1995). *Gender and Crime: An Introduction*. London: Prentice Hall.

Walklate, Sandra (2001). *Gender, Crime and Criminal Justice*. Cullompton, Devon: Willan Publishing.

Warshaw, Robin (1988). *I Never Called it Rape: The Ms. Report on Recognizing, Fighting and Surviving Date and Acquaintance Rape*. New York: HarperPerennial.

Waugh, Alec (1994). 'A Case Study of Policewomen's Experience in New Zealand'. Master of Public Policy Dissertation. Wellington: Victoria University of Wellington.

Weis, Kurt and Borges, Sandra S. (1975). 'Victimology and rape: The case of the legitimate victim'. In Leroy G. Schultz (ed.), *Rape Victimology*. Springfield, IL: Charles C. Thomas.

Wells, Robert C. (1991). 'Your best evidence'. *The Law Officers' Magazine*, 15 (9): 47.

White, Rob and Perrone, Santina (1997). *Crime and Social Control: An Introduction*. Melbourne: Oxford University Press.

Wiehe, Vernon R. and Richards, Ann L. (1995). *Intimate Betrayal: Understanding and Responding to the Trauma of Acquaintance Rape*. Thousand Oaks, CA: Sage.

Williams, L. S. (1984). 'The classic rape: When do victims report?' *Social Problems*, 31: 459–67.

Williams, T. (1998). *The Bad, the Very Bad and the Ugly: Who's Who of New Zealand Crime*. Auckland: Hodder Moa Beckett.

Wilshire, Donna (1994). *Virgin, Mother, Crone: Myths and Mysteries of the Triple Goddess*. Rochester: Inner Traditions.

Wilson, C., Nettelbeck, T., Potter, R. and Perry, C. (1996). 'Intellectual Disability and Criminal Victimisation'. *Trends and Issues*, No. 60. Canberra: Australian Institute of Criminology.

Wilson, Margo and Daly, Martin (1992). 'Till death us do part'. In Jill Radford and Diana E. H. Russell (eds), *Femicide: The Politics of Woman Killing*. Buckingham: Open University Press.

Wilson, Paul (1978). *The Other Side of Rape*. St. Lucia: University of Queensland Press.

Winkel, Frans W., Vrij, Aldert, Koppelaar, Leendert and Steen, Jaap (1991). 'Enhancing the quality of police–rape victim encounters through reducing secondary victimisation risks and skilled police intervention'. *Journal of Police and Criminal Psychology*, 7 (2): 2–10.

Wolf, Naomi (1997). *Promiscuities: A Secret History of Female Desire*. London: Chatto and Windus.

Wolfthal, Diane (1999). *Images of Rape: The 'Heroic' Tradition and its Alternatives*. Cambridge: Cambridge University Press.

Wood, Linda A. and Rennie, Heather (1994). 'Formulating rape: The discursive construction of victims and villains'. *Discourse and Society*, 5 (1): 125–48.

Wriggins, Jennifer (1998). 'Rape, racism, and the law'. In Mary E. Odem and Jody Clay-Warner (eds), *Confronting Rape and Sexual Assault*. Wilmington, Delaware: Scholarly Resources.

Wright, R. (1984). 'A Note on Attrition of Rape Cases'. *British Journal of Criminology*, 24 (4): 399–400.

Young, Alison (1998). 'Violence as seduction: Enduring genres of rape'. In Howe, Adrian (ed.), *Sexed Crime in the News*. Leichhardt, NSW: The Federation Press.

Young, Warren (1983). *Rape Study: A Discussion of Law and Practice. Volume I*. Wellington: Institute of Criminology and Department of Justice.

Young, Warren and Cameron, Neil (eds) (1989). *Effectiveness and Change in Policing*. Wellington: Institute of Criminology, Victoria University of Wellington.

Index